To Em!.

With best wishes

[signature]

Shared Identities

Shared Identities

*Medieval and Modern
Imaginings of Judeo-Islam*

AARON W. HUGHES

OXFORD
UNIVERSITY PRESS

Oxford University Press is a department of the University of Oxford. It furthers
the University's objective of excellence in research, scholarship, and education
by publishing worldwide. Oxford is a registered trade mark of Oxford University
Press in the UK and certain other countries.

Published in the United States of America by Oxford University Press
198 Madison Avenue, New York, NY 10016, United States of America.

© Oxford University Press 2017

All rights reserved. No part of this publication may be reproduced, stored in
a retrieval system, or transmitted, in any form or by any means, without the
prior permission in writing of Oxford University Press, or as expressly permitted
by law, by license, or under terms agreed with the appropriate reproduction
rights organization. Inquiries concerning reproduction outside the scope of the
above should be sent to the Rights Department, Oxford University Press, at the
address above.

You must not circulate this work in any other form
and you must impose this same condition on any acquirer.

CIP data is on file at the Library of Congress
ISBN 978–0–19–068446–4

1 3 5 7 9 8 6 4 2
Printed by Sheridan Books, Inc., United States of America

*To the memory of
Muhammad Ali ibn Khalil Najdi (aka "Bud Alley")
and to all those who transgress boundaries,
whether imagined or real*

*Identity is our legacy and not our inheritance
our invention and not our memory.*
—M. DARWISH

*The real question is whether in the end we want to
work for civilizations that are separate or whether
we should be taking the more integrative but perhaps
more difficult path, which is to see them as making
one vast whole whose exact contours are impossible
for any one person to grasp but whose certain existence
we can intuit and feel.*
—E. W. SAID

Contents

Preface   ix
Acknowledgments   xiii

Introduction   1
1. Symbiosis: Rethinking a Paradigm   17
2. Origins   36
3. Messianism in the Shadows   62
4. The Manufacture of Orthodoxy   82
5. Et in Arcadia Ego   104
6. Re-frame   125
Conclusion: Two Solitudes   145

Notes   151
Bibliography   191
Index   213

Preface

THIS STUDY SEEKS to reread the relationship between Judaism and Islam that originated in the late sixth century, a period of flux and uncertainty in the larger context of the late antique world. It extends to the twelfth century, a period that represents a supposed stability perhaps best symbolized by the so-called golden age of Muslim Spain. Between these two bookends resides a poorly documented and understudied period of transformation in both traditions. Rather than retroactively read the stability of later centuries back onto the material, my aim is to examine, taxonomize, and analyze the period in question. In so doing, I provide a set of often technical vignettes as a way to think nontechnically about how we imagine and describe the intersection between these two, for lack of a better term, religions. The traditional narrative that describes their historical relationship is as simplistic as it is telling. It runs something like the following: Judaism functioned as a midwife to Islam in the late sixth century before Islam returned the favor in the tenth to twelfth centuries—including the aforementioned "golden age" of Muslim Spain—by facilitating the rise and florescence of, among other things, Hebrew belles-lettres and Jewish rationalism. Informing the dominant narrative is the fiction of a creative and stable Jewish essence that gives life to Islam (as it had to Christianity several centuries earlier) and that later borrows from a now equally creative and stable Islam what it needs. Both essences are assumed to remain untouched by this encounter. Often marginalized in that narrative are a series of difficult questions. Who, for example, were "the Jews" with which Muhammad interacted? Who were the "pre-Islamic Arabs"? How exactly did Judaism transform during the so-called golden age? What exactly happened to Jewish–Muslim relations between these chronological bookends?

Perhaps the metaphor most invoked to characterize this interrelationship is "symbiosis," which was originally coined by the late Shlomo

Dov Goitein in the 1950s. This metaphor, derived from the field of biology, describes the mutually beneficial relationship between two or more species or organisms. Judaism and Islam, using this narrative, are imagined as two distinct "species" whose borders touch in such a manner that their centers, their perceived internal cores of stability and self-definition, remain unscathed by the exchange. Jews and Arabs are seen as races or nations, and it was inconceivable for Goitein, as it was for countless others who followed in his wake, that nations or ethnicities can be imagined and unimagined by sociopolitical circumstances. Yet, rather than simply retain the metaphor of symbiosis and all that informs and is informed by it here, I want to systematically rethink it. This means subjecting the intellectual agendas that manufacture symbiosis and the narratives that reproduce it to critical scrutiny. Much of what follows, then, is about wrestling with the meta or theoretical legacy of Goitein's path-breaking work. I do not claim to bring any new text to light here that will definitively change our understanding of the "parting of the ways" between Judaism and Islam in the late antique period because frankly I am not convinced that such texts exist. I do, however, submit both primary sources and secondary literature to critical and creative rereadings to help us rethink the relationship between Jews and Muslims, Judaisms and Islams, in their first centuries together.

I focus on the Jewish–Muslim encounter, since this encounter has fascinated me ever since I was an undergraduate, and it is the technicalities of this relationship that has sustained both my personal and scholarly interest since then. I am aware that both Jews and Muslims, both in the period examined here and in other periods, have interacted with other and often equally underdefined groups. Perhaps this is another way of saying that Christianity is largely absent from my narrative. This lacuna is certainly not meant to deprive the dynamic exchanges between either Jews and Christians or Muslims and Christians in the period I here examine. If anything, it is an admission that much systematic rethinking is needed when it comes to all of these diverse encounters. I offer what follows not so much as a definitive statement, but as a suggestive and critical intervention that seeks to overcome the ways we customarily talk about the intersection of religions in general and of Judaism and Islam in particular.

The story I wish to tell is ultimately one of boundaries, and of their simultaneous porosity and fixity. Group definition, at the risk of pointing out the obvious, can only take place on boundaries, since the consciousness of a collective ultimately demands an outsider, those who are "not us."[1] But such consciousness of identity, a form of what anthropologists call ethnogenesis, reminds us that identity is not a static marker of some genetically related kin group, but instead is a developing and changing idea that is ultimately a product of historical forces.[2] Borders—the desire for separation, the need to keep alterity outside, the emotional (not to mention financial) cost of erecting fortified walls, and the ultimate price of their transgression—are not just modern ways to define the relations between Judaism and Islam, now imagined as Israel and Palestine. Although in the concluding chapter I will return to security fences, "apartheid walls," and the futility of trying to keep people inside or outside, the borders I am most concerned with in the pages that follow are the ones that medieval thinkers sought to erect and the ones that modern scholars who work on this material emulate.

I have been thinking about the relationship between Judaism and Islam for much of the past thirty years. Until recently, however, my thinking could be described as being of the "symbiotic" variety. It was only when I began to write, at the behest of the Jewish Publication Society of America, a general and accessible volume on the history of Jews and Muslims in the medieval period that I began to resist. As I started that project, it occurred to me that what they expected and indeed the way I started to frame the narrative simply retold the same old story that Jews have been telling themselves since at least the eighteenth century. Who needs, I asked myself, another book that paraphrases and further reinscribes the standard narrative of symbiosis? Sustaining that narrative, I now realize, is the assumption that Judaism possesses an essence that exists removed from the light of history and that functions as the midwife present at the birth of Islam, as it did to the birth of Christianity several centuries earlier. Even though Judaism will subsequently take from a later creative and now equally stable Islam what it needs, Judaism's essence is again perceived to remain unblemished or undisturbed. This is the narrative that the trope of "symbiosis" structures and ultimately reproduces. I am no longer convinced that this is the most helpful let alone analytical model to use.

I soon realized that I could not write that volume. Instead what was supposed to be a nontechnical introduction meant primarily for an undergraduate and interested lay readership began to transform into a study of language and ultimately one of comparison. But there is a problem here. Comparison, as any good scholar of religion well knows, is a carryover from a different era of our discipline.[3] Comparison, after all, has been used and abused to attain often predetermined conclusions as to which religion (one's own) is better and to justify or legitimate why such a subjective assessment is "scientific." Whether we like it or not, or even whether we admit or not, the study of Judaism and Islam is and always has been a comparative project often used to elevate one (Judaism) over the other (Islam). A guiding question then becomes: what is the most appropriate way to talk about the intersection of religions? While those who work in the often highly technical study of late antique Islam and/or medieval Judaism are rarely interested in this "big picture," as a scholar of religions I am. Much of what follows, then, is about trying to find a new vocabulary that permits comparison and facilitates a way to talk about the historical and social connections between religions in a nuanced manner. If I have done my job properly, then others engaged in the academic study of religion and who deal with the intersection and comparison of religions will hopefully find my endeavors to be of some value.

The study that follows seeks to chart a new way to think about Judaism and Islam by temporarily removing the boundary—or borderline or hyphen or whatever else we want to call it—that separates them. Such an exercise reveals a proliferation of localized interactions between various sets of, for lack of a better term, Jewmuslims and Muslimjews that take place in the shadows of history. These shadows, often intentionally ignored or unconsciously bypassed because of their lack of luminescence, can however be accessed fleetingly and often in the most unlikely of places. A creative reading of the material, both primary and secondary, that we do possess is not just a historical exercise in complexity, I hope, but a way to add much needed nuance to a narrative between two traditions in a highly contested present.

Acknowledgments

THIS BOOK HAS, quite literally, been inside me for my entire life. I am grateful that, at long last, it has decided to reveal itself. Identities, like the boundaries erected to keep trespassers at bay, are ultimately as fixed as they are fictive. As the locus of self-imposed meaning, identities welcome with one hand as they simultaneously exile with the other. This is, to be sure, a messy process, one that—fiats of the status quo to the contrary—underscores the fragility of human existence. Much of this, as the present study seeks to explore in more detail, takes place on the margins. There, the fluidity of identity, coupled with the ephemeral imaginings of the center, inspires an unheralded creativity and freedom to transgress what the center seeks to label "normative." Without margins, in other words, there can quite literally be no center. Perhaps this is another way of saying that the struggle for self-definition has animated much originality and inventiveness over the centuries. I hope that what follows is no different.

Luckily I have been indulged by a set of wonderful conversation partners over the years. These include, in alphabetical order: Bill Arnal, Shahzad Bashir, Kalman P. Bland, Willi Braun, William Scott Green, Francis Landy, Laura Levitt, Shaul Magid, Russell McCutcheon, Josef Meri, Jacob Neusner, James T. Robinson, Hava Tirosh-Samuelson, Matt Sheedy, Steven M. Wasserstrom, Don Wiebe, and Elliot R. Wolfson.

I also wish to acknowledge Cynthia Read and her expert team at Oxford University Press. Her belief in my work is greatly appreciated, and her professionalism is a credit to the field.

Finally, I thank my dear wife, Jennifer, and my children Rebecca and Gabriel, for their love and support that enfolds me on a daily basis. I dedicate this book to the memory of a man I never knew, to someone who passed away in a small village in South Lebanon, a place that knows all too well the nightmare that borders can bring, nine months before I was born.

An earlier version of chapter 3 appeared as "Messianism and the Shadow of History: Judaism and Islam in a Time of Uncertainty," in *Islamic Studies Today: Essay in Honor of Andrew Rippin*, edited by Majid Daneshgar and Walid Saleh (Leiden: Brill, 2016), 145–163.

Shared Identities

Introduction

THE GREATEST TASK for those of us who work in religious studies is to translate between the highly technical specifics of our chosen subfield and the often too general framework provided by our disciplinary home. If the former is detail-driven and cautious, the latter often encourages us to transform something as amorphous or inchoate as a religion (e.g., "Islam," "Judaism") into a category of analysis. The discipline of religious studies, torn between the particular and universal, is not surprisingly caught in a complex web of contested entanglements. At what point is a study too technical, of interest to only a few other specialists, or when does it become too general and unrecognizable to fellow specialists outside of religious studies? Balancing these two opposing sides of the continuum is never easy. The present study is my attempt to address two audiences at once: those who work in the field of Jewish–Muslim relations in the early Islamic period and those interested in questions supplied by a field of study that frequently goes by the name of Religious Studies or the History of Religions.

This is not a history book that retells the story of Jewish–Muslim interactions. On the contrary, my aim is to examine what we realistically know about, say, the Jews of Arabia at the time of Muhammad in the late sixth century CE, what we do not, what we make up, and why. Indeed, even the very term Arabia or Arabness, as Peter Webb has recently argued, might well have been a later post-Islamic attempt at ethnogenesis.[1] We are, then, quite literally on uncertain terrain. In like manner, I do not recount, for example, the so-called golden age of Muslim Spain, but I do put the trope of "golden age"—what it is, how it came to be used, and what sort of intellectual heavy lifting it purports to do—under the analytic microscope. Each chapter that follows provides one of a set of interlocking vignettes that, when taken as a whole, reorients a narrative that has performed a great deal of extracurricular work over the past two centuries.

If I have done my job properly, I will have signaled to those in religious studies that the topic on which I work—the complex set of relations between so-called Jews and so-called Muslims—is but a subset of a larger issue or set of issues in the academic study of religion, to wit, what happens when what are assumed to be discrete religious traditions intersect and interact with one another? What gives? What does not? How does each serve as the catalyst for the other's self-definition? The relationship between Jews and Muslims, Judaism and Islam, is certainly amenable to the types of questions that some religionists ask, assuming, of course, we can break out of a traditional national or ethnic model that wants us to think about religions as hermetically sealed units and one that invokes terms such as "symbiosis" or "convivencia" to describe their interactions.

Unfortunately, for the study of religion, the majority of scholars who work on Jewish–Muslim relations especially in the earliest centuries are primarily historians (social, intellectual, economic, and so on). Their stimulating and data-driven works provide much useful material, but they are of limited use to the types of questions that interest scholars of religion. Writing over twenty years ago, Steven M. Wasserstrom remarked, "the glaring fact remains that [Shlomo Dov Goitein's] *A Mediterranean Society*—and Jewish-Islamic scholarship in general—infrequently deals directly with fundamental questions in the critical study of religion."[2] This is an assessment that, it seems to me, has not changed dramatically over the years. While the recent past has witnessed many important works devoted to micro topics in Jewish–Muslim relations, works that have done much to increase our knowledge of localized interactions between Jews and Muslims in specific geographical locales, they tend to be historical as opposed to theoretical.[3] Even though I maintain that history provides one of the most important antidotes against essentialism, we should also recognize that a strictly historical positive framework certainly carries its own set of concerns.

But if there is to be a study of religion, then surely it is incumbent upon the scholar of religion to demonstrate both her skill and her raison d'être. Namely, if Judaism and Islam are indeed two religions and if social actors who have appealed to these religions have historically interacted and continue to interact into the present, how can a scholar of religion contribute to understanding these interactions? What kind of theoretical issues, for example, do these interactions raise and what insights can a scholar of religion provide to understand and analyze them? It is worth mentioning in the present context that the religious studies I have in mind is not the feel-good, ecumenical, and liberal Protestant version that so often masquerades as critical study, but the more theoretical and critical approach found in the works of J. Z. Smith, Bruce Lincoln, and Russell McCutcheon.[4] Yet, this more theoretical tradition of the field is largely uninterested in the specifics of, say, late antique interactions, medieval poetry, or the Platonizing Aristotelianism (often anachronistically given the name of "Neoplatonism") that is the dominant form of philosophy in the Middle Ages. In like manner, those who work, say, in the documents associated with the Cairo Genizah are for the most part completely uninterested in the types of questions that professional religionists ask. Despite what should be an obvious set of connections, it is not easy to bring these two intellectual worlds into conversation with one another.

A historian, for example, might object that such a large or grandiose model that purports to deal with something as mammoth as "Jewish–Muslim" or as monolithic as "Judaism/Islam" too neatly sweeps over or bypasses various local and individual interactions. I would respond that that is certainly true, but simultaneously note that it was a detail-orientated historian, Shlomo Dov Goitein—who trained a generation of scholars at Princeton, who in turn trained the current generation of young scholars primarily at that same institution—who first coined the trope of "symbiosis" to refer to Muslim–Jewish relations, a trope that, as will be seen in the following chapter, continues to be recycled in one way or another into the present. Goitein, then, had no reservations about speaking of these two traditions as if they were discrete and commensurable. In like manner, a theoretician of religion might speak in general terms about religion, but leave the collection and collation of data to others. Yet, if religious studies is to exist as an independent and autonomous field of study, then surely it must be able to illumine meaningfully questions that are relevant to a large cross-section of scholars in other fields.

In this vein, I have decided to follow the path illumined by Wasserstrom, one of the few scholars to take Jewish–Muslim relations seriously from the perspective of the History of Religions. He writes, for example,

> If there is little dispute concerning the general significance of the Jewish–Muslim symbiosis, there is enormous uncertainty concerning its specific anatomy. The obscure history informing this apparently hyperbolic assertion, that is, is both too well known and too

little known: too well known, I believe, because its status as a rarely disputed historiographic assumption allows us to forget that the symbiosis was creative, indeed, that it even created us. And, on the other hand, it is too little known, insofar as the details of this creative symbiosis remain obscure beyond exaggeration.[5]

Although Wasserstrom is correct to submit the term "symbiosis" to full analytic interrogation, the term nevertheless remains his default model, and it is ultimately left intact at the end of his analysis.[6] Yet symbiosis is a made-up term. It was, as we have seen, lifted from the domain of biology, and it is my concern that it is a term that maintains, if not further reifies, boundaries between distinct entities or species. These boundaries, however, are neither natural nor written in stone. They emerge at particular moments, and the questions we need to ask are: When? Why? How? And for what purposes? The study that follows seeks to lay the groundwork for what a post-symbiotic relationship might look like.

Rather than claim that there has existed two unique and separate entities called Judaism and Islam locked in an originally creative (in the late antique and medieval periods) and subsequently pernicious (in the modern period) relationship, I want to suggest a different model. In the early period, as we shall see, no characteristics could be described as singularly Jewish or Muslim, primarily because neither group existed or at least not on the Arabian Peninsula (*jazīrat al-ʿarab* or *arḍ al-ʿarab*). "Islam," for example, would only be worked out much later and what "Judaism" looked like on the Arabian Peninsula in the sixth and seventh centuries is anyone's guess.[7] Instead, invoking the suggestive language of Daniel Boyarin who works on the interrelationships between Judaism and Christianity in the late antique period, what we may well have is groups of actors, only subsequently defined as Jewish and/or Muslim, who inhabited a shared social and intellectual space in which a wide variety of beliefs—messianism and apocalypticism in response to growing political instability, the religious contours of law, a belief in one deity, and so on—were widely distributed.[8] The eventual creation and maintenance of border markers to separate these beliefs into "Judaism" and "Islam" only occurred much later. The creations of theological ateliers in the caliphal center of Baghdad, rabbinic Judaism and Sunni Islam eventually became signified as orthodox and normative. Other groups and their beliefs subsequently became marginalized as heterodox or at the very least awkwardly folded into what was slowly emerging as "orthopraxy" or "orthodoxy." Ideas, beliefs, individuals, and groups could then later be neatly arranged on one side or another of this artificial border. But before such later categorization, the situation was much more complex.

Contrary to our theological sources, this separation did not occur overnight. Instead it took centuries as various Jewish and Muslim "heterodox" groups existed on the margins of the caliphal court and they did so in such a manner that drew inspiration and sustenance from one another. Rather than adopt the narrative that has Judaism as a "midwife" present at the birth of Islam, I wish to argue that, at least in the context of the Arabian Peninsula, they emerged dialectically with and from one another. Each would then become the catalyst of self-definition for the other. This self-definition, of course, has never stopped and continues—as even a cursory look at the news attests—well into the present. Only the terms and stakes have changed.

This now, at least for me, leads to a classic question of religious studies. Jewish–Muslim relations—the language used to describe them, the categories deployed to understand them, and the political ramifications that emerge from them—become an exemplum of larger issues in the academic study of religion. These can be as basic as what does it mean to engage in something we might problematically label as "comparative religion" or as local as issues of translation. What does it mean, for example, for the late-ninth and early-tenth-century Saadya Gaon to write a Muʿtazila-inflected theology of Judaism? Or how do we categorize the twelfth-century Judah Halevi's Ismāʿīlī-inspired defense of Judaism? Are these "symbiotic" thinkers? Are they Jewish thinkers writing in Arabic or Arabophone intellectuals applying Muslim ideas to Jewish data? Or, do they represent, to revert to the language of biology, some other species that is altogether different?

Just as I have done for other problematic categories—such as "Abrahamic religions"[9] or "Jewish philosophy"[10]—my goal here is to provide a full-scale interrogation and even deconstruction of the category "Jewish–Muslim." This means that it is incumbent to examine the various models or paradigms hitherto employed or deployed; trying to ascertain the political and/or ideological assumptions that inform them; and arguing that our traditional paradigmatic frame can and in fact does blur data. Having analyzed and undermined previous paradigms, the goal is to try to reimagine interactions from the bottom up, as it were, as opposed to from the top down.

The Dominant Paradigm

With very few exceptions, the basic narrative, framed either popularly or historically, of Jewish–Muslim relations goes as follows. "In the beginning," Judaism gave birth to Islam. Judaism is older than Islam therefore the former must have been responsible for the latter's genesis. This birth can be explained mythically or biblically in the sense that Ishmael was the son of Abraham through Hagar, his wife's maidservant. After being expelled from Abraham's house on account of Sarah's discomfort, Hagar and Ishmael cross the Negev desert and end up somewhere in Arabia. With the help of an angel sent by God, Hagar and Ishmael survive the harsh conditions and the descendants of Ishmael, like those of his half-brother Isaac, are promised to become a "great nation." According to much later tradition, Ishmael becomes the founding father of the Arabs, later to be recast as Muslims. There is, of course, not a shred of historical evidence for such a model.[11]

The other explanation, presumably more historical than this biblical model, locates a set of Jewish tribes living in the Ḥijāz, the westernmost region on the Arabian Peninsula and the home of the Muslim holy cities of Mecca and Medina, and in the South (modern-day Yemen). These Jewish tribes, according to the narrative, functioned as a monotheistic "midwife" by providing Muhammad and his earliest followers with the terms, categories, and basic apocalyptic narrative that would in the coming centuries transform into Islam.

These two narratives, the one based on the Bible and the other on some form of midwifery, as we shall see in the coming chapters, are historically problematic and based more on modern need than historical evidence. They are the product of nineteenth-century notions of identity and nationhood based on racialist paradigms. We thus need to look to more recent notions of communal consciousness. While we might be more convinced of the chronistic bona fides of the midwife model, it soon becomes apparent when we look at the evidence that we have absolutely no idea what or who these "Arabian Jews" were (were they, for example, "ethnically" Arab and "religiously" Jewish—with the understanding that both of the terms in quotation marks are modern constructs) let alone who the "pre-Islamic Arabs" were.

Returning to the narrative: After a few ambiguous centuries that are often simply bypassed, we arrive at the so-called golden age of Muslim Spain. This period witnessed Jews adopt and adapt a variety of scientific, philosophical, and literary arts from Muslims. Then after the "fundamentalist" Berber invasion from North Africa, matters begin to deteriorate gradually and then rapidly. The narrative then switches to those Jews living in Christian lands (medieval Iberia, Renaissance Italy, early modern Amsterdam, and so on). Eventually, with the rise of Zionism in the late nineteenth century and the formation of the State of Israel in 1948, relations hit rock bottom. Jews of Arab lands either leave or are forced out, and after a Six Day War, a Yom Kippur War, annexations, occupations, and mutual recriminations we arrive at the unsavory present.

As even the quickest of glances will reveal, this is a narrative embroiled in a host of political, ideological, even ethnic machinations that shows the Western world in need of Judaism. Just as Judaism gave birth to Christianity in the first century CE, it gave birth to Islam in the sixth. When we breach the parapet of this narrative, however, we see the emergence of counter or at least different narratives. We encounter instability where before stability was posited; we witness messiness in the place of a previously perceived order; and we see a set of contested skirmishes when before we imagined two unified religions working aside one another with no transgression or infraction.

Centers and Margins

Recent scholarship, inspired by the postmodern turn and its mistrust of inherited narratives, cautions us to be wary of dominant paradigms.[12] Such paradigms often serve political ends and protect the well-being of the status quo. This status quo, as seen in the previous section, often eschews complexity and ambiguity in favor of chronological, religious, and even ethnic tidiness. A dismantling of the regnant narrative briefly noted in the last section should help us to rethink the nature of the encounter between Judaism and Islam as it simultaneously illumines the larger issue of the historical interaction and intersection of religions. Rethinking the paradigm also permits a shift in traditional emphases that focus on "normative" and "orthodox" expressions at the expense of other voices that are subsequently dismissed as heterodox. This later heterodoxy is all too often retrofitted onto the earlier period whereupon it can be mislabeled as such. Although this is certainly anachronistic, it is all too often and unfortunately a common feature in the study of religion.[13] Too much time is spent at the center and much academic energy is expended in reproducing theological locutions as if they were historical fact. The view from the edge, as

Richard Bulliet so eloquently puts it, looks considerably different than it does at the center. Although his interests are in medieval Islamic history, Bulliet's observations are certainly germane to my discussion. According to him,

> The view from the center portrays Islamic history as an outgrowth from a single nucleus, a spreading inkblot labeled "the caliphate." But what other than a political label held Islam together? And why did its political cohesion evaporate after little more than two centuries, never to reoccur? The view from the edge holds out the possibility of addressing questions like these. It starts from the fact that most Muslims outside the Arabian peninsula proper are not descendants of the Arabs who participated in the Islamic conquests. ... Most of them learned about Islam after they entered the community, not before; and what they learned never assumed a homogenous character, though from the fourteenth century onward there was a strong impulse toward homogeneity.[14]

Whereas the view from the center begins with political institutions and religious dogma, often overlooked is the fact that such phenomena are often of a much later provenance and the result of real intellectual skirmish and ideological struggle. The view from the edge, however, is often the place where we can witness such skirmishes and struggles. A centripetal as opposed to a centrifugal model thus has the distinct advantage of demonstrating how centers are created, often in response to margins, as opposed to assuming that they exist de facto and that they simply express their will by divine fiat, at which point this will or consensus automatically becomes binding on all and sundry. In Bulliet's phraseology, a view from the edge "starts with individuals and small communities scattered over a vast and poorly integrated realm, speaking over a dozen different languages, and steeped in religious and cultural traditions of great diversity."[15] Doctrinal cohesion and theological proclamations only emerge slowly, the products of considerable political manipulation that responds to the dialectic that occurs between center and margins. Yet, the margins, as Bulliet does so well to articulate, exist "wherever people make the decision to cross a social boundary."[16] These margins, to return us to Jewish–Muslim relations, are everywhere and nowhere in the first centuries. They are everywhere in the sense that the doctrinal and political center of each religion has not yet formed or, even if they exist in some inchoate form, there is no central authority to make it binding on others. They are nowhere in the sense that there is such fluidity and instability between often amorphous social groups that appear, on a phenomenological level, to be indistinct from one another and that will only emerge at a much later time as discrete religions, namely, "Judaism" and Islam."

Take, for example, the Jewish tribes of the Ḥijāz at the time of Muhammad, to be discussed in greater detail in chapter 2. Despite scholarly appeals to the contrary, we know nothing about them: who they were, what they believed, or how they worshipped. They left no writings and we have no material remains—no synagogues, no cemeteries, no ossuaries, and no mikvahs. Their tribal names, as Margoliouth mentioned years ago, are neither identifiably Jewish nor even Jewish sounding.[17] Later Muslim sources made them into rabbinic Jews and a foil to Muhammad and his early followers, and much Jewish scholarship from the nineteenth century on has also made them into *pure laine* and ethnic Jews, perhaps to establish the genetic purity of Jews from biblical times into the present.[18] But the fact remains: we have no idea who they were. All we possess is a series of later projections.

Taxonomically, we encounter a culture delineated not by religions or ethnicities, those essential characteristics by which we in the modern period divvy up our world, but by tribes. Rather that assume a uniformity of some pan-Arabian tribal culture of which so-called Jewish tribes partook, we need to imagine what Webb calls "zones of fragmentation."[19] Such zones account for the different allegiances some tribes had with larger Empires in the region (e.g., Ghassān with the Byzantines and the Lakhm with the Sasanians) that, in turn, reflected or produced different models of kingship, patronage rituals, and other traditions. Some of these tribes may well have identified in some way as "Jewish," emphasizing some vague monotheistic or apocalyptic message. As Muhammad's call would have spread throughout the Peninsula, it would certainly have absorbed some of these tribes and their messages.[20] But, and this is worth underscoring, this was not something that was predicated on borrowing, influence, or midwifery. If anything, we encounter what Donner calls a "community of believers" though the exact contents of that belief are rather vague, only to be codified and theologized in later centuries.[21] Those who did this later codifying and theologizing were precisely the ones who marked the territory whereupon subsequent borders would be constructed. At this point and in their and our textual memory, the undistinguished and indistinguishable "Jewish" tribes became transformed into orthodox, rabbinic Jews.

Context

This study is not interested in adding to the scholarly discussion about the conflicts or contrasts between Jews and Muslims so much as it is in reflecting on the notion of Muslims as Jews or Jews as Muslims. Rather than reify a later boundary that is projected onto an earlier period, I wish to demolish it and imagine its porosity before, during, and after its construction. Owing to the gravity or novelty of this utterance, let me explain. I certainly do not want to downplay what distinguished Jews from others in the late antique and early medieval periods. The fact remains, however, that biblical and other ancient Jewish apocalyptic literature provides the catalyst for the earliest Muslims to think about themselves and their movement. At the same time, early Islam provided the functioning context for virtually all early Jewish literature from the seventh to the ninth centuries. The language of "borrowing" or "influence," so often invoked for a host of extra scholarly reasons, however, does little to account for this creativity.

My project simultaneously derives energy from and seeks to contribute to a growing number of studies that are interested in showing the ambivalences of Jewish cultures, and on how Jewish differences are frequently predicated on similarities with the cultures in which Jews found themselves, just as similarities between them are predicated on difference. The study of Palestinian Judaism, for example, has recently been recalibrated as an example of, as opposed to an aberration from, Roman provincial culture.[22] This means that the cultural, textual, and hermeneutical strategies that the Palestinian rabbis employed had much in common "with Greek, Syrian, Egyptian, and other sub-elites who simultaneously subverted, absorbed, and manipulated Roman norms."[23] There is a need, then, to resist the romantic narratives of the past, narratives that seek to create dramatic differences or even firm boundaries between Jews and their neighbors, Judaism and other religions, all in the name of apologetically protecting Jewish difference.

Yet, rather than focus on difference, a task upon which much energy has been expended, it is time to turn to the similarities that make such difference not only possible but also necessary. Rather than posit Judaism and Islam as discrete yet commensurable entities that bump up against one another and rather than worry about priority and directionality of "borrowings" or "influences," this study seeks to investigate the construction of mutual identities through the discourse of alterity. Just as Jewishness aids in the formation of multiple and overlapping Muslim identities,

Muslimness serves a similar function in the construction of Jewish identities. Rather than reflect on these mutual productions, much scholarship has succeeded in producing a totalizing discourse that reifies "Jew" and "Muslim." Dismantling such discourse means that we must try to deconstruct or at the very least undermine our categories.

The book claims to be illustrative, not exhaustive. It does not pretend to cover the subject in all its various manifestations and ramifications. I am not interested, for example, if Jews were better served under the tenth-century Buyids than they were under twelfth-century Ayyubids. I will leave such comparisons to historians. Of necessity, the study that follows must be highly selective. It does not engage with fragments or isolated ruminations, but with major texts that should be familiar to anyone with even a passing interest in the subject. My aim is to show how too much contemporary scholarship on these works is rarely interested in using them as a window onto earlier mentalities than it is in using such works to reify boundaries only imagined after the fact. My goal, in other words, is not to provide another contribution to the genre, so prevalent in recent years, of the history of Jewish–Muslim relations. Rather, as I trust is clear by now, it is to interrogate a paradigm and a regnant discourse. I aim to show the conception of collective identity, to use the language of Erich S. Gruen, "in terms of (rather than in contrast to) another culture forms a significant ingredient in the ancient outlook."[24] This admixture of cultural forms and identities is a complex one that demands scrutiny. In Gruen's formulation,

> When ancients reconstructed their roots or fashioned their history, they often did so by associating themselves with the legends and traditions of others. That practice affords a perhaps surprising but certainly revealing insight into the mentalities of Mediterranean folk in antiquity. It discloses not how they *distinguished* from others but how they transformed or reimagined themselves for their own purposes. The "Other" takes on quite a different shape. This is not rejection, denigration, or distancing—but rather appropriation. It represents a more circuitous and a more creative mode of fashioning self-consciousness.[25]

Applying Gruen's conceptual apparatus to Jews and Muslims in the seventh and eighth centuries, it is safe to say that how we imagine difference in late antiquity or even the medieval period rarely falls along modernist lines. Different social groups—groups we may today conveniently label using anachronistic concepts such as "ethnicity" or even "religion"[26]—certainly interacted with one another. However, they did not necessarily construct or imagine difference or imagine alterity in the same manner that we do today.

The story of Jewish–Muslim relations, then, is really two stories. The first is what actually happened and the second is what modern commentators wanted to happen. The latter, when compounded by the paucity of sources and sources that claim to be earlier than they actually are, makes it difficult if not impossible to access the former. When we take as normative the process of defining the self through the exclusion of difference, however, we gloss over some of the complex internal dynamics that helped shape both Judaism and Islam throughout their diverse and lengthy historical interactions with one another. The totalizing language that we have adopted to create a dominant narrative of Jewish–Muslim relations while desiring to create stable boundary markers instead masks persistent—I would suggest even necessary—instability. In his *Christ Circumcised*, Andrew Jacobs seeks to use the circumcision of Jesus, the stereotypical mark of the Jewish covenant, to examine identity and difference in early Christianity. He writes,

> No boundary between self and other persists, except as a fantasy of identity. Because my subjectivity emerges out of a scene of imaginary boundaries between my "self" and "others," it is inherently unstable: it shifts and reconstitutes itself according to myriad psychic and material pressures and forces. It desires wholeness and a sense of permanence—thus the insistence on "myself," a coherent subjectivity that can speak in the first person—but that desire is constantly, and sometimes thrillingly, frustrated. The sense of self is therefore always accompanied by anxiety and ambivalence.[27]

Jacobs's analysis, like my own, is less interested in the internal psychology of this process than it is on its role in the realm of social relations. "When we think of boundaries of community along these same lines," he continues, "as fantasies that both create and uncreate communal cohesion, we view the formation of such identities, and their disruption, quite differently."[28] Again, while I am less interested in examining the psychological ramifications of the boundary that Jews and Muslims—both in the past and in the present—erect between themselves, I find Jacobs's language helpful in showing how our desire to bound and define, in many ways, constitutes a hidden act of dissolution and blurring.

This study, in the final analysis, is about the fantasy of boundaries. They can be as porous as a line in the sand or as massive and ugly as the security wall that snakes betwixt and between the so-called Green Line.

Contents

After a theoretical chapter that frames some of the approaches traditionally used to describe the intersections of Judaism and Islam, the work falls roughly into three unequal parts that can best be characterized as analyses of "before," "during," and "after" the construction of the wall, hyphen, or whatever other metaphor we invoke to describe the boundary separating these two religions.

In chapter 1, my goal is not historical but historiographical. I seek to tell a relatively modern story about the language we employ to think about boundaries—their construction, their maintenance, and the price of their transgression. What political baggage, what ideological contexts, and what rhetorical moves, in other words, function as scholarly aids to help us imagine the historical relationship between Judaism and Islam? This chapter interrogates "symbiosis" and shows how it is but one paradigm used to study the relationship between the two religions. Although it is certainly the predominant one—indeed, it may even be the one from which the others (such as commensalism, convergence/divergence, convivencia, and even parasitism) derive.

Chapter 2 begins at the beginning, as it were. Just when did Jewish–Muslim relations begin? While some point to biblical precedent, I opt for the more historically grounded narrative of the seventh-century Ḥijāz. However, there is a real problem with this narrative, grounded as it is in the nineteenth-century tradition of German-Jewish Orientalism that sought to show how Islam derived from Judaism. The latter, it is assumed, is the stable entity that gives birth to a fledgling Islam. Rarely broached, however, is just how little we actually know about the Jews of the Arabian Peninsula in the fifth and sixth centuries CE. If we assume that Islam is fledgling at this juncture since it had yet to be worked out theologically or doctrinally, why are we content to make Judaism normative? It is for ideological and not historical reasons that we project later Judaisms and Islams back onto the period in question. There was not, then, a clearly defined break between the two religions, one wherein certain beliefs and practices would have been easily identifiable as "Jewish" or Muslim." Rather, on my reading, both emerged at the same time, and often in ways that were indistinct from one another.

At the current moment, we lack both the conceptual and material tools to draw the boundaries between these two religions in the earliest period. We think we do, however, and this is why we fall back on the default language of "borrowing," "influence," or even "theft"—but it is always assumed that this movement is unidirectional from Judaism to Islam. My goal in this chapter—as it is in this study more generally—is to develop a vocabulary that allows us to account for this plurality and complexity in more accurate terms. This approach refuses to see Jew and Muslim, Judaism and Islam, as fully formed, bounded, and in the possession of discrete identities or essences.

Chapters 3 and 4 function as a diptych. They both argue, in a manner that inverts the dominant narrative, that the political and doctrinal instability associated with the early Islamic Empire functioned as a catalyst for Judaism from the very earliest period. Chapter 3 deals with the decades immediately following the death of Muhammad and examines an inchoate set of overlapping Islams that use a number of Jewish themes and motifs (e.g., messianism) without attribution or even awareness. Such Islamically underdefined social groups paradoxically created a number of diverse and equally underdefined Jewish responses that run the gamut from the apocalyptic to what would only later emerge as normative. This, once again, is a far cry from the regnant narrative that imagines a normative and stable Judaism on the Arabian Peninsula in the late antique period. This certainly does not rule out that a normative Judaism was being developed in the workshops associated with the rabbis in Babylonia. What it does mean, however, is that many scholars from the nineteenth century onward have put the proverbial cart before the proverbial horse and assumed that what was happening in Babylonia was simply and straightforwardly representative of the entire Jewish world.

Chapter 4 begins with the notion that after the rise of Islam and its political dominance in the region, Judaism was poorly or underdefined, with many groups exploring different paradigms of leadership and structures of authority. All of this was to change with the career of Saadya Gaon (882–942), who tried to establish a theological clarity when it came to what Judaism was or ought to be. In so doing, however, he adopted the literal (Arabic) and metaphorical (Kalāmic) language of Islam. This adoption, I suggest, facilitated the creation of an "Islamic Judaism." This was not only phenomenologically similar to what Muslim thinkers were creating at the same time, in the same place, and in response to similar threats to authority, but also historical in the sense that Judaism was fundamentally "Islamic" in its description and orientation.

Chapters 5 and 6 provide another diptych, this time dealing with the so-called and overused golden age trope of al-Andalus (Muslim Spain). As mentioned, my interest is less in ascertaining whether or not this was in fact a golden age than in examining its uses and the work to which this trope has and continues to be put. To this end, chapter 5 continues a discussion broached initially in chapter 1 about the often extracurricular needs of establishing a "golden age" to talk romantically about a past that will hopefully be future again. Only now the focus is on how "reason" played an integral part in this relationship. It begins by showing how and why nineteenth-century German-Jewish scholars created the trope of the "golden age" of Muslim Spain and how their construction has now largely become our truth. Just as nineteenth-century German scholars looked to the Orient as the place of intellectual repose, German-Jewish scholars did something similar when it came to Muslim Spain. The locus of al-Andalus now functioned as a utopia, the mirror inverse of their dystopian present.

Chapter 6 seeks to re-frame or redescribe this so-called golden age by arguing that Islam provided the intellectual and religious context for the florescence of Judaism at a formative moment in its development. In this, the context was little different from what went on in the late antique period. I doubt many would disagree with this premise. But I then go a step further and argue that the border separating Jew from Muslim in this period may still be more retrofitted from the present than real. To do this, I examine a number of key Jewish thinkers—Judah Halevi, Baḥya ibn Paqūda, Abraham ibn Ezra, Moses Maimonides—with the aim of showing how they continued to destabilize the line between Judaism and Islam. Even in the late twelfth century, in other words, we still have the existence of an "Islamic Judaism" subsequent to that fact that rabbinic Judaism had been historically overdetermined as normative. Indeed, so much so that rabbinic Judaism continued to absorb many elements of Islam to change not only its margins but also its center.

The conclusion takes us to the present. It begins with the erection of the "security barrier" (from the Israeli side) or the "apartheid wall" (from the Palestinian). It uses this structure as a way to think about the intersection of Judaism and Islam in the modern period. Although much of the analysis in previous chapters focused on the premodern period, it should be quite clear already that my premise is that we cannot get at the past except through our own present. Unfortunately, we all know too well what

"Jewish–Muslim relations" means at the current moment. While my goal is not to solve the unsolvable, it is to point out what I trust will have been obvious from previous chapters, namely, that Jews and Muslims continue to think from, with, and about the other.

Violence: From Taxonomic to Bloodshed

I am aware that I write at a time when the line between Jew and Muslim is perhaps more fixed and impermeable than it has ever been. When I wrote the first iteration of this Introduction in January 2016, the news had come out of Israel that a novel by the author Dorit Rabinyan, born to a Persian-Jewish family, entitled *Borderlife* had been disqualified for inclusion in the list of required reading for high school literature classes in Israel. The novel recounts the story of Liat, a translator from Tel Aviv, and Hilmi, a Palestinian artist from the West Bank, who meet in New York City and fall in love. According to the Israeli newspaper *Haaretz*, senior education ministry officials rejected the book for inclusion because "intimate relations between Jews and non-Jews, and certainly the option of formalizing them through marriage and having a family—even if it doesn't come to fruition in the story—is perceived by large segments of society as a threat to a separate identity."[29] The Israeli Education Ministry is but the latest iteration of border-makers who desire a firm boundary because they seek to imagine a purity that exists nowhere else than in their own mind.

Perceived threats to imagined identities form the mise en scène in which this study has taken shape. The violence that takes place daily along the borderlines separating Jews and Muslims has unfortunately become increasingly bloody and no longer simply discursive and taxonomic. The pages that follow trace the history of these borders from their complete absence to their subsequent origins in the need for self-definition to the erection of an "apartheid wall" that pays no heed to geographical boundaries. It is a tragic story, to be sure, but I retell it to remind us that Judaism and Islam, Jews and Muslims, have always been intimately intertwined with one another.

I

Symbiosis

RETHINKING A PARADIGM

IN A SPEECH to commemorate the official signing of the 1993 Oslo Accords in Washington, then President William Jefferson Clinton remarked,

> Let us resolve that this new mutual recognition will be a continuing process in which the parties transform the very way they see and understand each other. Let the skeptics of this peace recall what once existed among these people. There was a time when the traffic of ideas and commerce and pilgrims flowed uninterrupted among the cities of the Fertile Crescent. In Spain and the Middle East, Muslims and Jews once worked together to write brilliant chapters in the history of literature and science. All of this can come to pass again.[1]

I begin with this anecdote because it is illustrative of so much of the emotional and wistful longing that occurs when we put the terms "Judaism" and "Islam" or "Jewish" and "Muslim" in counterpoint. I am not aware of similar longings when we juxtapose other religions that have interacted closely and historically—say, Hinduism and Buddhism, or Christianity and Islam. Judaism and Islam for some reason seem to possess an interwoven narrative in our collective imagination with themes that are simultaneously scholarly, political, and romantic. Back "then," so this narrative goes, relations were better and the solution to today's problems between Muslim and Jew, Arab and Israeli, can be solved or at least better understood when set against the longue durée of their perceived historical cooperation.² Previous "historical" interaction would, in other words, seem to offer an antidote to today's problems.

Yet, how we choose to describe this interaction, including the descriptors we use to delineate it, are based less on the past than they are on the present. Metaphors lifted from the realm of biology to describe the interaction of species—for example, "symbiosis"[3] and "convergence"[4]—are frequently invoked. Moreover, terms that emphasize the decidedly irenic—such as "commensality,"[5] "*convivencia*,"[6] and even the universal sounding "Mediterranean"[7]—are used. All these terms are neither innocent nor value neutral. Rather, they betray the quest for an illusive essence behind a historical relationship that has been anything but stable. We seem to have no problem invoking the language of history, in other words, to make a non-historical point.

My goal in this first chapter is to think theoretically about how we have traditionally described the relationship between Muslim and Jew, Islam and Judaism. Whereas I shall argue in the following pages that there is a real fluidity, and thus perhaps no distinct border at all, up to and including the tenth century, many instead prefer to imagine an "interface," a "boundary marker," a "space" between species, or some other natural line of demarcation from the beginning. But, assuming for the moment, that such a border exists between them, can it be broached? Are there sentinels who patrol this border? Does it open and shut? Is it localized or general? For how we imagine or conceptualize this border subsequently dictates the terms, categories, and other metaphors that we use to analyze it. Instead of being a natural marker, I want to suggest that the "history" of the border between Judaism and Islam has primarily been interpretive and that what brings it into existence is a set of imaginative acts. Returning briefly to President Clinton's remarks in 1993, we see how the terms he uses (e.g., "mutual recognition," the two-way "traffic of ideas and commerce," the working and living "together"), in addition to the general contextual frame—a past that implies a "convivencia" or an "interfaith utopia," a dystopian present, and the hold out for some sort of messianic future that will revisit the distant past—all come from somewhere.[8] Clinton, in other words, did not conjure these concepts and terms of reference into existence. Rather, these terms and tropes, and the narratives into which they fit, all have histories and many of them were manufactured in scholarly workshops. Understanding these histories ought to aid us to think about the various ways in which these two religious traditions have been situated, contextualized, put in counterpoint or, again, whatever metaphorical language we care to use. Only by examining the genealogies of these terms and narratives will it hopefully be possible to reevaluate our traditional paradigms instead of assuming that they are axiomatic let alone descriptive.[9] Rather, we need to acknowledge that they are of our own making and remember that often they serve a number of politically and ideologically (and not necessarily academically) motivated ends. They must, as the chapters that follow seek to argue, be systematically rethought.[10]

My story in this opening chapter is a relatively modern one about the language we employ to think about boundaries. The "boundary," "interface," or whatever else we choose to call it in the present, is largely of our own construction. Even as late as the twelfth century, the great Maimonides (1135–1204) did not see himself as a "*Jewish* philosopher" writing something that we today problematically but all too easily refer to as "*Jewish* philosophy" in an Arab-Islamic environment. If anything, he seems to have seen himself as a *faylsūf*, a practitioner of *falsafa*, a way of trying to reconcile monotheism and Greek-inflected rationalism.[11] He was, in other words, someone who redefined what he imagined Judaism to be using the literal and metaphorical language of Islam. We could also say the same for the *mutakallim* (theologian) Saadya Gaon (882–942) or the *shāʿir* (poet) Moses ibn Ezra (ca. 1060–ca. 1138). If such towering medieval thinkers did not see a clear boundary between Judaism and Islam, why should we assume that those who preceded them in the late antique period, a period that witnessed even greater fluidity, be any different?

Antiquity

Although the reflection on the borderline between Judaism and Islam is, for the most part, a modern activity, we cannot deny that historically there certainly were Muslim and Jewish discussions of the Other, something that the following chapters will discuss in greater detail. Perhaps it should not surprise us that in Islam this discussion tended to be legal, and in Judaism exegetical. Muslims, in other words, were interested in defining the legal status of Jews and other non-Muslims (including Muslim heterodoxies) that they ruled over, whereas Jews were primarily interested in understanding why and how they were subservient. Yet, even this tells us but part of a much larger and more complex story. Prior to Judaism and Islam morphing into religions that could be imagined as distinct and discrete, there existed manifold and overlapping Muslim and Jewish subcultures that shared a common vocabulary and set of taxonomies. Aspects of these vocabularies and taxonomies could be emphasized or invoked as a way to make sense of selves and others in the light of the chaotic social worlds that coincided with Islam's ascendency in the mid-seventh century.[12]

Since my goal is less with historical interactions in this chapter than the manner in which such interactions have been interpreted in the present, allow me a few comments that I trust are relevant to my narrative—comments that will be picked up in subsequent chapters. As early as the Qur'ān, for example, we see the classification of "the Jews" with whom Muhammad had contact into factions: "a faction [tā'ifa] of the Banū Isrā'īl believed [in Jesus], and a faction disbelieved" (61:14). Such an utterance is revealing because it hints at the inchoate nature of "Jewish" belief on the Arabian Peninsula at the time of Muhammad.[13] Some Jews, according to this locution, believed in Jesus whereas other apparently did not. Why should we not assume, moreover, that some believed in the Torah of Moses and others did not or did so along with other oral teachings and traditions? Muslim heresiographers subsequently taxonomized Judaism (and Christianity and even their own tradition) based on the *ḥadīth* (saying) in which Muhammad said "The Jews are divided into seventy-one sects, the Christians into seventy-two; my community will be divided into seventy-three sects."[14] Such a *ḥadīth* seems to show a certain homology between Judaism and Islam, since the categories used to show Jewish heresies were not qualitatively different from those used to compose the heresiography of Muslims.[15] Within this broader context, it might be worth noting that Muslim heresiographers never shied away from trying to connect Muslim heterodoxies to what they considered to be historical Jewish individuals—the *ghulāt* tendency to deify Ali in Shī'ism was traced to the Jew, Abd Allah ibn Sabā';[16] the origins of Ismā'īlism to Maymūn al-Qaddahm;[17] the idea of the "created" Qur'ān to Labīd,[18] and so on.

Unlike their Muslim counterparts, Jews did not classify or categorize the various Islams they encountered. Perhaps this is because the project of comparison—or, at least, comparative religion—is often the conceit of the dominant group. This is not unlike the way Protestant Christianity positions itself in the contemporary field of religious studies by providing a set of guidelines by which other religions measure themselves or are measured by others.[19] "The discipline of comparative religion," to use the words of David Chidester speaking about the rise of comparative religion in the context of southern Africa in the nineteenth century, emerged "not only out of the Enlightenment heritage but also out of a ... history of colonial conquest and domination."[20]

Wissenschaft des Judentums

My concern in the present chapter is less with medieval heresiologists and theologians than it is with how—and why—we take our modern constructions of the perceived border between Judaism and Islam and then imagine it retroactively in past times and places. This is not a completely modern phenomenon, however. Indeed, its origins would seem to date to the formation of Jewish Studies (*Wissenschaft des Judentums*) as an academic discipline in Germany in the middle of the nineteenth century.[21] Our forbearers, in other words, established the narrative and it should come as little surprise, given our collective inheritance that still largely structures our understanding of Judaism in the academy, that we continue to envision the relationship between these two religions as predominantly positive. Not infrequently this involves reproducing the trope of Judaism as a midwife and that of some sort of "interfaith utopia" in places like the "golden age" of Muslim Spain. Although the non-Jewish Hebraist Franz Delitzsch was the first to coin the term "golden age" to refer to Muslim Spain,[22] Jewish scholars subsequently picked it up as a counterpoint to the traditionalism and talmudism that, for them, characterized so much of nineteenth-century European Jewry.[23] Alienated from their own tradition, lacking political emancipation in Germany, positive Jewish–Muslim relations—at the time of Muhammad and then later in Muslim Spain, among other places—began to symbolize romantically all that their home in Germany was not.[24]

This newly created "golden age" could then be used to perform a great deal of intellectual heavy lifting. It could show, on the one hand, non-Jewish Germans the heights to which Jews could aspire with political emancipation and, on the other, it could show Jewish contemporaries, whom the young scholars associated with the new Wissenschaft movement accused of being backward and overly legalistic, the beauty of their own tradition.[25] Reconstituted medievals such as Judah Halevi, Shlomo ibn Gabirol, and Moses Maimonides became mirrors onto which a generation of German-Jewish scholars—Abraham Geiger, Heinrich Graetz, Moritz Steinschneider, among others—projected and subsequently saw their own reflections. Many of these scholars, influenced by the then newly created denominations within Judaism, were interested, simultaneously, in reforming Judaism and creating a positive Jewish identity.[26]

Heinrich Graetz (1817–1891), for example, could write of the Jews at the time of Muhammad:

> Wearied with contemplating the miserable plight of the Jews in their ancient home and in the countries of Europe, and fatigued by the constant sight of fanatical oppression, the eyes of the observer rest with gladness upon their situation in the Arabian peninsula. Here the sons of Judah were free to raise their heads, and did not need to look about them with fear and humiliation, lest the ecclesiastical wrath be discharged upon them, or the secular power overwhelm them. Here they were not shut out from the paths of honor, nor excluded from the privileges of the state, but, untrammelled, were allowed to develop their powers in the midst of a free, simple, and talented people to show their manly courage, to compete for the gifts of fame, and with practiced hand to measure swords with their antagonists.[27]

In like manner he could wax poetic about the Jews who lived in al-Andalus. Like him and his generation, these Jews

> were not narrow specialists. . . . If not poets themselves, they found pleasure in the rhythmic composition of the new Hebrew poesy. . . . The prominent men, who, either through their political position or their merits stood at the head of Jewish affairs in Spain, were for the most part noble characters imbued with the highest sentiments. . . . Their religious life was elevated and idealized through this higher culture.[28]

Here Graetz compares the *mentalité* of the medieval Sephardic Jews with the manly honor of Bedouin-like Jews found on the Arabian Peninsula in the sixth century. Both sets of Jews possessed aesthetic and rational sensibilities that were "imbued with the highest sentiments." They were proud and religious, but their religious motivations were not fanatical (as they were among contemporaneous—read: Ashkenazic—Jews); rather, they were informed by the "higher culture" in which they lived and which they helped to produce. Untouched by the "bad" traits of late antique (Christian) persecution, medieval obscurantism, or the flights of fancy of kabbalah, these "good" Jews could be constructed as "just like us." In his 1878 history of the Jewish people, Samuel Bäck (1834–1912), wrote that the medieval Spanish Jews

> cultivated all areas of intellectual activity and nevertheless maintained a steadfast fidelity to their religion; they observed every statute that the Bible and the Talmud prescribed, and never forgot that they were Jews. These Spanish Jews occupied the highest state offices and yet adhered lovingly to Judaism; these Jewish scholars immersed themselves in the depths of philosophy and were also familiar with the most secret branches of the Talmud. Jewish physicians, travelers, and merchants maintained a love and zeal for Jewish scholarship.[29]

This seems to be more about wishful thinking in the present than anything historical.[30] Just as Germans were attracted to a romanticized notion of "the Orient," German-Jews used the same language to rhapsodize about the "Sephardim," that is the Spanish Jews and their descendants.[31] Although German-Jews were themselves Ashkenazic, they imagined the "Sephardic experience" that glorified the philosophical, cultural, aesthetic, and theological superiority of Spanish Jews who thrived under the orbit of Islam. In the non-scholarly world, this coincided with the rise of Moorish-styled synagogues in places like Leipzig, Cologne, Frankfurt, Mainz, Budapest, Berlin, and Vienna.[32] Sephardic style liturgy replaced what was considered to be the artless and, by extension, unedifying prayer books associated with Ashkenazic practice. In the scholarly Jewish world, it saw the creation of critical editions of texts by individuals now imagined and constructed as the great medieval rationalists, the creation of good Judaism (which was rational and philosophical, never mystical nor Kabbalistic), and the rise of terms and narratives to describe Jewish florescence under Islam.[33] We continue, for a variety of reasons, to recycle much of this in the present.

This romantic narrative—invented by a group of German-Jewish scholars for a number of internal reasons, most of which had nothing whatsoever to do with Muslims or any particular historical period—will, as we shall see in what follows, become the dominant narrative that we have inherited to describe Jewish–Muslim relations. It is the one that Clinton recycled and one that we continue to use in the classroom and even in our scholarship. Framed simply: Jews did well under Islam and not so well under Christianity, until, of course, the twentieth century sets in and we near 1948, when matters begin to deteriorate.

Goitein's Symbiosis

A conduit of sorts between the German-Jewish scholarship associated with Wissenschaft des Judentums and that movement's new home in the United States was Shlomo Dov Goitein (1900–1985).[34] Goitein was trained at the University of Frankfurt under the famed Arabist Josef Horovitz, writing his doctoral dissertation on prayer in Islam, before immigrating to Palestine with Gershom Scholem in 1923.[35] He subsequently founded the School of Asian and African Studies at the Hebrew University in Jerusalem, and the Israel Oriental Society, with his main research focus being the language and culture of the Jews of Yemen, a relationship that, for him, constituted "the most genuine Jews living amongst the most genuine Arabs."[36]

In 1948 he began his work on the Cairo Geniza, which saw him leave Israel and move to the United States, first to the University of Pennsylvania and then to the Institute for Advanced Study at Princeton.[37] It was his pioneering work on the Geniza documents—written by Jews in an Arabophone environment primarily between the ninth and thirteenth centuries—that showed on a local as opposed to just an intellectual level the social and economic integration of Jews within their surrounding Muslim environment in those regions in and bordering the Mediterranean. He considered this to be a universalist culture, one that Muslims, Jews, and others shared, and to which he gave the name, in his six-volume magnum opus, *A Mediterranean Society*, subtitled *The Jewish Communities of the Arab World as Portrayed in the Documents of the Cairo Genizah*.

Based on his work with the Geniza documents, Goitein coined the term "symbiosis" to describe the relationship between Jews and Muslims. This term subsequently became part of the dominant narrative used to describe the interaction of Jews and Muslims. It has been picked up, for example, by Bernard Lewis in his *The Jews of Islam* (1984) and recycled,[38] in one way or another, by Goitein's own students. Goitein borrowed "symbiosis" from the field of biology where it is used to refer to the close and often long-term interaction between two distinct biological species. It is a trope, moreover, that has a distinctly positive and irenic valence, as opposed to say its biological antonym "parasitic." As far as I can tell, Goitein never taxonomized "symbiosis," but perhaps we can. There are at least three different types of symbiotic relationships: *mutualism*, where both the symbiont and host, or the two symbionts, benefit; *commensalism*, where the symbiont benefits with little effect on the host; and *parasitism*, where the symbiont benefits to the detriment of the host. What does "symbiosis" allow Goitein to do? Unfortunately, he neither problematizes nor theorizes the term, at least in ways that a professional religionist might like. It seems to just exist for him, and it does so, moreover, in a manner that implies "mutualism," that is, a *mutually beneficial* relationship between the symbiont and the host. There are certainly other biological metaphors he could have used, like evolution or co-evolution, if in fact religions evolve or history is teleological. In co-evolution, according to Wasserstrom, we have a "stochastic system of evolutionary change in which two or more species interact in such a way that changes in species A set the stage for the natural selection of changes in species B. Later changes in species B, in turn, set the stage for the selecting of more similar changes in species A."[39]

If we retain the trope of symbiosis, and I am not at all convinced that we should, we need to ascertain what constitutes both "mutual" and "beneficial?" Maybe a better term for this process, one with less wistful baggage, is Hodgson's "Islamicate," although even this term assumes a symbiotic relationship predicated on commensalism.[40] All of these models, moreover, work on the assumption that Judaism and Islam are two distinct species. My argument here is that they are not, and that both developed in tandem with one another and using a common structure and vocabulary. What would eventually become two distinct and discrete religions—Judaism and Islam—took considerable time to coalesce and in such a manner that each gained definition from, with, and by the other. What is decidedly not the case, and this is the assumption of many who reproduce the "symbiosis" thesis, is the interaction of two fully developed religions that, although sharing certain superficial phenomena (language, literature), retained their separate essences.

Goitein, it seems, was attracted to the concept of "symbiosis" because it facilitated a conceptual framework that preserved Judaism's unique features, its ahistorical essence, within a dominant culture while still enabling Jews to be full participants within it. The Jewish–Arab/Muslim symbiosis, however, was not the only symbiotic relationship of which Goitein spoke. He distinguished it, for example, from the "Greek–Jewish symbiosis," which occurred in the Greek New Testament and in Philo of Alexandria;[41] and what he called the symbiosis between Jews and "the Romanic and Germanic peoples," which lasted for over a thousand years, and reached its climax around 1900.⁴² These other two symbioses differ in kind from the Arab/Muslim–Jewish version, however, because they have not "influenced the personal inner life of every Jew to the profound degree as did the great Jewish writers who belonged to the medieval civilization of Arab Islam."⁴³ "The reason for this is self-evident," he could write, because "modern Western civilization, like the ancient civilization of the Greeks, is essentially at variance with the religious culture of the Jewish people. Islam, however, is from the very flesh and bone of Judaism."⁴⁴ Or, again: "Judaism could draw freely and copiously from Muslim civilization and, at the same time, preserve its independence and integrity far more completely than it was able to do in the modern world or in the Hellenistic society of Alexandria."⁴⁵

Goitein envisaged the symbiotic relationship between these two "species" as one of mutualism, albeit at two very different stages in the historical record. In the late antique period, a nascent or fledgling Islam needed Judaism for its genesis on the Arabian Peninsula. Then, several hundred years later, Judaism needed Islam to thrive. To use his own words: "During the first half of which Muslim religion and Arab nationhood took form under Jewish impact, while in the second half traditional Judaism received its final shape under Muslim-Arab influence."⁴⁶ Let me take up briefly each of these in turn since my study is an attempt to nudge us beyond it. The first stage of this symbiotic relationship occurred in Muhammad's Arabia, when it would seem, for Goitein as for so many others, Judaism functioned as the "midwife" for the birth of Islam.⁴⁷ He describes Islam as "an Arab recast of Israel's religion."⁴⁸ Like so many others, however, Goitein makes Judaism into something stable, already articulated, and well defined in the sixth century Ḥijāz. This Jewish conceit creates the basic and still largely regnant model wherein Jews shape Islam, and the Qur'ān simply recycles midrashim and other Jewish literature of the period. It is a model, however, that always assumes that the influence moves in one direction. But who, as the next chapter asks, were these "Jews?" What did "Jew" signify in sixth-century Arabia? We have to be cautious of assuming an orthodoxy of stable Jewish identity and practice based upon what the rabbinic academies of Babylonia were producing at this time. What "Arab Jewishness" consisted of, in other words, might have looked considerably different than other forms of Jewishness in the larger context of the Mediterranean basin.⁴⁹

In the second phase, according to Goitein, the direction shifts and we now see the influence of medieval Islam upon Judaism. Now "the vital contributions made by the cultural elements inherent in one civilization [that is, Islam] to the autonomous spiritual life of the other."[50] This second-phase of the symbiotic relationship was characterized by (1) the use of Arabic, which led to Arabic ways of thinking and forms of literature, "as well as of Muslim religious notions";[51] (2) the rise of Jewish philosophy, which reveals "the impact of Muhammadan spiritual life on the Jewish mind";[52] (3) mysticism; and (4) Hebrew poetry, which he calls "the acme of Jewish-Arab symbiosis."[53] "The Hebrew poet," Goitein writes, "could draw in full measure from a civilization which was closely akin to his own, while at the same time cherishing a strong transcendental belief in the mission of Israel."[54] Sometimes, as with poetry, for example, he will argue that the Jews had it first, that is, before the advent of Islam, and that the Muslim interest in ornate speech only reentered Judaism in the high Middle Ages.[55] The anxiety of influence and the politics of who had what first, are never far from the surface in this literature. And while "Judaism" becomes, on Goitein's reading, a midwife to the birth of Islam, the best that Islam can do for Judaism is to function as a mnemonic, a reminder of its poetic and democratic birthright. It is not at all clear to me, however, that medieval Jewish poets, philosophers, belletrists, or others clearly distinguished between what was "Jewish" and what was "Islamic" in ways that we do today, post-1948.

Convergence and Commensality

In the editorial introduction to their 2011 *The Convergence of Judaism and Islam*, Michael M. Laskier and Yaakov Lev try to avoid the term "symbiosis" and instead opt for "convergence" to describe the relationship between Judaism and Islam.[56] Although they never really define, let alone theorize, what they mean by the term, we can. Convergence, perhaps not coincidentally, is also a biological term, one that refers to the process whereby unrelated species, often geographically distant from one another, evolve superficially homologous characteristics based on similar biomes or environmental conditions. New world monkeys, porcupines, tree-anteaters, marsupial opossums, and chameleons, for example, all share the trait of prehensility in their tails despite the fact that they are all unrelated to one another. Similarly, koalas of Australasia and humans have evolved fingerprints that are indistinguishable from one another. Again, we might ask the question: Why are we so attracted to biological metaphors, especially those predicated on the interrelationships between species, to describe Jewish–Muslim relations?

If we are going to employ such biological metaphors, however, we must be aware of the ramifications and the full array of cognitive or intellectual assumptions that they bring to the analysis. I worry, however, that this is rarely done. If we follow through on the implications of "convergence," something that Laskier and Lev never do, it would seem to be that while Judaism and Islam are unrelated, they developed similar characteristics independent of one another. This model, however, is no less difficult to endorse because, without getting into contemporary theological categories such as "Abrahamic," there is little evidence that there was independent development. Maimonides, for example, read Arab-Muslim philosophers and engaged in *falsafa* in a way that was very much dependent on Muslims. He did not, in other words, develop his theory of, for example, prophecy independently of Muslim philosophers such as Alfarabi or Avicenna.[57] "Convergence," like "symbiosis," is an ahistorical term that we have tried to make perform historical work.

Laskier and Lev have also edited a companion volume to the aforementioned, *The Divergence of Islam*, which would seem to imply a different metaphoric orientation.[58] Once again, though, they are not interested in the semantic fallout of their choice of metaphors. Presumably they invoke the trope of "divergence" as the opposite of their previous volume's "convergence," and as a way to signal the so-called parting of the ways between Judaism and Islam after a certain period that, for them, is tantamount to "the end of the nineteenth century to the onset of the third millennium."[59] They fail to note, though, that once again their term is not something that exists naturally in the world and thus has to be theorized or, at the very least, they need to show both the heuristic utility and/or cognitive relevance of transcribing a biological metaphor onto a religious study register. In biology, genetic divergence is used to speak of ancestral species that develop genetic mutations independent of one another across time, after they have become isolated from one another. In ophthalmology, to use another example, "divergence" signifies the simultaneous outward movement of both eyes away from each other, with the aim of maintaining single binocular vision when viewing an object. If we followed through with what the metaphor implies, it would seem to suggest that the two religions move away from one another involuntarily in order that they may create a single and better vision. Binocular vision is, after all, more effective than monocular vision.

Laskier and Lev show the danger of not thinking through the range of meanings when it comes to the metaphors we choose to describe the relations between Jews and Muslims. Such metaphors are not mere poetic indulgences or window dressing; rather, they simultaneously structure and produce the "facts" we choose to emphasize or, as the case may be, simply ignore. The transference of such metaphors from the realm of biology to the study of religions may very well obscure or taint our understanding of the latter. Perhaps unconsciously aware of this, midway through their introduction to their first volume, on convergence, they switch metaphors, and invoke that of "commensality." They write that

> At the same time, however, we contend that the positive convergence was not consistently idyllic. . . . While not denying the vitality of Goitein's "symbiosis," we [propose] the term *commensality* . . . as being a more suitable expression of coexistence derived from mutually advantageous gains.[60]

In one paragraph, we see the editors move, simultaneously, from "convergence" to "symbiosis" to "commensality." Although we have not seen commensality invoked hitherto, we have seen that "commensalism" is one type of symbiosis, namely, a class of relationship between two organisms where only one organism benefits without affecting the other. The organism that does not benefit is presumably neutral. Sociologically, however, "commensality" refers to the practice of eating together, something that definitely has irenic or, *pace* Laskier and Lev, "idyllic" overtones, and is related to the notion of *convivencia*, which I shall discuss next. I have spent some time with their two rather uneven volumes not because of their contents but because they are exemplary of the cognitive problems associated with framing metaphors.

Convivencia

The term *convivencia*, or "coexistence," is another term that has been used, especially in recent years, to describe Jewish–Muslim (and often Christian) relations in the premodern world, especially in the so-called golden age of Muslim Spain. Although avoiding the biological language of the interaction of species, it nevertheless has a distinctly irenic dimension to it. It implies a period of religious tolerance in the past that can be neatly contrasted with our own present-day religious intolerance, especially in the post-9/11 period. Américo Castro (1885–1972) first used the term in his 1948 *The Spaniards*, which was subsequently translated into English in 1971.[61] Castro used *convivencia* to describe what he considered to be the everyday interactions between Jews, Christians, and Muslims. Although an invented term, it subsequently became part of Spanish academic vocabulary as attested by the term's perhaps uncoincidental inclusion in the 2001 dictionary produced by the Real Academia Española, which defines it simply as "acción de convivir" (the act of living together).[62]

Perhaps the most forceful use of the term may be found in the late María Rosa Menocal's award-winning 2003 *The Ornament of the World: How Muslims, Jews and Christians Created a Culture of Tolerance in Medieval Spain*.[63] We would do well to remember, however, that "tolerance," at least as we have come to understand it in the West since the time of John Locke, was not necessarily a virtue in earlier periods and in other places. To quote Bernard Lewis's forthright statement, "For Christians and Muslims alike, tolerance is a new virtue, intolerance a new crime. For the greater part of the history of both communities, tolerance was not valued nor was intolerance condemned."[64] Despite his warning, many insist on searching for better times and better places for the existence of interfaith dialogue (another modern concept). For Menocal, the antidote to our contemporary "clash of civilizations" is an imagined al-Andalus, which she describes as nourished by a "complex culture of tolerance," something that she subsequently associates with a distinctly "Andalusian ethic."[65] Such an ethic, as nostalgic as it is invented, is meant to stimulate interest in examining the past as present or, simultaneously, the present as past. If we could only escape our present age of intolerance, so the narrative goes, we might be able to return to a future that is past again.[66]

The Third Term

The history of the study of religions is full of covert apologetical agendas in the service of the comparative enterprise. Whether it be the traditional comparisons of Christianity and Judaism in late antiquity, Protestantism and Catholicism in the early modern period, or more recent attempts to compare a liberal Islam with more militant versions—we must remind ourselves that none of these have been or even remain purely intellectual activities. On the contrary, all have invoked extra-historical terms or categories to show that one of these terms, often the first of the aforementioned, is superior to the other. Comparison, in other words, tends to revolve around ontology and ontological uniqueness as opposed to simple intellectual interest or taxonomical concern. Indeed, one could even go so far to say that much comparison in the field of religious studies has, since the formation of our discipline, used Protestant Christianity as its lodestar.[67] Comparison is thus a potentially deeply flawed endeavor despite the fact that it plays such a central role in the discipline of religious studies. No comparison is natural—it is always done for a reason—and making ourselves and our readers aware of our intentions and the reasons behind our engagement with the comparative enterprise is both important and necessary. One of the most recent and articulate theorists of comparison is J. Z. Smith, who argues that every comparison (x is like y) implies, but rarely receives, a third term (with respect to z). This means that, for Smith, comparison is not based on natural affinity or even historical process, but personal utility. He argues that "the statement of comparison is never dyadic, but always triadic; there is always an implicit 'more than,' and there is always a 'with respect to.' In the case of an academic comparison, the 'with respect to' is most frequently the scholar's interest, be this expressed in a question, a theory, or a model."[68]

Every comparison, on Smith's analysis, requires a third term for its successful execution. "A," for example, can never simply be the same as or like "B." "A" can only be similar to "B" with respect to "C." It should probably come as no surprise that the hidden third term in comparing Jews and Muslims is often Christianity. That is, we always work on the assumption that Jewish–Muslim relations, at least in the premodern period, are necessarily better than Jewish–Christian ones with respect to concepts such as tolerance and persecution. While Jews and Muslims, so the narrative goes, were sitting down at the same table in a symbiotic relationship, Christians were persecuting Jews as Christ-killers, money lenders, and so on.[69] Such a comparison, however, not only ignores the cultural, intellectual, and religious florescence of Ashkenazic Jews,[70] it also reduces the Christian–Jewish relationship, especially in the medieval period, to one that is drenched in blood.[71] Perhaps not surprisingly this construction, the polar opposite of the "golden age" of the medieval Jewish–Muslim encounter, is also the product of those associated with Wissenschaft des Judentums. Heinrich Graetz, someone we have already encountered, could neatly differentiate, for example, between "the Church" and "the [Moorish-inspired] Synagogue,"

> The Church was the seat of monastic ignorance and barbarity, the Synagogue was the place of science and civilization. In Christianity every scientific effort was condemned by the officials of the Church as well as by the people as the work of Satan; in Judaism the leaders and teachers of religion themselves promoted science, and endeavored to elevate the people.[72]

Bernard Lewis in his important survey *The Jews of Islam* picks this motif up and, writes, for example, that in Jewish–Muslim relations

> there is little sign of any deep-rooted emotional hostility directed against Jews—or for that matter any other group—such as the anti-Semitism of the Christian world. ... On the whole, in contrast to Christian anti-Semitism, the Muslim attitude toward non-Muslims is not [one] of hate or fear or envy but simply of contempt.[73]

Caught between a "clash of two civilizations,"[74] Lewis maintains that Jews fared better under Islam.[75] "With few exceptions," writes Lewis, "whatever was creative and significant in Jewish life happened in Islamic lands. The Jewish communities of Europe formed a kind of cultural dependency on the Jews of the far more advanced and sophisticated Islamic world, extending from Muslim Spain in the west to Iraq, Iran, and Central Asia in the east."[76] For Lewis, as indeed for so many, medieval Islam becomes synonymous with Jewish creativity, whereas medieval Christianity is tantamount to religious persecution.

In an attempt to counter this narrative, predicated as it is on aesthetic as opposed to historical considerations, Susan L. Einbinder remarks that a

> bias has prevented scholars from seeing the liturgical poetry from Rhenish or northern French communities as either beautiful (meriting attention for its literary excellence) or cultured (defined largely as a secular term). This bias was reinforced by an underlying sense that communities under siege could hardly have been characterized by a thriving or vital degree of interaction with the cultural developments around them. Certainly persecution and social disruption are not recipes for flourishing literary creativity. But we would do well to remember that violence against the Jewish communities of northern Europe was sporadic and rarely dealt a deathblow to

an entire local population. In the end, the systematic policies of harassment, repression, and ultimately expulsion had more of a deleterious effect than isolated outbreaks of violence on literary and cultural activity.[77]

Again our historical preference for Jewish–Muslim relations revolves around our own aesthetic demands. If medieval Jewish belles-lettres was constructed as "secular" and "nationalistic," medieval Ashkenazic literature was signified as "religious" and "liturgical." The latter was produced by anonymous individuals, whereas the former are associated with the "great men" of Judaism, such as Shlomo ibn Gabirol, Moshe ibn Ezra, Judah Halevi, and Moses Maimonides. Such terms, however, are our own—terms that we have inherited from our nineteenth-century German-Jewish predecessors and terms that we still largely buy into, as even the quickest glance at a program from the Annual Meeting of the Association for Jewish Studies (AJS) should reveal.[78] The Andalusi standard was and continues to be upheld as aesthetically superior. This is why we have critical edition upon critical edition, translation upon translation, of Andalusi works but relatively few from medieval Ashkenaz. Whereas the Judeo-Arabic material is assumed to show Judaism at its most universal or open to other cultures, the other assumption is that the Jewish poetry produced in Christian lands was internal, particularistic, and not in conversation with neighboring Christian motifs and forms. Why would Jews, so it is assumed, use the forms of expression popular among their persecutors? We are only now—thanks to the work of people like Einbinder, Fudeman, among others—beginning to realize that patterns of influence are more complicated.

Medieval Jewish philosophy, the area in which I was trained, is another case in point. Far too many studies work on the assumption that it was the Jews of Islam that did all the important philosophical work, and that the rest is but a series of footnotes produced by Maimonidean epigones.[79] Within this context, we have examined ad nauseam the intersection between medieval Islamic philosophy, on the one hand, and medieval Jewish philosophy, on the other, and, in the process, have largely excluded the intersection between, say, medieval scholasticism and Jewish philosophy. We know a tremendous amount about Maimonides and his relationship to Alfarabi and Avicenna, for example, but relatively little when it comes to, say, Isaac Pulcher's or Abner of Burgos's relationship to Christian philosophy in Castile, not to mention Provençe and other places.

To the End of the Land

Lewis ends his *The Jews of Islam* in the 1940s with (1) a discussion of Ḥajj Amīn al-Ḥusaynī, the mufti of Jerusalem, and his desire for German-Arab cooperation to achieve the ominous sounding "common ends"; and (2) anti-Jewish violence in Arab countries such as Iraq, Syria, Egypt, southern Arabia, and northern Africa.[80] The establishment of the State of Israel in 1948 signals for Lewis the slamming shut of a vital and creative period in Jewish history. What is left are a set of memories and a relationship that, for Lewis at least, seems to be marked by tension and bloodshed.[81]

Lewis's cynicism has been picked up by a host of scholars, whom Mark Cohen labels "neo-lachrymose."[82] Several individuals have modified Lewis's carefully expressed ideas; however, their political motivations are much more overt and a direct reflection of present anxieties over Islam. The American-Israel Public Affairs Committee (AIPAC), for example, issued a "Myths and Facts" supplement in its *Near East Report* just after the Six-Day War in 1967 to let readers know that Jewish–Muslim relations were not what many assumed them to be.[83] The historian of the Holocaust, Saul S. Friedman, whose obituary refers to him as a "tireless advocate of the Jewish community" and "a leader in the Youngstown [OH] chapter of the Zionist Organization of America,"[84] writes of the "fable of the Semitic brotherhood." Writing in 1970, he argues that "current Arab propaganda insists that the basic cause of antagonism between Jews and Arabs is political Zionism, which is depicted as a fanaticism born of European persecution that has destroyed a Middle Eastern harmony hitherto existing for a thousand years."[85] This is repeated by numerous historians, including Cecil Roth, who warned Jews of romanticizing the "halcyon days under the pallid light of the Crescent [and] of the purgatory in the shadow of the Cross."[86] Interesting, Roth located the real Jewish "golden age" not in Muslim Spain, but in the Italian Renaissance.[87] One of the more recent iterations of this approach is Dario Fernandez-Morera's *The Myth of Andalusian Paradise*, which, complete with blurbs on the back from the likes of Daniel Pipes, provides subheadings saturated in modern and far from value-neutral terminology: "The Destruction of a Nascent Civilization"; "Inquisitions, Beheadings, Impalings, and Crucifixions"; and "Female Circumcision, Stoning, Veils, and Sexual Slavery." In such hands, the "golden age" is now transformed into Islamic dystopian fiction that, while set in the past, does little more than represent an Islamophobe's worst fears for the future.

Conclusions

We primarily talk about Muslim–Jewish relations in the modern world and, with especial urgency, in the years post-1948. Medieval Jews and Muslims certainly thought about one another, but, for the most part, they did not erect a grand theory of "symbiosis and parasitism" or "convergence and divergence" to make sense of their interactions. All of these latter terms, to reiterate, are modern and imported from the realm of biology to explain the interaction of species. Why do we insist on using such terms? The answer, as I have tried to show here, has something to do with a need that frequently has very little to do with scholarship. They allow us to construct a narrative—things were better in the past and can become so again, if we appreciate that past—that offers us (as scholars, as journalists, as politicians, and so on) hope that there is a way out of the current malaise. Like all grand narratives, however, it conceals as much as it reveals.

I certainly do not wish to deny the many important works—by Goitein, by his students, by their students, and others—dealing with specific Geniza or other texts or on the social, economic, religious, and intellectual interactions between Jews and Muslims. The data that they study is important and illuminating. My goal is, quite simply, to get us to think more broadly about the general terms and rhetorical moves used to frame their specific studies and, for us in religious studies, to engage and interpret their rich studies. Twenty years after Wasserstrom's path-breaking study, I still agree with his assessment that "Jewish-Islamic scholarship in general . . . infrequently deals directly with fundamental questions in the critical study of religion."[88] My goal in what follows is to make these interactions into an intellectual problem that ought to concern those of us in religious studies, regardless of whether we are scholars of Judaism or Islam or both.

2

Origins

THE PAST LOOMS large in our imaginations. It functions as a reminder of whence we came as it simultaneously holds out hope for what might again be.[1] In these imaginative acts, antiquity is not infrequently coupled with an assumed authenticity, both of which are used to adumbrate a past that is as sanitized as it is fictive. Bookended between beginnings and ends, we ask of history that which it cannot possibly provide: a model or a paradigm for the future.[2] Yet, the sheer weight of the historical record betrays the complexity of the past and ought to undermine our confidence in the project of a strict historicism. The past, in other words, is never simply nor solely about the past, but almost always about the present. We frequently map histories from the vantage point of our unmoored present so that beginnings masquerade as ends, and vice versa. This anachronism means that we imagine a point, located in the distant past, upon which is projected any number of presently constructed virtues. Origins become a mnemonic necessary for self-understanding just as they illumine the path for self-preservation into the future.

Perhaps on account of the geopolitical moment in which we currently find ourselves, Muslim–Jewish relations are not infrequently bound up with a putative sibling rivalry between Isaac and Ishmael. Their shared patrimony and their subsequent estrangement provide a neat and tidy story that explains the current animosity between those who define themselves alternatively as Jew and Muslim or as Israeli and Arab. Despite the antagonism, such a story nevertheless holds out hope for some sort of future reconciliation between these two sons of the patriarch of all monotheisms, Abraham. Those who desire biblical models against which to situate the present find comfort in this "Abrahamic" descent of Judaism and Islam.[3] The terror of history, the backdrop against which Jewish–Muslim relations take place and through which they are presumed to have devolved, can now be neatly bypassed through such ahistorical categories and narratives.[4] The incandescence of ahistory is thus used to illumine the dark and cavernous aspects of history. The quest for the originary, that moment of imagined repose, functions as a type of modern authorization to recall the traces, inherited or invented, of the past.[5]

So when did Jewish–Muslim relations originate? The answer to such a question is dependent upon the person, the need, and the desired outcome. Some want, as we have just seen, to put their origins mythically in biblical times.[6] This is problematic for a number of reasons. First, their common origin in the progeny of Abraham, while tidy, is historically problematic. Second, Ishmael, assuming for the moment that he actually existed, was not a Muslim, since Islam as a historical force does not enter the stage of world history until Muhammad in the sixth century CE. The more historically minded want to put the origins of Muslim–Jewish relations more sensibly in the late antique period at the time of Muhammad. The latter's appeal to being more historical, however, is quickly undermined. Implicit in the late sixth/early seventh century CE dating is the superiority of Judaism (or alternatively Judeo-Christianity), now imagined as stable and normative, and the inferiority of Islam, which it is assumed can be reduced to the sum of its monotheistic parts. This usually takes the form of the question, so succinctly put by Abraham Geiger in his 1833 doctoral dissertation: "Was hat Mohammed aus dem Judenthume aufgenommen?" Namely, "What did Muhammad take from the Jews?"[7]

Both of these models—let us call them the "Abrahamic" and the "larcenous"—nevertheless prove problematic. While the latter would seem to be more historical than the former, situated as it is in real as opposed to biblical time, it is equally bound up in essentialism. As this chapter seeks to explain in greater detail, however, if we are to rethink the dominant paradigm concerning the origins of Jewish–Muslim relations, we first have to wade through the political uses for which these origin narratives have been deployed. In particular, there has been a systematic attempt since the emergence of German-Jewish Orientalists in the nineteenth century to try to show how Islam derived from Judaism.[8] The latter, it is assumed, is the stable entity that produces from its own loins a fledgling Islam.[9] Lost in this discussion, which still largely functions as the normative account of the origins of Islam, is just how little we actually know about the Jews of the Arabian Peninsula in the fifth and sixth centuries CE.[10] Before I examine the problems that the Jews of Arabia present us, let me first take up the other regnant paradigm, that of sibling rivalry. Though ahistorical, it still performs a great deal of intellectual work, to which the recently invented term "Abrahamic religions" should alert us.[11]

The "Abrahamic" Paradigm

This paradigm usually takes the form of one of two narratives. For the sake of convenience, allow me to label them as the phenomenological and the historical. The phenomenological approach begins with the notion that Judaism and Islam (and, of course, Christianity) are so-called Abrahamic religions.[12] This usually involves the assumption that Jews and Muslims developed a strong notion of covenant between their prophetic figures (Moses and Muhammad) and Abraham. In Judaism, Abraham's willingness to enter into a covenantal relationship with God, symbolized by the physical act of circumcision, established a promise of land and of peoplehood. This was handed down from Abraham to Isaac, from Isaac to Jacob, from Jacob to his twelve sons, and from them to the ancient Israelites and then to the Jewish people. In Islam, the situation is similar: the relationship between Abraham and Muhammad—through Ishmael, to be discussed shortly—is foundational since, as a direct descendent of Abraham, Muhammad is given access to prophecy.[13]

The other narrative, not content to have such a vague or nebulous framework, actively seeks to show "historical" connections between the two religions, by returning, among other things, to the Genesis narrative. There we read,

> Now Sarai, Abram's wife, had borne him no children. But she had an Egyptian slave named Hagar; so she said to Abram, "The Lord has kept me from having children. Go, sleep with my slave; perhaps I can build a family through her." Abram agreed to what Sarai said. So after Abram had been living in Canaan ten years, Sarai his wife took her Egyptian slave Hagar and gave her to her husband to be his wife. He slept with Hagar, and she conceived. When she knew she was pregnant, she began to despise her mistress. Then Sarai said to Abram, "You are responsible for the wrong I am suffering. I put my slave in your arms, and now that she knows she is pregnant, she despises me. May the Lord judge between you and me." "Your slave is in your hands," Abram said. "Do with her whatever you

think best." Then Sarai mistreated Hagar; so she fled from her. The angel of the Lord found Hagar near a spring in the desert; it was the spring that is beside the road to Shur. And he said, "Hagar, slave of Sarai, where have you come from, and where are you going?" "I'm running away from my mistress Sarai," she answered. Then the angel of the Lord told her, "Go back to your mistress and submit to her." The angel added, "I will increase your descendants so much that they will be too numerous to count." The angel of the Lord also said to her: "You are now pregnant and you will give birth to a son. You shall name him Ishmael, for the Lord has heard of your misery. He will be a wild donkey of a man; his hand will be against everyone and everyone's hand against him, and he will live in hostility toward all his brothers." She gave this name to the Lord who spoke to her: "You are the God who sees me," for she said, "I have now seen the One who sees me." That is why the well was called Beer Lahai Roi; it is still there, between Kadesh and Bered. So Hagar bore Abram a son, and Abram gave the name Ishmael to the son she had borne. Abram was eighty-six years old when Hagar bore him Ishmael. (Gen. 16:1–16)

Here we witness the circumstances of the birth of Ishmael, who would subsequently be superseded by Isaac, born to Abraham with his wife, Sarah. Bothered by the presence of Hagar and Ishmael, Sarah asks Abraham to cast the two of them out. He does, but only after assurances from God, who informs Abraham that "I will make the son of the slave into a nation also, because he is your offspring" (Gen. 21:13). After Hagar and Ishmael depart, they find themselves in the Negev desert. On the verge of dehydration, God sends an angel to them who supplies them with a well of water, whereupon He once again informs Hagar about Ishmael's future, "Lift the boy up and take him by the hand, for I will make him into a great nation" (Gen. 21:18).

If we fast-forward to the Qur'ān, we learn that Abraham (Ibrāhīm) did not simply dismiss Hagar and Ishmael (Ismāʿīl), he went with them to the Arabian Peninsula, via the Negev desert. There Abraham and Ishmael built the Kaʿaba,[14] the cubed, stone structure that to this day stands in the heart of Mecca and, thus, of Islam. Although Abraham returned to Sarah, the later Islamic commentary tradition has him return periodically to Mecca to visit Ishmael and his family.[15] Back home, God asks Abraham to sacrifice his son:

> God put Abraham to the test. He said to him, "Abraham," and he replied, "Here I am." And He said, "Take your son, your favored one, Isaac, whom you love, and go to the land of Moriah, and offer him there as a burnt offering on one of the heights that I will point out to you." (Gen. 22:1–2)

Here we see a difference of opinion in the two traditions. According to the Hebrew Bible, as we see here, it is clear that Abraham has been asked to sacrifice Isaac. While the Qur'ān references this story (Q 37:102–111), it leaves the son ambiguous. The later commentary tradition, however, transforms him into Ishmael.[16] This is undoubtedly because later Muslims identified Ishmael as the ancestor of the Arabs, although it seems unlikely that Muhammad himself made this connection.[17] In this respect, it is worth noting, as Peter Webb reminds us, that we should not simply believe that everything that the early Islamic sources tells us is historically true. One classic theme of later sources is that the Muslims simply emerge on the world historical stage as the descendants of ancient Arabian Bedouin. Like so much in early Islamic history, he warns us, such narratives are anachronistic: "Arabs" could become convenient placeholders for Muslims of later centuries to articulate their identity and to explain the rise of Islam. According to him,

> The inhabitants of the geographical area now known as Arabia did not call themselves Arabs, they struggled with divisive political alignments, they neither possessed a common religious creed nor shared similar lifestyles, and they did not speak one standardized language.[18]

Despite this, for some reason we insisted on making the "pre-Islamic Arabs" into a monolith, an ethnic group that shared a common identity and destiny. Such an assumption, however, overlooks the paucity of material evidence and ignores the uses to which imagined identities can be put.

So whence does the connection between Muslim/Arabs and Abraham originate? It would seem in early Jewish sources. According to the second-century BCE *Book of Jubilees*, for example, we read, that Ishmael settled "between Pharan and the borders of Babylon, in all the land to the East, facing the desert. And these mingled with each other, and they were called Arabs and Ishmaelites" (20:11–13). The Roman-Jewish historian, Josephus (ca. 30–100 CE) picks up this theme in his *Antiquities*. Therein, he informs his readers that after the divinely sent angel saved Hagar and Ishmael, the latter went on to be the founding figure of the "Arab nation":

> When the lad was grown up, he married a wife, by birth an Egyptian, from whence the mother was herself derived originally. Of this wife were born to Ismael twelve sons; Nabaioth, Kedar, Abdeel, Mabsam, Idumas, Masmaos, Masaos, Chodad, Theman, Jetur, Naphesus, Cadmas. These inhabited all the country from Euphrates to the Red Sea, and called it Nabatene. They are an Arabian nation, and name their tribes from these, both because of their own virtue, and because of the dignity of Abraham their father.[19]

What, then, do we learn from these stories? For one thing, early Muslims sought to connect themselves—not unlike the earliest Christians—to the monotheistic message of ancient Israel just as they sought to reimagine themselves as "Arabs." Second, the ancient Israelites also sought to make sense of neighboring tribes using the genealogical terms supplied by their sacred scripture. Third, despite the fact that these are mythic narratives of Israelites and Arabs, it was subsequently used to refer specifically to Jews and Muslims.

But while this myth of origins may well connect Jews and Muslims, Judaism and Islam, in a convenient narrative, it is decidedly ahistorical. While attempting to provide a genealogy to a relationship, it paradoxically confuses the situation by imagining two distinct groups that emerge from Abraham. It is surely more accurate to examine the complex intersections between these two traditions as opposed to mistaking later theological projections as historical facts. In addition, both these narratives are, of course, theological as opposed to historical. This is facilitated by the fact that later generations of Muslims invoked the biblical story as a way to legitimate their monotheistic message and by the fact that many late antique and early medieval Jewish communities referred to Arabs/Muslims as "the sons of Ishmael." But just because later theological accounts did so does not mean that we should simply import biblical terms of references into our analysis. It is, in sum, a mistake to take biblical mythopoesis or salvation history as historical fact.

Nevertheless, this does not stop many scholars from assuming some sort of historicity to the contents of these stories.[20] In his 1955 *Jews and Arabs*, for example, Shlomo Dov Goitein was very interested in the biblical period. Although he coined the term "symbiosis" to refer primarily to Jews and Muslims in the late antique and medieval periods, he also imagined the special relationship between the two as extending back to the period prior to the rise of Islam. Writing against pan-Arabists such as Wellhausen and Robertson Smith, who desired to see the ancient Israelites as an offshoot Arab tribe, Goitein writes:

> What is there to be said about this theory which regards Israel as an Arab tribe coming out of the Arabian desert and Israel's religion as the creation of an Arabic mind? This theory is nothing but a series of misconceptions. The sooner we get rid of it the better we shall be able to evaluate the actual common background of Israel and the Arabs.[21]

What is this "common background"? For him, Ancient Israel as it appears in the Bible and the "original Arabs" as they emerge from early Muslim sources share what he called "a primitive democracy." Before I discuss this concept in greater detail, let me mention how problematic his argument is from a historical point of view. If we assume that the biblical materials dealing with the tribal structure of ancient Israel dates to roughly 500 BCE, the early Muslim literature of which he speaks dates to around the period of 750 CE.[22] Not even factoring the romance that Muslim writers had for the pre-Islamic Arabs that may have made their remarks more mythic than historical, this is a timespan of roughly 1,250 years. Yet, Goitein persists because he wants to make a series of connections between Jews and Arabs—"cousins"[23] in his locution—that extend from his own day back in time to the biblical period via the late antique Arabian Peninsula.

Goitein, as we have seen, conceived of a deep spiritual and historical bond between Jews and Arabs, who shared a set of common traits that "can best be described as those of a *primitive democracy*."[24] This political orientation that presumably biblical Jews and late antique Arabs shared is what seems to have differentiated them, at least on his reading, from the great and tyrannical civilizations that surrounded them in the ancient Near East. He writes further:

> Against the background of the civilization of the ancient Orient, which crystallized chiefly in the mighty kingdoms of Mesopotamia, Egypt, and Asia Minor ... Israel and the Arabs present the type of a society which is characterized by the absence of privileged castes and classes, by the absence of enforced obedience to a strong authority,

by undefined but nonetheless very powerful agencies for the formation and expression of public opinion, by freedom of speech, and by a high respect for human life, dignity and freedom.[25]

For Goitein, however, Israel and the Arabs have a deep-rooted connection that extends beyond the realm of just the political.[26] These two people, though distinct from one another (lest we conflate them as the pan-Arabists tried to do), "alone preserved their primitive democracy ... when both peoples became bearers of religions which were destined to mold the development of a great part of the human race."[27]

Establishing the "Larcenous" Paradigm

The other paradigm—and I think it safe to say, the central one—used to describe the origins of Jewish–Muslim relations has the sixth century Ḥijāz (that is, the western part of modern-day Saudi Arabia that borders the Red Sea) as its mise en scène. The home to both Mecca and Medina, this region, so the master narrative goes, was also home to a sizeable Jewish population. However, using today's parlance that is certainly steeped in the rhetoric of authenticity it is unclear just how "kosher" these Jews were. Where, for example, did they come from? What kind of Judaism did they practice? Despite the fact that we do not know with any modicum of certainty the answers to these and related questions, a good majority of secondary scholarship wants to make these Jews normative, that is, rabbinic. This, however, is impossible to prove given the nonexistence of any contemporaneous textual sources (including rabbinic or Talmudic ones that might mention them) or material remains. Even the names of their tribes, for example, are Arab-sounding as opposed to anything recognizable as Hebrew or Jewish. Yet, for some reason secondary literature—a brief survey of which will follow—assumes that it is precisely this "normative" Judaism that gave birth to Islam.

This regnant paradigm has Jewish tribes arrive in the Ḥijāz in the aftermath of either the destruction of the First Temple (587 BCE) or the Second Temple (70 CE)—though each date would certainly imply a different type of religious expression. The religious forms and idioms of ancient Israel would have looked considerably different in the sixth century BCE, for example, than would that of any type of Judaism practiced in the second century CE, both of which would look considerably different from medieval or modern forms. Yet, this does not stop scholars from positing a direct line of religious or ethnic identity that stretches, in the words of Walter Sobchak in *The Big Lebowski*, "from Moses to Sandy Koufax."[28]

So what do we know? While this will be elaborated later in the present chapter, it suffices to mention now: we know that at some point in the mid-fifth century CE, a king of Yemen (roughly 1,000 km to the southeast of Mecca) adopted some form of Judaism as the official religion of his kingdom—again I underscore *some form*—which remained in the area even after Judaism ceased to be the state religion; we know that when Muhammad had political problems in Mecca, for example, he sent some of his followers to Yemen for protection, presumably so that they would be close to other communities of monotheists; we also know that Jews of some sort lived or at least had lived at some point on the Island of Elephantine in the Nile River.[29]

There were, then, certainly Jews in the Arabian Peninsula and the larger Mediterranean Basin prior to the rise of Muhammad's prophetic career. We just do not know what kind of Jews they were. Were the *pure laine* or "old stock" Jews, to whom various local tribes might have been drawn? Were they "converts" (if so, to what type of Judaism?)—in which case, were they just individuals or whole tribes? But even these may be the wrong types of questions, especially at a time when ethnic, tribal, and religious divisions may not have been as stable or fixed as they would later become. At any rate, according to this basic narrative as Muhammad was beginning his career he borrowed heavily from these Jews, presumably on the assumption that all monotheists in the area (including Christians) would recognize his still largely inchoate apocalyptic and monotheistic message. Although the so-called normative Jewish tradition forbade the existence of new prophets, lawgivers, or messianic figures, this certainly did not stop certain Judaisms, as we shall see in the following chapter, from gravitating to such individuals. If we assume that the Jews of the Ḥijāz were rabbinic, and again we have absolutely no reason to believe that they were, then we would imagine they would naturally be hostile to Muhammad's message.[30] This, to reiterate, is the dominant paradigm. However, if we assume that some or indeed all of these Jews were not rabbinic, as I want to here, then there is no reason to believe that they would not have been attracted to and subsequently subsumed within his fledgling community, perhaps even providing some (but certainly not all) of the prime matter that Muhammad and the early community used to form what would eventually become Islam.

The main narrative usually then moves to focus on several of these Medinan Jewish tribes conspiring with Muhammad's enemies in Mecca.[31] According to later Muslim tradition, Muhammad confronted these tribes and gave one, the Banū Qurayẓa, a choice between "conversion" or death. I put conversion in quotation marks because it is unclear what people could convert to at this early stage of Muhammad's career other than a generic apocalyptic message with many monotheistic elements that would have resembled those of the "Judaism" or "Judaisms" practiced or imagined by so-called Jewish Arabs. This is why this is most likely a later story, from when Islam would have been a theological program as opposed to just an apocalyptic slogan, projected back onto this period. These later accounts tell how all the men of the Banū Qurayẓa were murdered and the women and children sold into slavery. However, other sources, again later, mention the existence of Jewish tribes in Medina long after the Banū Qurayẓa's alleged treason.[32] What happened to these other tribes? Did they leave Medina and the Ḥijāz to join what was developing as normative Judaism in Babylonia? Or were they gradually absorbed into Muhammad's growing and at this point still largely inclusive message?[33] Did what became Islam, then, begin as a regional variation of Judaism? Still other sources tell of Muhammad deciding the fate of the Banū Qurayẓa with elders of these Jewish tribes.

It is also around this period, again according to later tradition, that Muhammad began to separate his message from the Jews of the region. He switched the *qibla* (direction of prayer) from Jerusalem to Mecca, told his followers not to rest on the Jewish Sabbath, and instituted the month-long fast of Ramadan to replace Yom Kippur. It would seem that up until this point, Muhammad and his followers considered themselves to have been "Jewish," once again though with the caveat that we have no idea what this term signified or denoted within the context of the sixth-century Ḥijāz. They were monotheists, believing in the God of the ancient Israelites, they prayed facing Jerusalem, rested on the Sabbath, and fasted during Yom Kippur. Once Muhammad changed these practices, he now began to differentiate his message from those Jews who did not join him. But, again, we cannot rule out that such stories were the creations of later theologians trying to work out the doctrinal differences between Judaism and Islam and that they subsequently projected onto the past. Regardless, some version of Judaism—to later Muslim interpreters it would be the normative rabbinic Judaism encountered in cosmopolitan centers such as Baghdad—thus functioned for these later framers as the quintessential "other" in Muslim self-definition.[34]

One thing we do know is that the Jewish tribes of Medina and the Ḥijāz posed an existential problem for later (including contemporary) Jewish and Muslim interpreters. The latter do not want to mention them because if too many of these Jews became part of Muhammad's community, then it might be too "Jewish."[35] Such a position might well reinforce the later Orientalist narrative, the one still operative in most circles today, that Muhammad's message is but a pastiche of earlier monotheisms, particularly that of a stable Judaism. In like manner, many Jewish interpreters and historians do not want to entertain the wholesale "conversion" of Jews to another religion, which would be tantamount to apostasy. Either way, however, the problem remains: What did Judaism look like on the Arabian Peninsula in the sixth and seventh centuries? Since we have no idea, how and why do we continue to claim that a normative rabbinic Judaism was present at the "birth" of Islam.

Abraham Geiger and Problems with the "Larcenous" Paradigm

It should now be clear why the "larcenous" paradigm is so problematic. Most worrisome is the assumption that at the birth of Islam in the late sixth and early seventh centuries, Judaism was fully formed and stable and functioned as Islam's "midwife." The biggest proponents of this argument were German-Jewish scholars, the most famous of whom was Abraham Geiger (1810–1874).[36] In his previously mentioned *Was hat Mohammed aus dem Judenthume aufgenommen?*, he sets out his task: "It is assumed that Mohammed borrowed from Judaism, and this assumption, as will be shewn later, is rightly based."[37] Like many of his Jewish Orientalist colleagues, Geiger ascribes a certain stability and orthodox-inflected existence to these Arabian Jews, assuming that they were somehow rabbinically normative. The Jewish tribes of Arabia, for Geiger, are descendants of those Israelites who fled Jerusalem (though he never specifies if this flight took place after the destruction of the First Temple in 587 BCE or the Second Temple in 70 CE, I assume that he meant the latter). According to him,

> That the Jews in Arabia at the time of Mohammed possessed considerable power is shown by the free life of many quite independent tribes, which sometimes met him in open battle. ... The

want of settled civil life, which continued in Arabia till the rule of Mohammed, was very favorable to the Jews, who had fled to that country in large numbers after the Destruction of Jerusalem, in as much as it enabled them to gather together and to maintain their independence.[38]

Here, once again, we see the Jews of late antique Arabia embody a set of manly virtues ("free," "independent," ability to "fight in battle"). It is also an attempt on the part of Geiger to show an important chapter in the book of Jewish history: the Jews of Arabia represent both the geographical and spiritual link between the Jews of the Land of Israel in biblical times and those of Babylonia in rabbinic times. Here we should remember that Geiger, not unlike Graetz, whose views we will encounter shortly, was interested in writing a large and sweeping history of *the* Jews.[39]

Geiger, like others, operates with a set of nineteenth-century assumptions about race, identity, and nationality. For some reason, this triangulation continues into the present when we should really know better. It is assumed, for example, that although these Jewish tribes had assimilated into the political and intellectual culture of the non-Jewish tribes of Arabia, religiously they remained distinct. It is against this larger backdrop that Geiger sets out to show how Islam was derivative of Judaism. Muhammad was, on his reading, in awe of the Jews and sought to legitimate his message by harnessing it to theirs. In his own words,

> While the physical power of the Jews inspired partly fear, partly respect in Mohammed's mind, he was no less afraid of their mental superiority and of appearing to them as ignorant; and so his first object must have been to conciliate them by an apparent yielding to their views. That the Jewish system of belief was even then a fully developed one, which penetrated the life of each member of the community, is proved both by its antiquity and by the fact that the Talmud had already been completed.[40]

While the Talmud most certainly was completed by the sixth century, we have absolutely no idea if and when it became binding on the Jews of Arabia (or, if we prefer, Arabian Jews or Jewish Arabs). Geiger further claims that Muhammad borrowed or stole certain biblical terms both to authenticate his own message and to differentiate it from earlier ones. In so doing, however, Geiger overlooks the shared vocabulary between the two traditions, and what he envisages as "theft" or "borrowing" may well amount to nothing more than Muhammad and the early framers of Islam drawing on a common Semitic vocabulary.[41] Geiger also never entertains the fact that Judaism in seventh-century Arabia might have been just as inchoate as this fledgling Islam was, and that each functioned as the catalyst for the other's development. The problem with Geiger and other commentators that followed him is the assumption that Judaism, his own religion, is stable and is something that can be neatly juxtaposed against Islam's instability.

What is so problematic in these constructions is the reification of terms like "Jew" and "Muslim," or "Judaism" and "Islam." None of these terms would have emerged fully formed from the Bible or the Qur'ān. Instead, as I will suggest in the following chapter, both of these social groups developed historically and isomorphically in relation to one another. We make a categorical mistake, *pace* Goitein and others, when we use language to describe these interactions that invoke biological and related metaphors because they imply the interaction of discrete groups. Such metaphors posit stability in the face of instability and imply a set of surface-level interactions that never penetrate an assumed core or essence. While the narratives created by such metaphors reproduce tropes of influences or borrowings, they tend to marginalize the often localized skirmishes that occurred on other fault lines, often at the margins and often involving contested notions of leadership, eschatology, and so on. These skirmishes, I maintain, subsequently became the sites of theological, religious, and intellectual genesis that helped to establish centers. Too often, however, the margins are ignored in favor of centers.

The narrative that wants to make Islam derivative of Judaism, it seems to me, is based on a variation of the "Jewish pride" thesis, the one that makes Judaism responsible for all subsequent monotheisms.[42] However, we have to seriously doubt—or, at the very least, treat with significant skepticism—just what inroads so-called Talmudic or rabbinic Judaism had made into Arabia by the sixth century. The Babylonian Talmud, redacted in the seminaries of Iraq in the century before, did not become binding overnight on Jews throughout the Mediterranean Basin.[43] Geiger's reading of the religious forms and expressions of Medina's Jews, like so many who construct and perpetuate this narrative, is ultimately betrayed by a paucity of contemporaneous historical sources. Those who picked up Geiger's thesis in the ensuing years include I. Gastfreund (1875),[44] R. B Smith (1889),[45] M. Grünbaum (1893),[46] J. Barth (1903 and 1915),[47]

H. Speyer (1923–1924),[48] I. Ben-Zeev (1931),[49] J. J. Rivlin (1934),[50] J. Oberman (1944),[51] H. Z. Hirschberg (1946),[52] A. I. Katsh (1954),[53] and most recently G. Newby (1988)[54] and H. Mazuz (2014).[55] It is also worth noting dissenting opinions, many of which claimed that Muhammad's knowledge of Jewish texts was superficial at best. Yet even such outliers still ascribe to these Jewish Arab tribes a much later normativity. Instead of positing a Jewish origin for Islam, such dissenters often imagine a Christian one. These include the likes of J. Wellhausen (1897),[56] H. P. Smith (1897),[57] C. H. Becker (1907),[58] A. Moberg (1930),[59] K. Ahrens (1930),[60] and C. Brockelmann (1950).[61] Either way, it is always assumed that influence is unidirectional and that earliest Islam, and by extension later Islam, is but the sum—often the confused sum—of other and much more stable monotheisms in the area.

Any discussion of sixth-century Arabia as the point of origin for Muslim–Jewish relations must address this problem of sources.[62] Many of these sources, while claiming to be contemporaneous with the events that they recount, are often much later projections. This all too often means ignoring the fact that a heavy ideological patina covers many of these later sources since they are the propagandistic products of various sectarian groups trying to legitimate their own authority against competing claims. The issue may well be not that the Medinan Jews were normative, but that later Muslim sources insisted in transforming the Jews that Muhammad had contact with into what they considered to be normative Jews. The Jews on this reading function as a trope of treachery—not unlike that of the Pharisees in early Christian literature—that threatens to undermine the apparent fragility of Muhammad's pristine message. The authors of these later sources, familiar with the rabbinic Jews with whom they interacted in cosmopolitan centers such as Baghdad, in other words, might well have used "Jews" as a model to imagine the identities of the Jews of Medina and juxtapose them against the perceived purity of the Bedouin Arabs, their own imagined ancestors.

Despite some pioneering work in the literature and history of the Arabian Peninsula at the time of Muhammad, the basic narrative of Jewish–Muslim relations at this time has progressed very little over the past two hundred years. We do not possess, for example, a miqva (a ritual bath), an ossuary, let alone a cemetery, or other archeological features or structures that would suggest a Jewish presence in the area. Certainly later sources tell us of Jewish tribes there, but we have no idea what these Jews believed, practiced, wrote, or thought. We have absolutely no idea what their relationship was to the Jews of Jerusalem, Babylonia, or other centers. The texts produced by these latter Jews make no mention of these Jews in Arabia. Was this because they did not consider them to be "Jewish" enough? Indeed, they may well have been Arab tribes that considered themselves to be somehow Jewish—keeping in mind that the very notions of ethnicity and religiosity are modern constructs—who otherwise differed very little, if at all, from pagan tribes.[63] So rather than assume that a rabbinically normative Judaism influenced the rise of Islam, we have to revisit the narrative to rethink the paradigm.

"Larceny": The History of an Idea

The "theft" narrative has proven to be indefatigable on account of its usefulness especially among Jewish historians. Like Geiger, Graetz, the father of modern Jewish history, also maintained that the Jews of Arabia were thoroughly Jewish and granted them "a superiority over the heathen tribes" in the area that "soon granted them [to be] their masters."[64] Although he admits that how the Jews got to the Ḥijāz is "buried in misty tradition," he surmises that their origins in the region may well be the result of an Israelite colony created by King David or related to the expulsion that occurred after the destruction of the First Temple in 587 BCE.[65] Not surprisingly, these Jews, whom are imagined by most nineteenth-century German-Jewish historians to play such an important role in the rise of Western monotheism, are given a noble pedigree that is traceable to the Davidic monarchy. Descendants of such individuals, Graetz surmises but without offering any historical evidence or providing any useful analytical model, were the various Jewish tribes of both Yathrib (later to be renamed Medina) and Yemen at the time of Muhammad. Graetz, however, does acknowledge certain similarities between Jews and Arabs:

> In consequence of their Semitic descent, the Jews of Arabia possessed many points of similarity with the primitive inhabitants of the country. Their language was closely related to Arabic, and their customs, except those that had been produced by their religion, were not different from those of the sons of Arabia. The Jews became, therefore, so thoroughly Arabic that they were distinguished from the natives of the country only by their religious belief.[66]

Graetz again assumes that these Jews were religiously and presumably ethnically normative, although he acknowledges that they were most likely culturally indistinct from the Arabs. They may have been Arabs on the outside, in other words, but they remained pure Jews on the inside. Since they looked indistinct from their Arab neighbors, he must then explain how they performed their Jewishness, which he does as follows:

> In the form in which it was transmitted to them, that is to say, with the character impressed upon it by the Tanaim and Amoraim, Judaism was most holy to the Arabian Jews. They strictly observed the dietary laws, and solemnized the festivals, and the fast of Yom Kippur, which they called Ashura. They celebrated the Sabbath with such rigor that in spite of their delight in war, and the opportunity for enjoying it, their sword remained in its scabbard on that day. Although they had nothing to complain of in this hospitable country. . . . they yearned nevertheless to return to the holy land of their fathers, and daily awaited the coming of the Messiah.[67]

This romance and wistfulness, however, is based solely on conjecture of what Graetz wants the Jews of Arabia to be, since we do not possess a shred of historical evidence for anything that he recounts. Like Geiger, he transforms these Arabian Jews into pious individuals who otherwise shared in the manly poetic culture of the Arabs. He further relates that on account of "the Arab mind, [which was] susceptible to intellectual promptings, [and which] was delighted with the simple," the Arabian Jews were able to teach them something of biblical lore.[68] This assumption that the monotheistic prowess of the Jews, on the one hand, and Arabian simplicity (or simple-mindedness), on the other, accounts for much late-nineteenth and twentieth-century Orientalist speculation about the origin of the Qur'ān and early Islam.

This narrative was not unique to the German Orientalist tradition. The English Orientalist D. S. Margoliouth (1858–1940)—someone whose father had converted from Judaism to the Church of England, whereupon he subsequently engaged in proselytism to the Jews—provides yet another iteration of this approach to Jewish–Muslim relations at the time of Muhammad. In his *Relations between Arabs and Israelites Prior to the Rise of Islam* (1924), for example, he again mentions the mythic origins of how the Jews came to Arabia, but acknowledges that such myths are impossible to verify independently.[69] However, unlike those already examined, he does raise questions about the connection between these individuals and the ancient Israelites, since the former possess no identifiably Jewish or Jewish-sounding names. This leads him to conclude that what tradition passes down to us concerning the Jews of Medina, something that virtually all of the secondary literature I have discussed accepts at face value, is historically problematic.[70] He suggest that the Arabian Jews might not be "Jewish" at all, but Arab converts to Judaism—though, again, he bypasses the problem concerning to which type of Judaism such converts would have converted. "We do not even know," he writes, "whether they were Judaized Arabs or Arabized Israelites."[71]

Here Margoliouth builds on the pioneering work of Hugo Winckler (1863–1913), a German Orientalist, who had argued that had the Jews of Arabia originated from Israelite colonists "they would not have sunk from their higher civilization to the primitive tribal organization in which they appear in the Prophet's biography."[72] Winckler had argued that although these Arab tribes may well have changed their religion, they were either unable or unwilling to change their habits or way of life. Whereas Geiger and Graetz were happy to maintain an inner/outer distinction so that Jews could remain Jewish internally even though they may have physically resembled Arabs, the likes of Winkler and Margoliouth worry that such a dialectic did not remain for long. Nevertheless, both are willing to still grant some sort of superiority to "the Jews." Margoliouth, for example, argues:

> Against this it may be noticed that their civilization seems to have been somewhat higher than that of their neighbours; their cultivation of the soil was somewhat more scientific, and they appear to have themselves disliked fighting, but to have been forced into their neighbours' quarrels. ... Whether this implies a higher or lower degree of intelligence than that of other Arabs must be left to the individual judgment to decide.[73]

Despite their hesitation as to the ethnic makeup of these tribes, both Winckler and Margoliouth privilege Judaism and assume it to be more stable at this period than it probably was. Although Margoliouth doubts how fully "Jewish" the Arab-Jewish tribes of Arabia actually were, he concludes that "Judaism cannot indeed be removed from the doctrines of Mohammed himself, since the Qur'an consists largely of material taken either from the Old Testament or the Jewish Oral Tradition."[74] He never mentions, however, where this material might have come from. Did these Jews of Arabia possess the Mishnah? Did they have access to the recently canonized Babylonian Talmud, or oral traditions derived therefrom? Differences between the Qur'ān and the Hebrew Bible, as is typical of this literature, are reduced to the "woeful ignorance" on the part of those who did the copying.

As I argued in the previous chapter, many of these ideas were brought to America via Goitein. The first stage of his symbiotic model between Jews and Arabs, it will be recalled, occurred in Muhammad's Arabia. For him, it was Judaism that gave birth to Islam. Like Geiger, he imagines rabbinic literature, such as non-legal midrashim, as playing a large role in this process of Islam's formation. Although he can provide no actual texts that these Jews of Arabia, or Arabian Jews, possessed, the assumption is always that what became Islam needed some sort of help, which will be repaid in the golden age of Muslim Spain.

It is always assumed, however, that the theft (or borrowing or influence) moves in one direction. But, again, who were these "Jews"? What did "Jew" signify in sixth-century Arabia? Even though the existence of Jews in Arabia would certainly seem to predate the codification of the Babylonian Talmud, it is assumed that by the time of Muhammad they had somehow miraculously transformed into rabbinic Jews. Yet, we are never informed about the process whereby this took place. We cannot assume an orthodoxy of fixed and ascertainable Jewish identity and practice based upon the rabbinic academies of Babylonia, which, to use Bulliet's inkblot metaphor, is imagined to have simply spread out through the Jewish communities of the Mediterranean basin overnight. We must also be aware that the positing of sharp ethnic, racial, and religious distinctions—all terms with fairly modern provenances—between "Jews," "Arabs," and "Christians" at that time might draw more upon our concerns and preoccupations than those we purportedly discuss and analyze.

Modern Takes

If recent years have witnessed many disciplines in the Humanities interrogate traditional notions of identity, including the manifold ways in which it is created, maintained, and patrolled, such discussions have unfortunately largely bypassed the discussion of Islamic origins. Critical theory—from fields as diverse as anthropology and sociology—is largely ignored even in more recent attempts to write this history of the Ḥijāzī Jews. Writing in 1988, for example, Gordon D. Newby admits to the problem of sources: "We do not know enough. We do not have the personal records, autobiographies, and letters that would really let us glimpse the lives of individual Arabian Jews."[75] However, this does not stop him from attempting to explicate from this aporia by proclaiming that "we can only look at these long-dead Jews at a communal level. Even with that limitation, we can learn much about Jewish courage and survival in a harsh environment after the destruction of the Temple."[76] Jewish "courage" and "survival," it is worth noting, are modern tropes, ones certainly in vogue in our post-Holocaust world, but not necessarily germane to the late antique period. Despite his assurances, Newby, like his predecessors, brings no new evidence, neither textual nor archeological, to light in his analysis. "Islamic literature is rich in traditions and stories," he informs us, "that can be used to reconstruct the history of the Arabian Jewish communities."[77] He fails to mention, however, that all of these sources are later—often much later—than the events on which they purport to relate. This is the problem we confront time and again in the secondary literature: reflections of later authors are either taken to be eyewitness accounts or history becomes largely unimportant because it gets in the way of a good story. In terms of the latter, we often hear the claim that, while even though these texts might be from a later period, they nonetheless tell us what later Muslims wanted to happen.[78]

While Newby admits that the origins of the Jews of Arabia are unclear, he does not refrain from positing that "they identified with Jewish interests and concerns outside Arabia and expressed their interests in correct practice to authorities beyond their local rabbis and community leaders."[79] I find the term "correct" disconcerting here for many reasons, not the least of which is "correct" to whom? Newby then goes on to use, for example, an obscure verse from the Mishnah, *Shabbat* 6:6, to prove his point:

> A woman may go out with a *Sela* [a coin worth four *Dinar*] fastened on a corn [on her foot]; girls may go out with ribbons, and even with chips in their ears; Arabian women may go out in their veils, and Median women in their mantillas. So [indeed] may anyone, but the Sages speak of common custom.

The Mishnah passage, compiled in the second century CE, tells us very little, however. He deduces from this one sentence:

> From the Mishnah we know that the concerns of Arabian Jewry were sufficient to attract the attentions of the Babylonian rabbis.

Issues of kosher dress, clothing, and food in the Arabian context were debated by the rabbis. Jewish women, and presumably men, wore veils when outside to protect themselves from the windborn sand, a custom adopted from the Arabs and allowed by the rabbis.[80]

Newby, however, provides no compelling evidence that makes these Jews either "rabbinic" or even "ethnically" Jewish. The only thing he can do, as indeed everyone has done, is use later sources as if they are accurate projections.[81] In a more recent formulation, Jonathan Brockopp admits that even though we know very little about the early Islamic period, we are nevertheless able to use the later sources to imagine how later Muslims imagined the earlier period and thus themselves.[82] Fair enough, but once again, this is of limited value when it comes to reconstructing factually the earliest period with which we are ostensibly concerned. This reconstruction proves impossible largely on account of the fact that Muslim sources, the very sources Newby and others use non-problematically, not only are much later but also cast "the Jews" in a largely adversarial position.[83] This literature is less interested, I submit, in historical Jews than in literary ones. Such literature, to use the words of Wansbrough, seeks to establish "'the isolation of semiological space' into which may be inserted a selection of themes and symbols intended to recall the event of revelation."[84] The Jew in the text, in other words, is a metaphor for what the potential rejection of Muhammad's message might look like. These Jews, to continue with Wansbrough's semiotic metaphor, function as a placeholder that while necessary for syntactic restraints, offers little or no semantic information.[85]

We also see this hermeneutic at play in the recent work of Haggai Mazuz.[86] Although he too argues that Medinan Jews were kosher in the sense that they were "religiously" and "spiritually" authentic, unfortunately he nowhere problematizes authenticity, ethnicity, and identity—let alone religion or spirituality—nor does he bother to mention that all the aforementioned terms are modern constructs.[87] While such terms can be perhaps potentially useful as heuristic models, they need to be employed with caution. Although he freely acknowledges that "there are no—and perhaps never were any—Jewish or Christian sources documenting the history of the Hijazi Jews,"[88] this acknowledgment does not stop him from reaching the conclusion that they "were Talmudic-Rabbinic Jews in almost every respect."[89]

Since Mazuz produces no new sources, he must use the same ones that we all do. To maintain his argument that the Medinan Jews were somehow authentic, he must take at face value those sources that suit him, and either ignore or try to interpret away those that do not. If a later source, for example, mentions that Abu Bakr, Muhammad's successor, asked some of the Jews to convert to Islam, he assumes it is true.[90] He never asks, however, convert to what? How could one convert to a largely inchoate message especially given the fact that the Qur'ān had still not reached its final form?[91] If the text that mentions Abu Bakr and the conversion request is a much later source, however, and one that had a clearer sense of what Islam consisted of when it came to doctrine and practice, then his source is surely compromised.

To get around these and related problems, Mazuz proposes what he assumes to be a "unique methodology" based upon the Arabic principle of *mukhālafa* (opposition). He develops this hermeneutic by relying on a saying attributed to Muhammad, "do the opposite [*khālifū*] of the Jews."[92] Mazuz elevates this saying to a methodological principle by claiming that since (later) Islamic sources obsess about differentiating Islamic practices from Jewish ones, we must assume that when (again, much later) Muslim sources say Muslims do something, then the actual Jews of Medina did the opposite. "The juxtaposition of Islamic sources together with Jewish sources," he maintains, "often demonstrate Islam's attempt to differentiate itself from Talmudic law in many areas."[93] Again, though, there is no evidence of Talmudic law, let alone the physical existence of the Talmud, in Arabia at this time. In Mazuz's hands, however, it is clear that since Muhammad did not have access to the Talmud, then the Jews of Medina function metonymically for Talmudic law. This is a difficult way to proceed because the customs, laws, practices, and beliefs of the Medinan Jews are essentially constructed in absentia. Just as he shows no awareness of modern scholarship querying identity, he does not reflect theoretically on the permutations and limitations of his methodology.

The bulk of Mazuz's analysis is then spent trying to ascertain the laws, customs, and religious practices of the Jews of Medina. Mazuz, writing a century and a half after Geiger, still subscribes to the unhelpful and unproductive Orientalist assumption that Judaism and Christianity at the time of Muhammad are somehow stable entities that influence and shape a fledgling Islam. Why, I wonder, is it so important to Mazuz—writing in 2014 as opposed to 1914 or 1814—that the Jews of Medina be normative? Like Geiger and Graetz he seems to want to maintain some continual and "authentic" Jewish identity that stretches out from the ashes of the destruction of the Second Temple and moves directly through to the codifiers of the Babylonian Talmud (and beyond).[94] The Jews of Yemen and Arabia, now imagined as true rabbinic Jews, form a missing piece of the puzzle of Jewish continuity.

Returning to the Sources

The main narrative, as witnessed in this chapter, works on two levels, with Jews functioning, depending upon the audience, as either heroes or villains. In terms of the former, it was the Jews of the Ḥijāz that provided Muhammad the terminological wherewithal for his monotheistic message (the Jewish "take-away"). In terms of the latter, it was the Jews in Medina who not only were the main holdouts to Muhammad's monotheistic message but also the ones who actively plotted to undermine it (the Muslim "take-away"). In both cases, however, the historical record gets in the way of the mythopoeic one. Both accounts are based on later sources and projected back onto the period in question. Certainly there would have been some Jews who resisted Muhammad's message, just as there would have been Jews who became part of his still largely inchoate and as yet highly inclusive message. But, in each case we really have no clear idea what "Jew" means and because of this we really can make these Jews into anything we want. If we assume, as Bernard Lewis does, that no Jew would have accepted Muhammad's inchoate teachings, we again come back to the question, if these were not "normative" or "rabbinic" Jews, why would they have resisted this message? Why might they not have simultaneously informed and been informed by Muhammad's messianic apocalypticism. Once again, we confront the reality that Jewish identity in the sixth-century Arabian Peninsula might well be more fluid than we would like. Such an admission, however, gets in the way of the narrative that Jewish scholars have been telling themselves since at least the 1850s, namely, that Judaism gave birth to Islam in the seventh century, just as it had given birth to Christianity in the first.

But if Judaism and Jewish were fluid and evolving, so too, of course, were both "Islam" and "Arabness." Our underlying assumption that there existed some pre-Islamic and pan-Arabian ethnos that was unified—whether politically, socially, or religiously—under the rubric "Arab" would seem to be a much later projection. As Robert Hoyland puts it, later Muslims were "strong on religion, but short on identity," and they needed to fashion a religious pedigree for themselves. Perhaps it was only natural that they turned to the nomadic Arabs, "who were short on religion, but strong on identity."[95] This may be witnessed by the fact that pre-Islamic Arabians did not even use the term "Arab" to refer to themselves. Even their neighbors did not use such a term, but instead referred to them using the Latin *Saraceni* (Saracens) or the Syriac *Ṭayyāyē*.[96] Indeed, some of the earliest extant, non-Muslim sources—such as the seventh-century anti-Jewish polemical treatise *Doctrina Iacobi*—refer to Muhammad as preaching some version of Jewish messianism.[97] As Crone and Cook argued close to forty years ago, we have to understand the earliest Islamic message as an apocalyptic movement focused on Jerusalem.[98] Moreover, Stephen Shoemaker has recently argued that later apocalyptic Jewish works, such as the mid-seventh-century *The Secrets of Rabbi Shimon bar Yoḥai*, envisage Muhammad "as the leader of the Ishmaelite army that was believed to be the agent of Israel's divine deliverance from Roman oppression in Palestine."[99] This so-called Jewish text, in other words, speaks very highly of Muhammad, describing him as an "Ishmaelite messiah" and as someone whose followers included "an inter-confessional, eschatological religious movement focused on Jerusalem and the Holy Land that welcomed Jews and other monotheists."[100]

This is certainly not to make the case that all Jews in Arabia—whatever they might have believed or whomsoever they considered to be their authoritative leaders—would have endorsed the vision articulated in the *Apocalypse of Rabbi Shimon bar Yoḥai*. However, it is to make the point that to imagine the Jews of Arabia as a monolith—as the group which resisted Muhammad's message—is equally problematic and is again based on much later theological, typological, and historical desires. Rather than use later Muslim and or Jewish sources that make sharp distinctions between the two groups, however, we must situate both groups in Arabia against the larger and more fluid backdrop of the late antique Mediterranean world. We do not even know, for example, if the Arabian Jews saw themselves in terms that we would today describe as "ethnic Jews." They may well have seen themselves as Arabs (though this seems unlikely given the fact that the term is rarely used prior to the advent of Islam) or *Saraceni* or *Ṭayyāyē* who happened to be "religiously" Jewish. Any attempt to map the relations between Muslims and Jews in this period must take this fluidity into account.

One of the major problems is that secondary interpreters either want to make Islam into an incoherent spinoff of Judaism by assuming that

Judaism in the sixth-century Arabian Peninsula was the same Judaism of the Babylonian Talmud. Or, they want to adopt the viewpoints of later sources that make Islam at the time of Muhammad into something that it could not have been. There is instead the desire to use the empirical accuracy of these later sources with an eye to extracting contemporaneous data to reconstruct the pre-Islamic Arab way of life.[101] Too many attempts to get at what really happened between Muhammad and the Jews of Arabia—to say nothing of Islam at the time of Muhammad—have run roughshod over the sources. What is needed is a set of diachronic analyses that will help us examine the many voices and genres that developed over centuries.

Islam at the time of Muhammad was still very much fluid. Confessional boundaries, today so important and ones that have been retroactively projected onto the late antique period, were likely not as important.[102] Certainly there was the notion of a small-i "islam" (i.e., submission [to God]), but what we now recognize as Islam—its theological, liturgical, and legal content, for example—were still centuries from being worked out. What Islam meant at the time of Muhammad, which probably amounted to little more than a generic apocalyptic and eschatological message would have looked very different from that of the twelfth century.

In like manner, what Judaism looked like on the Arabian Peninsula in the sixth century would have been radically different from Judaism of the Geonic period (the mid-eighth to eleventh centuries), when the Rabbis of Babylonia made their version of Judaism, centered on the Babylonian Talmud, presumably normative for all Jews. We, thus, have to be careful of imposing later theological differences, including our own in the present, onto this period. Terms like "ethnicity" and "religion," while part of our conceptual and analytical frameworks today—were constructed very differently in the premodern world in general and sixth-century Arabia in particular.

It might well be worth mentioning the so-called Constitution of Medina in this context. This Constitution, often attributed to Muhammad (who was, according to tradition, illiterate) and which has been described as "The First Written Constitution in the World,"[103] is often assumed to date to the first year after his *hijra* (622 CE), or "exodus" of Muhammad and his followers from Mecca to Medina. However, as is so often the case in dealing with early Islamic history, the earliest copy we possess dates to at least a century after Muhammad's presence in Medina.

In his *Constitution of Medina*—which he assumes to be authentic—Michael Lecker notes that although eleven "Jewish" tribes are mentioned, the three main ones (Naḍir, Qurayẓa, and Qaynuqāʿ) are not. Ever since Wellhausen, it has been assumed that the document included all the inhabitants of Medina.[104] Lecker, however, argues that by this time the Jews of Arabia were included in the "Constitution" as clients of the Anṣār, among whom they lived. However, one of the tribes mentioned in the "Constitution," the Thaʿlaba seem to have been a "Jewish" tribe composed of Arab converts.[105] Lecker also maintains that the Constitution has relatively little Jewish participation in it because the Jews had made up their own non-belligerency treatises with Muhammad.[106] We, of course, have no evidence of this—let alone that the Constitution was authentic. If it was in fact later, then it would have contributed to the subsequent creation of Jewish difference.[107] Another way of slicing all of this, of course, is to say that many of these "Jews" had been folded into the umma whether as "Muslims," or some sort of hybrid "Jewish-Muslims" or "Muslimjews," or some other multi-layered identity.

According to Uri Rubin, the Jewish participants in the "Constitution" were not the main Jewish tribes but nameless Jewish groups that, unlike the main tribes, had neither a territory of their own nor a distinct tribal affinity. Again, they would have functioned as clients to the various Arab tribes in whose territory they dwelt and by whose names they used to be called.[108] Once again, the contours of these "Jewish" groups or clients are impossible to ascertain with any historical clarity.

Conclusions

This chapter has started at the beginning of Jewish–Muslim relations and tried to show just how difficult any sort of historical, let alone doctrinal, reconstruction is. Despite claims to the contrary, we have no idea who the Jews of late antique Arabia were—where they came from, what they believed, where they went after the advent of Muhammad's message— let alone that they were somehow normative. This aporia, however, has not prevented many from attempting to write their history and providing us with detailed contents of their beliefs, even reconstructing their "spiritual" lives. My argument, to the contrary, is that this has been done for a host of non-scholarly reasons. Such reconstructions have filled a basic need on the part of many Jewish (and even non-Jewish) scholars to imagine Judaism as the original monotheism, from which other and much larger ones originate.

Just as problematic is the attempt to know with any degree of certainty just what "Islam" consisted of in the early- and mid-seventh century. Once again, we are in the shadow of history. If we want to know what and how later Muslim thinkers thought about and interpreted this period we are on relatively firmer ground. However, if we want to know what "really happened" we are at a complete loss.

What we can conclude, however, is that "Jews" and "Muslims" at this juncture of history would have looked considerably different than they would, say, two centuries later. It is sources from this later period, however, that all too frequently masquerade as eyewitness accounts. Yet, we gullibly accept them as such. Rather, as the next chapter will explore in greater detail, we should instead imagine "Jews" and "Muslims" as existing on a common cultural map, one wherein many ideas, vocabularies, beliefs, and worldviews were held in common.

3

Messianism in the Shadows

DESPITE THE FACT that we know next to nothing about the Jews with whom Muhammad ostensibly interacted, this has not stopped many, as just witnessed, from making historical pronouncements about them. There exists no material or other archeological remains that tell us how they lived, no contemporaneous textual evidence of what they believed, and thus little to no idea who they were, let alone how they conceived of Judaism. This historical aporia, however, has not prevented the subsequent projection of a later ethnic and religious normativity onto these "Jews." The transformative result of this Orientalist imaginary further sustains the myth of a monolithic "Judaism" present at the birth of "Islam," nudging it along and providing the prime monotheistic matter for its subsequent genesis. Indicative of this are the comments of Shlomo Dov Goitein, who could proclaim, against the evidence, "that Judaism was a fully developed system at the time when the Arab Muslims made their first conquest."[1] Rather than simply repeat such an utterance here, I have tried to step back and examine some of its political contexts.[2]

Here it is important to remember that Goitein inherited a basic narrative scripted by a generation of German-Jewish intellectuals intent on showing the universal significance of Judaism. The goal of this narrative was to demonstrate how Judaism functioned as the bedrock from which Christianity and Islam were hewn.[3] Judaism, it is frequently assumed in this literature, bequeathed its message of unadulterated monotheism to these other religions, and today it can stand alongside them as a primus inter pares.[4]

However, if scholars of Christian origins have begun to show how the emergence of Christianity and Judaism (i.e., and not Christianity from Judaism) was much more complex than our traditional narratives would have us believe, there has been a surprising reluctance when it comes to "the parting of the ways" between Judaism and Islam in the century or so following the death of Muhammad.[5] This is not to say that there have not been pioneering works devoted to the study of Islamic origins,[6] only that it is a topic that is surprisingly moribund within the larger context of Jewish studies.[7] Yet, if the field of Jewish studies is unwilling to examine the Arab-Jewish or Judeo-Arabic tribes of Arabia—or even if such tribes existed in the first place—in its historical context, why is it content simply to recycle nineteenth-century tropes that reveal more about the people who coined them than the actual historical record?

Why, for example, do some scholars insist on maintaining that the Jews of Arabia were normatively rabbinic and that their religious and ethnic stability somehow provided the catalyst for Muhammad's message? Not only is it impossible to know who these Jews were, it is not possible to know with any better certainty who the "Muslims" were, since Islam was un- or at the very least underdeveloped at that point. So while Judaism may well have been a "fully developed system" in some places and for some Jews in the sixth century, there is no evidence that this was the case for those with whom Muhammad came into contact. Rather than claim that "the influence of Judaism on early Islam must have been very considerable, if not decisive,"[8] we need a new paradigm—one that acknowledges and taxonomizes the fluidity of religious and ethnic identity. The present chapter begins this process.

Unfortunately, however, the dark shadows of history do not dissipate any time soon. The period emerging after late antiquity, from roughly the death of Muhammad in 632 CE to the death of Saadya Gaon, one of the most important framers of rabbinic Judaism and someone who wrote primarily in Arabic, in 942, are equally obscure. Despite his earlier confidence in the contours and contents of Arabian Judaism, even Goitein quipped, "the centuries both preceding and following the rise of Islam are the most obscure in Jewish history."[9] This, however, has not stopped others, Goitein included, from projecting later ideas onto this obscurity.

Another way to bypass this historical aporia is simply to ignore it, and pick up Islamic-Jewish relations in the so-called golden age of Muslim Spain. This, for example, is the approach of S. Katz,[10] Y. Baer,[11] R. D. Barnett,[12] E. Ashtor,[13] B. S. Bachrach,[14] N. A. Stillman,[15] B. Lewis,[16] H. Beinart,[17] J. S. Gerber,[18] and M. R. Cohen.[19] Many of these otherwise informative studies prefer to begin, not surprisingly, with more historically reliable sources that date to the ninth and tenth centuries. Gerber's comments may be apropos here. She describes how the Jews arrived in what would eventually become Muslim Spain, "the beginnings of Jewish life in Spain are cloaked in myth and legend," but she then goes on to remark that such "legends do not entirely violate historic truth."[20] Myth and history intersect and when there is a lack of understanding of the latter, there is a tendency to supplement it or embellish it with the former. Not only has scholarship proved unable or unwilling to account for the plethora of beliefs and doctrines of Jews under early Islam, it has very little idea how these Jews moved around and where they settled. Despite the fact that well over three-quarters of world Jewry lived within Islamic lands until the tenth century, there is no getting around the disconcerting fact that we know next to nothing about the Jews during the late antique period.[21]

Perhaps the one thing that can be safely said is that Judaism, not unlike Islam, was poorly or underdefined, with many groups—later written off as heterodox—exploring different paradigms of leadership and structures of authority.[22] Through later rabbinic and Muslim sources, we know of the existence of several of these paradigms, which ranged from the highly messianic and apocalyptic to that which would eventually become normative. We know names of individuals, groups, and institutions—Isawiyya, Karaites, Exilarchs, Geonim—but since the latter carried the day and often treated their rivals using argumenti ex silentio,[23] we do not know nearly as much about them as we would like. Whereas the Karaites produced a relatively large body of literature, most of which still exists in manuscripts,[24] we possess nothing from groups like the Isawiyya except what we can cobble together from Muslim heresiographers.[25] While this chapter examines the contours of these groups, it does not seek to provide histories of them. Rather, I use them as discursive sites to examine how Jewish or even Judaizing groups struggled with the rise and spread of Islam and did so, moreover, using the vocabularies provided by sectarian Muslim groups, so much so that on the surface they are almost identical to one another. If the assumption has been that a stable Judaism gave birth to Islam in the seventh century—an assumption I tried to correct in the previous chapter—one could now make the opposite case, namely, that an unstable Islam created further instability in various Jewish and Judaizing groups by providing vocabularies and tropes, many of which had been adopted and adapted, reused and recycled, from earlier Jewish messianic circles. The result, again, is a chaotic system of messianisms that do not tell us who had what first, but rather reveal a porosity between numerous Jewish and Muslim social groups responding, often in the same way, to the social, religious, and intellectual turmoil brought about by the rapid spread of a still largely inchoate Islam and the concomitant process of Islamicization.[26]

The cloud only begins to lift gradually as the medieval period approaches.[27] This period will witness, for example, rabbinic florescence, the emergence of a set of interlocking Judeo-Arabic cultural forms, and the rise of Jewish philosophical and other sciences that are usually defined, as already witnessed, by the default metaphor of "symbiosis."[28] However, often passed over in these more general narratives are the struggles and contestations that went into making rabbinic Judaism normative in the first place.[29] We cannot simply assume that there existed a normative Judaism to which Jews throughout the Mediterranean world simply assented and did so overnight. These early contestations and struggles not only took place against an Arab-Muslim backdrop but also actively employed Arab-Islamic terms and categories. Even Saadya's *halakhic* redefinition or, what Steven Wasserstrom calls "retrenchment,"[30] is written in Arabic and done so using the terms and categories that he inherited from the Muʿtazilites, a group of rationalist Muslim theologians in whose ranks he must certainly be situated.[31] It is necessary to be cautious, once again, of assuming that one side of the Jewish–Muslim dyad is somehow more stable than the other or that one somehow derives its monotheistic or any other sustenance from the other.

What is needed is a paradigm that can both account for and taxonomize the stochastic developments between two underdefined and amorphous entities—"Judaism," "Islam"—each of which subsumes numerous and often contradictory elements. How, in other words, do we if not actually account for then at least engage consciously with the messiness of interactions between a host of Judaisms and a host of Islams in what was becoming one of the largest empires that the world had seen in the late antique period? Whereas subsequent centuries would write much of these movements off as "non-normative" or as "heterodox," during these dark and obscure times they would have been anything but. On the contrary, such groups and their self-understandings were precisely what would make normativity possible in the coming centuries. Only by defining themselves by what they were not was it possible for rabbinic Judaism, orthodox Sunnism, and orthodox Twelver Shīʿism to emerge from the shadows of history as normative.

Once again, we are mired in the thorny problem of influences. Influence, and its synonym borrowing, has long plagued the study of religion. "Judaism is older than Islam (or Christianity)," so the narrative goes, "and, therefore, it must have influenced it." The naiveté of such an utterance should, I trust, now be readily apparent. Instead of such simplicity,[32] it is necessary to acknowledge the instability of both parts of the "Jewish–Muslim" dyad, including perhaps just as important the hyphen that links them to one another.[33] Another way of saying all this is that if both sides of the dyad "Jewish–Muslim" are underdefined in the late antique period and in the period immediately thereafter, how is it then possible to posit a set of relations based on borrowings or influences?

Key to my analysis in this chapter and the following one is the towering rabbinic figure of Saadya Gaon (882–942). The conventional narrative transforms Saadya Gaon into the great consolidator of rabbinic authority in the light of numerous struggles with other groups who are then labeled as heterodox.[34] Keeping in mind the sparse nature of eighth-century Gaonic sources, and the problems associated with dating those that we do possess, such an interpretation may well be premature if not actually politically motivated as a way to make rabbinic authority universal or catholic under the Babylonian Gaonate.[35]

My argument here is that at the time just prior to Saadya there existed a real diversity of Judaisms vying for authority, but they were all too frequently and neatly obscured by the term "Judaism" in the singular. While rabbinic Judaism will eventually emerge as regnant, in part thanks to Saadya, it is important to be aware of these other groups and, of course, how they were all being forged in the intellectual, social, and religious crucible of early Islam, which was also undergoing its own developments and sectarian struggles revolving around a set of terms and categories shared in common with various Jewish and Judaizing groups. Rather than regard Saadya as protecting an already established normativity, I wish instead to step back and argue that his synthesis may well betray an attempt to patch over an inchoateness with a newly imagined normativity, one paradoxically supplied by Islam. Then in the following chapter, I seek to situate Saadya within his immediate Islamicate environment, arguing that what he is doing is identical to what Muslim theologians were doing at the exact same time. Despite this we often insist on appending the adjective "Jewish" to Saadya so that he becomes a "Jewish" *mutakallim*, assuming that this rubric exists as somehow distinct from a "Muslim" *mutakallim*.[36]

Saadya Gaon

Saʿīd ibn Yūsuf al-Fayyūmī (882–942) was born about one hundred kilometers to the south of modern-day Cairo,[37] and he would go on to distinguish himself as one of the most important rabbinic leaders (*geonim*; sg. *gaon*) associated with the academies of Sura and Pumbedita (both in Babylonia or modern-day Iraq)—hence the name Saadya Gaon. These academies, it will be recalled, were responsible for the codification of the Babylonian Talmud in the sixth century and subsequently for beginning the process of making it authoritative over Jewish communities throughout the Mediterranean. This process of rabbinic legitimation and consolidation did not happen overnight; rather, it represents an end process that witnessed many ideological struggles that included the existence of antagonistic institutions of authority. Saadya does not represent the end of this process so much as an integral part of its development. Rather than regard him simply as inheriting the mantle of orthodoxy, it might be more accurate to envisage him as a key figure in the very manufacture of that orthodoxy. The paradox, of course, is that this orthodoxy absorbed key elements both from Islam and what would soon be taxonomized as a variety of Jewish heterodoxies.

The medieval Jewish polymath, Abraham ibn Ezra (1089–1167) referred to him using the rabbinic title "the chief spokesperson in all matters of learning."[38] One of his modern biographers, Henry Malter, continues this trend by writing of him in equally glowing terms, all the while acknowledging that "the period in question is represented in Jewish annals by an almost blank page, and there is but little hope that the page will ever be written upon."[39] Malter continues,

> The man who was to inaugurate a new era in Jewish learning and literature springs out of the darkness to light the torch of reason in the gloom-encompassed camp of his brethren, and, his mission performed, darkness again engulfs him; for according to the records Saadia died "in melancholia."[40]

Saadya spent considerable time in Baghdad, the cosmopolitan center of the Abbāsid caliphate, and a hotbed of Islamic theological speculation (*kalām*) associated with the Muʿtazila school of thought, a feature that I shall discuss in greater detail in the following chapter. Within this larger context,

Saadya was among the first important rabbinic figures to write extensively in Arabic, and he is generally considered to be one of the founders of Judeo-Arabic literature, composing works on biblical and other interpretation,[41] linguistics,[42] and theology,[43] in addition to writing a Hebrew-Arabic dictionary known as *Sefer ha-Egron*[44] and translating the Bible into Arabic. For the purposes of the present chapter it is important to note that he was heavily involved, like all *mutakallimūn* (theologians), in religious polemics, seeking to articulate and defend an imagined normativity against the threat of others, especially the Karaites,[45] a sectarian movement that denied the validity and authority of the Oral Torah.[46]

In the secondary literature, Saadya is described as central to the formation of rabbinic Judaism. Graetz, for example, hails him as the one responsible for transferring Judaism to a "European ground":

> Judaism assumed, so to speak, a European character, and deviated more and more from its Oriental form. Saadiah was the last important link in its development in the East. . . . He was a man of extensive knowledge who had absorbed the learning of the Mahometans and Karaites, and impregnated it with Talmudic elements. More remarkable even than his knowledge was his personality. His was a religious spirit and deep moral earnestness. He had a decided character, and belonged to those who know how to render account of their actions, and who persevere in carrying out what they think right.[47]

While not quite as glowing in his characterization, Goitein writes of Saadya,

> Although of Egyptian origin, [Saadya] was so great a scholar that he succeeded in becoming Gaon, that is, the spiritual head of the Jewish community, who had his seat in Baghdad, in addition to his substantial greatness as a doctor of the Jewish law, Saadya excelled as a philosopher and theologian, as a linguist of great originality and even as a composer of religious poetry.[48]

This "renaissance man" of late antiquity was, depending on the assessment, the one who made Judaism European (as opposed to Oriental), stole from his rivals what he needed, and introduced reason into Judaism.[49] Saadya and the Babylonian Geonim were responsible for leading the great

Babylonian Jewish academies and, along with their Palestinian counterparts, represented the main religious and intellectual authority of world Jewry. Although tensions certainly existed between the Babylonian and the Palestinian Geonim over certain matters such as the calendar, it is important not to forget that there also existed another group, most notably the Exilarchs, who vied with the Geonim for power at this time. The Exilarch, leader of the exile (*rosh golah*; Ar. *ra'īs jalūt*), was the head of an institution that had a lengthy history in Babylonian Jewry that far predated the rise of Islam in the area.[50] This position was largely hereditary and based on presumed descent from King David. Under the Muslim caliphs, the institution was largely responsible for the collection of taxes to be paid to the royal court, wherein the Exilarchs made their home. As Wasserstrom notes, on account of their omnipresence in the court we possess many Muslim accounts of the Exilarchs, but virtually none of the Geonim.[51]

There existed numerous tensions between Geonim and the Exilarch in Babylonia despite the fact that the former officially appointed the latter. One Gaon refers to an Exilarch "who cannot control Bible or Talmud or make practical decisions but is powerful through money and closeness to the throne."[52] Another feud, with major intellectual consequences to be discussed later, arose when the Geonim overlooked Anan ben David (ca. 715–ca. 795), the oldest son of the recently deceased Exilarch, and instead appointed his younger brother, Haninah. Legend has it that when Anan refused to recognize the new Exilarch and instead contested the office, he was subsequently thrown into jail, and released only after Abū Ḥanīfah (the founder of the Muslim legal school that bears his name) convinced him to tell the Caliph that he would not only not contest the Geonic decision but also actively create his own religion.[53] Whether or not this story is historically accurate, it nonetheless shows how Muslim authorities, here symbolized by the Caliph himself, played an active role in inner Jewish religio-politics. Those associated with Anan ben David and his textual methods were subsequently called Ananites, the forbearers to the Karaites, and they offered a completely different paradigm of leadership and, indeed, of Judaism.[54]

Two important features emerge from this Gaonic–Exilarch tension. The first is that just prior to the rise of Saadya it is clear that there existed various understandings of Judaism that revolved around issues such as authority, definition of legitimacy, and the nature and function of the Oral Torah. Such matters, then, were not stable, but very much in a flux. Second, as Wasserstrom duly noted some twenty years ago, early Islam witnessed the creation of "the *only* important Jewish sects after the destruction of the Second Temple."[55] This is significant because it seems that in this larger context Islam permitted not only a proliferation of rival Judaisms but also the stability that would eventually witness one of these Judaisms, rabbinic, emerge as authoritative.

This is why Saadya's paradigm becomes so important. As we will see, he makes rabbinic Judaism normative by coopting many of the intellectual innovations of the Karaites and others, and he effectively marks the beginning of the so-called silent treatment that the Rabbanites gave to their rivals. What became rabbinic Judaism, then, was not imposed as normative overnight, but took centuries of contestation with rival groups at the center (e.g., the Karaites) to say nothing of other sectarian movements on the margins (e.g., groups such as the Isawiyya in Persia or the Khazars of Central Asia). Yet, and despite this complexity, our dominant paradigm of orthodoxy–heterodoxy or who is really "Jewish" (e.g., the rabbis) and who is not (e.g., Karaites, the Isawiyya, the Khazars) focuses almost solely on rabbinic Judaism, thereby ignoring these rival Judaisms. It is also worth noting that every single version of Judaism that emerges under early Islam is in some way, shape, or form beholden to Islamic expressions, which, of course, are also in a considerable degree of flux in this period. Again, the paradigm should less be one of "borrowing" or "influencing," and more one of porosity as rival understandings of authority and leadership are being developed by Jewish and Muslim social groups in response to similar political and social stimuli. If we are to rethink the paradigm here we must now move beyond such hackneyed narratives that posit anachronistic normativities. The burgeoning Islamic Empire, complete with the political uncertainty engendered by it, provided an instability that provoked numerous responses and, at the same time and perhaps paradoxically, a stability that nurtured the rise and fall of an inchoate set of Judaisms in the two hundred years after the death of Muhammad. Let me now examine a few of these Judaisms.

The Isawiyya

The late antique period was awash with messianic and apocalyptic speculation,[56] into which the originary message of Muhammad undoubtedly tapped.[57] As the likes of Israel Friedlander, and more recently Wasserstrom have argued, there was a common semantic matrix from which emerged various groups—Jewish, Muslim, Jewish-Muslim, or Muslim-Jewish—many of which would later be written off using some version on the theme of heterodox pietism.[58] Such groups, as Shlomo Pines argued, would have existed alongside Jewish-Christian communities in places such as Jerusalem at the time of Muʿāwiyah (r. 661–680), the founder of the Umayyad Caliphate.[59] Before all these groups were subsequently deemed heterodox, however, they were, of course, mainstream. The messianism that produced Muhammad and that would undoubtedly have led a large number of Jews—keeping in mind the underdefined nature of this term on the Arabian Peninsula—to accept his apocalyptic message gave way in the coming centuries to a variety of Jewish messianic movements that only make sense within the larger context of the sectarianism associated with early Islamic history. To use the words of Averil Cameron, "Islam took shape within a context of extreme religious and cultural tension."[60] To this we must certainly add that so, too, did Judaism. Yet, for some reason it seems to be preferable to keep Judaism out of this larger context by assuming it to be more normative or stable than it possibly could have been.

This early Islamic milieu, for example, witnessed the rise of proto-Shīʿī groups who were coalescing around the personality of Alī—the cousin and son-in-law of Muhammad—and his descendants.[61] In addition to these were a number of other groups with pro-Alid connections, such as the Khārijites and other ghulāt (extremist) groups, which again only in retrospect would be labeled as "heterodox." Indeed, the rise and ultimate success of the Abbāsid uprising against the Umayyad ruling dynasty was largely based on its ability to tap into this early Shīʿī messianism that included, among other things, the apocalyptic symbolism associated with the slogan "black banners from the East."[62]

The Isawiyya seem to have had their origins in the mid-eighth century, which corresponded to the fall of the Umayyad caliphate and the initial apocalypticism associated with the rise of the Abbāsid one. Against this backdrop, there existed a plethora of loosely connected and largely underdefined proto-Shīʿite ghulāt (extremist) movements.[63] Pines, for example, argued that Abū ʿĪsā al-Iṣfahānī, the leader of this—for lack of a better term—"Jewish sect," was most likely influenced by a combination of Jewish and Christian beliefs and that would have included a set of apocalyptic texts such as the *Doctrina Iacobi*, a seventh-century Greek Christian text that records a prophet in Arabia at the time of the birth of Islam.[64] But, again, note that Pines falls back on the language of "influences" and "borrowing." Moreover, he also wants to make this into an intellectual movement based on the reading of texts, when, if anything the Isawiyya seem to have been the apocalyptic rebellion of a lower class.[65] My brief analysis here relies on the pathbreaking analysis of Wasserstrom, who has done more than anyone else to show not only the filiations between the Isawiyya and various sectarian Muslim groups but also the far reaching consequences of this group. For Wasserstrom, following the earlier study by Friedlander,[66] the similarities between these Muslim or quasi-Muslim ghulāt groups, some of whom would be eventually folded into what would emerge as normative Twelver Shī'ism, and the Isawiyya, are more than coincidental, but most likely based on real historical circumstances and interactions. For Wasserstrom,

> Abu Isa is the most influential Jewish "prophet" between Bar Cochba in the second century and Shabbetai Tzvi in the seventeenth century. In fact, this charismatic sectarian played on Jewish Messianic expectations in an almost-successful attempt to create a new political Judaism along the lines of Shi'ism.[67]

Abū 'Īsā al-Iṣfahānī was born in the early eighth century in Persia, hence the name al-Iṣfahānī. Persia was a hotbed of messianic sentiment that witnessed, for example, the impetus behind the Abbāsid revolution. It was an environment wherein a variety of Jewish and Muslim messianic groups drew upon a wide range of figures and tropes that they held in common. In Wasserstrom's apposite formulation,

> The early Muslims did not borrow their Messiah from Judaism, nor was Jewish Messianic imagery lent by a Jew to a Muslim in the sense that a lender lends to a debtor. Rather, Muslims consciously and creatively reimagined the Messiah. These Islamic rereadings, consonant with the decentralized pluralism of the Jewish redeemer myths, never pronounced one image of the Messiah as definitive. There were, of course, no councils of Judaism or Islam to rule on the officially proper Messiah.[68]

With no monolithic or monothetic sense of what or who a Messiah was or should be, Jewish groups could rely upon a prophetic vocabulary supplied by Muslim sectarian groups (many of which would eventually be labeled as "Shī'ī"), just as Muslim groups sought to recycle Jewish motifs. Neither, of course, were historians and neither were interested in ascertaining what was authentically "Jewish" or "Muslim." Nor were either interested in saying who had what first or who borrowed from whom. Such questions, to reiterate, are modern questions, ones supplied by our largely Orientalist framework. If anything, we seem to have an environment that consisted of a common conceptual vocabulary and often shared systems of hermeneutics. Within such an environment it is difficult, if not impossible, to neatly untangle these messianic threads from one another. Abū ʿĪsā's quasi-political, quasi-religious sectarian movement, the Isawiyya, remained one of the most important sectarian movements in Judaism, along with the Karaites (to be discussed presently) until the seventeenth century. While they were by no means the only Jewish messianic movement of the period, they were certainly among the most important. According to the Muslim heresiographer, al-Shahrastānī (1086–1153), writing much later, Abū ʿĪsā claimed:

> He was a prophet [*nabī*] and a prophetic messenger [*rasūl*] of the awaited Messiah [*al-masīḥ al-muntaẓar*]; that the Messiah has five harbingers [*rusul*] who precede him one after the other ... that the Messiah is the best of the children of Adam; that he is of a higher status than the foregoing prophets [*anbiyāʾ*]; and that since he is his own apostle, he is the most excellent of them. He enjoined faith in the Messiah, exalting the mission [*daʿwa*] of the harbinger; he believed that the harbinger is also the Messiah.[69]

The Arabic terms transliterated in this paragraph have decidedly proto-Shīʿī valences, most of which would go on to become staples of normative Twelver ideology. We are thus able to see how Abū ʿĪsā combines "Jewish" and "Muslim" messianic vocabularies in such a manner that he is understandable to both groups. Rather than say that one "influences" the other, it might be more apposite to imagine them as intimately linked. The Isawiyya thus seem to be able to work on the margins of the hyphen in the phrase "Jewish–Muslim." Again, according to Wasserstrom,

> They could be recognized as Jews by (Rabbanite and Karaite) Jews because they seemed Judaically orthoprax, and could be recognized as believers (by Khārijite and Shiʿite) Muslims because they seemed Islamically orthodox. This was, perhaps, an unwieldy if not spurious symmetry.[70]

It is this paradox, the hyphen separating Jew and Muslim, which makes groups such as the Isawiyya—and perhaps even other groups that have not yet come down to us—so interesting. Both Muslim and Jew, neither Muslim nor Jew, they occupy the margins of history. They become the groups that give definition to the center while at the same time they were subject to further marginalization. So while the Isawiyya will rarely appear in surveys documenting the history of Judaism or in general classes on Jewish history, in the dark shadows associated with the late antique period they provided a valid socio-religious framework that only in retrospect became labeled as heterodox.

Abū 'Īsā, for example, claimed to be the last of the five heralds from God announcing the arrival of the Messiah and the end of days.[71] He acknowledged, for example, Jesus and Muhammad as true prophets, but only to their own followers—and here he seems to have been part of the same environment that produced polythetic and inclusive messianic works such as *Doctrina Iacobi* and the *Secrets of Rabbi Shimon bar Yoḥai*, to be discussed presently, though again I do not want to reduce this simply to borrowings or influences. Abū 'Īsā was not an antinomian and seems to have believed in some notion of Jewish law (*halakhah*). Insofar as it is possible to reconstruct his doctrines from later Muslim heresiologists (he was after all ignored by Jewish sources), he forbade meat, fowl, and wine, and instituted a cycle of ten prayers (which included the *shemoneh esrei*) in a twenty-four-hour cycle.[72] It is interesting to note that the early Karaites made similar pronouncements. Also, at least according to al-Shahrastānī, members of the Isawiyya were allowed to marry rabbinic Jews because they shared a similar commitment to the *halakhah* and holy days.[73]

After his messianic claims, legend has it that Abū 'Īsā led some sort of messianic uprising before perishing in battle. This, however, was not the end of the Isawiyya. Indeed, according to Wasserstrom, the Isawiyya existed as a discrete Jewish sect for at least another three centuries.[74] They were not, as some later scholars of Jewish–Muslim relations want to claim, a short-lived or anomalous messianic movement.[75] Indeed, they show up frequently in subsequent Muslim literature, especially heresiologies, where they receive a larger treatment than both Rabbanites and Karaites. However, as mentioned, one searches contemporaneous rabbinic literature in vain for any mention of them. Although the Isawiyya are frequently left out of the "Jewish" curriculum, the exemplar of rabbinic Judaism, Maimonides, writing in the twelfth century, could still write of Abū 'Īsā and the Isawiyya that there was an exodus of a multitude of Jews, numbering hundreds of thousands from the East beyond Isfahan, led by an individual who pretended to be the Messiah. They were accoutered with military equipment and drawn swords, and slew all those that encountered them. According to the information I have received, they reached the vicinity of Baghdad. This happened at the beginning of the reign of the Umayyads.[76]

Despite the fact the he mentions the revolt, Maimonides nowhere gives us the name of Abū ʿĪsā. Although Maimonides puts the date of the uprising earlier than al-Shahrastānī does (perhaps he meant the beginning of the Abbāsid dynasty?), the messianic forces—on Maimonides's reading—are stopped by the caliph on the outskirts of Baghdad with a group of (normative?) Jewish sages, who ask the leaders of the rebellion who their instigator was. They replied, "This man here, one of the descendants of David, whom we know to be pious and virtuous. This man whom we knew to be a leper at night, arose the following morning healthy and sound."[77] The sages subsequently inform Abū ʿĪsā's followers that they are incorrect in their interpretation and that, to them, he possesses none of the marks of the Messiah. The caliph then made them return home and "ordered them to make a special mark on their garments, the writing of the word *cursed*, and to attach one iron bar in the back and one in the front."[78]

Maimonides's retelling of the story neatly encapsulates the tensions between centers and margins in the Jewish world under early Islam. It is a rebellion too that foreshadows the Abbāsid revolution—an armed and messianic rebellion based on still inchoate Shīʿī doctrine then developing in the Eastern provinces of the burgeoning Empire.[79] Unlike the Abbāsid revolution, which did succeed in gaining power at the center, Maimonides presents the Isawiyya as ignorant of rabbinic sources—which by the thirteenth century are certainly normative—and when informed of their ignorance, they politely agreed with the rabbis whom they acknowledge to be in the possession of the correct understanding. It is a retroactive story to be sure, one that depicts Jewish sectarian movements as ignorant of rabbinic Judaism and as easily correctible. The situation, on the ground, however, was probably much more complex.

We get yet another glimpse of this Jewish-Islamic milieu in the apocalyptic *Secrets of Rabbi Shimon bar Yoḥai*, also composed in the mid-eighth century, apparently in a Persian environment.[80] This work, written at the end of the Umayyad caliphate and at the beginning of the Abbāsid one—to wit, a time of increased messianism and apocalypticism—identifies Muhammad as the fulfillment of Jewish messianic speculation. The work ends with the hope for the restoration of the Temple in Jerusalem and the beginnings of the Abbāsid revolution that will usher in an apocalyptic battle between Israel and Byzantium, followed by the Final Judgment. Near the beginning of the text, Metatron—an individual who figures highly in both Jewish and Islamic angelology[81]—informs Rabbi Shimon that

> because of their oppression of Israel, the Holy One, blessed be He, sends Ishmaelites against them, who make war against them in order to save Israel from their hands. Then a crazy man possessed by a spirit arises and speaks lies about the Holy One, blessed be He, and he conquers the land, and there is enmity between them and the sons of Esau.[82]

After Shimon asks Metatron if this is correct, the angel informs him in a passage worth quoting at length:

> The second king that will arise from the sons of Ishmael loves Israel; he repairs the breaches of the temples, makes war with the sons of Esau, and slaughters their armies. Then a king will arise whose name is Marwan. He will be a herdsman of asses, and they will take him from the asses and make him king, and the sons of Edom will come against him and kill him. Another will arise in his place, and he will have peace on all sides, and he will love Zion and die in peace. And another king will arise in his place, and hold firm the kingdom with his sword and his bow, and there will be strife in his days, sometimes in the east and sometimes in the west, sometimes in the north and sometimes in the south. He will make war on all, and when the Gairin in the west falls on the sons of Ishmael in Damascus, the kingdom of Ishmael will fall. And of that time it is said: "The Lord hath broken the staff of the wicked" (Isaiah xiv, 5). While the strong men of the sons of Kedar are still with him, a north-east wind will rebel against him and many armies will fall from him: the first on the Tigris, the second on the Euphrates, the third in between. He flees before them, and his sons will be captured and killed and hung on trees.[83]

The *Secrets of Rabbi Shimon bar Yoḥai* is remarkable in the sense that an ostensibly "Jewish" document recycles Muslim apocalyptic speculation, some of which had already been paradoxically recycled from Jewish sources by early Muslims. Again, rather than imagine this as borrowing or influence, we should see it as collective world-making in an environment wherein ideas moved freely between porous boundaries. The result is that it is impossible to know what is "Jewish" and what is "Muslim."

For Wasserstrom, sectarian groups like the Isawiyya and those responsible for the *Secrets*, if in fact they are different from one another, represent, what he calls, "a comparatively long-lived reaction to Islamicization."[84] I wish to challenge this thesis and to argue instead that rather than react to Islamicization, such groups were instead caught up in the very processes of Islamicization. The eastern reaches of the growing Islamic empire were a hotbed of messianic fervor and apocalyptic speculation, and in participating in this environment, Jews and Muslims, on the margins, did not differ when it came to both responding to and creating their social worlds. Indeed, if anything they seem to have been indistinguishable, since they both saw the other as invested in the same apocalyptic drama that focused on Jerusalem and the coming End of Days. They thought with, from, and to one another—recycling motifs, terms, and cosmologies without recourse to who had what first. In fact, contrary to many of the scholars examined in the previous chapter, even we in the present cannot work out who influenced whom or who borrowed from whom. In the shadows of history, our perspective, contrary to the claims of many, is obscured. Rather than celebrate this obscurity, there is an unfortunate tendency to paper over it.

We see this clearly in the *Secrets of Rabbi Shimon bar Yoḥai*, which shares a vocabulary of political uncertainty, messianic revolution, and armed revolt. Many of these motifs find expression in ghulāt narratives that revolve around the Shīʿī Mahdī ("messiah") figure. None of this was conscious, of course. It was the case of a well-worn stock of themes, vocabularies, and motifs crossing porous boundaries. If "the Muslims" become part of the messianic redemption of Jews in the Holy Land,[85] we not infrequently see "Jews" cast as the enemies of Islam in the cataclysmic upheavals associated with End of Days.[86] Alongside such prophesies, we also possess those volumes like the *Secrets of Rabbi Shimon bar Yoḥai* that see Muslims as part of the larger story of the deliverance of the Jews, just as we possess Shīʿī messianic topoi that link the Mahdī as emerging from the House of Alī, itself imagined as related to the House of Aaron.[87] Groups on each side of the imaginary hyphen thus seem to be using those on the other side—sometimes consciously, but most often not—for their own purposes and ultimately for their own self-definition.

These, of course, are not the traditional Jews and Muslims of history or even the ones that the field of religious studies is accustomed to imagine. Nor are they neatly defined and discrete species that interact with one another. Rather, they are meta-historical narratives that reveal a shared vocabulary that draws on a common stock of characters and ideas. Just as claimants to the throne of Jewish messianism drew upon themes in use by ghulāt and other pro-Alid and proto- Shī'ī groups, so too did the latter invoke Judaized or Judaizing notions of prophecy and prophethood. However, to return to the theme of the last chapter, there seems to have existed some sort of Near Eastern messianic "library" from which these messianic and apocalyptic doctrines could be checked out. Even as more normative versions of rabbinic Judaism, Sunnism, and Shī'ism began to develop and exert their authority over broad swathes of the Islamic Empire, these groups still existed and helped to provide definition at the center.

Karaites

The Karaites were yet another group that emerged in the pietistic and messianic environment associated with the eighth century. While this is certainly not the place to retell their story or get into their historical development, I mention them in the present context on account of their genesis within the aforementioned sectarian environment.[88] Karaism represents yet another response to Islam. If groups like the Isawiyya represented a messianic response to the social uncertainty associated with the spread of Islam,[89] the Karaite response was to ground authority in the Written as opposed to Oral Torah. While Anan ben David, encountered earlier in this chapter, is usually credited as the founder of this sectarian movement, it might be more apposite to refer to him, as Ben-Shammai notes, as the founder of a rival legal school (Ar. *madhab*) to that of the rabbis.[90] Within this context, it is worth noting that this was also the time of the codification of the four major legal schools in Islam (the Ḥanafī, Mālikī, Shāfi'ī, and Ḥanbalī).[91] Regardless, it seems that many of Anan's immediate followers, the so-called Ananites, envisaged him as creating a new sect. Whether or not we believe the apocryphal story that the only way he could get out of jail was to convince the caliph that he was part of a different religious group than the Rabbanites, it seems quite clear that he rejected the rabbinic tradition of scriptural exegesis and its use in the derivation of the law (*halakhah*) in favor of a new and independent legal system.[92]

The Karaites seem to have emerged at the same time as Anan, either as an offshoot of the Ananites or as an independent group. Unlike Anan, they began to polemicize overtly against rabbinic Judaism and its methods of interpretations, especially its development of the Oral Torah. One of its earliest leaders was Daniel al-Qūmisī (fl. late ninth century), who renounced the diaspora and blamed its existence on a corrupt rabbinic leadership. Instead, he joined "the remnant, who come from [every] land to Jerusalem in penitence, and in order to observe the religious commandments before [the advent of] the time of trouble."[93] Prior to Saadya's redefinition of rabbinic Judaism, early Karaite thinkers, such as al-Qūmisī, criticized the rabbis for their lack of rationalistic and philological interpretation of Scripture. They accused the Rabbanites of a human-made tradition and of claiming that the Bible possessed multiple meanings. The Karaites, in contrast, argued that there was only one correct interpretation articulated through the exercise of reason. Fast forward a generation, the subject matter of the following chapter, and we witness rationalism enter rabbinic Judaism and become its foundation stone.

Many of these early Karaites, writing in the Islamic East, sought to create a rational and systematic approach to the Bible. In so doing, they drew upon genres developed in early Islamic circles—such as grammars, dictionaries, theological summae, and biblical commentaries—and applied them to Judaism. It is important to note within this context that many of these genres appeared in the tenth century in the Islamic East. Salo Wittmayer Baron, aware of this, nevertheless warned us of a theory of "pan-Karaitism" that was prevalent in nineteenth-century scholarship. This "pan-Karaite vein," as he called it, was based on the mythology that "the rise of Karaism shook the Jewish community to its foundation, and that the great danger of a complete breakdown was averted only by the intervention of the militant and superlatively gifted Saadiah Gaon."[94] He continues:

> Before long all the revolutionary discoveries of that period in Hebrew philology, Bible exegesis, and philosophy were ascribed to Karaites or, at best, to Rabbanites reacting to the rise of the new sect. These exaggerations of literary history have, as we shall see, been effectively disproved by more recent painstaking research, which, at

times, went to the opposite extreme of denying even some indubitable pioneering merits of Karaite authors.[95]

While Baron sought to minimize the influence of the Karaites, it is no exaggeration to say that their literary genres and their rationalist program, both derived from largely Islamic sources, changed the shape of rabbinic Judaism. According to Rina Drory, for example, we see a disproportionate number of Karaite authors using many of these new genres in the tenth century.[96] One of the most important of these, as Daniel Frank has shown, was the Bible commentary[97]—a genre that would go on to define Rabbanism in later centuries.[98]

Conclusions

Saadya Gaon, as we shall see in the following chapter, was extremely critical of the Ananites and Karaites and he was among the most critical of their exegetical methods. However, in criticizing these groups—many of which were comprised of elite subsections of Islamic Jewry—he ultimately absorbed many of their teachings, especially those that involved the rationalist interpretation of Scripture. It was this absorption of Karaite ideas, which were themselves inflected with a Muʿtazilite rationalist apologetic, that enabled him to articulate rabbinic Judaism. It was an articulation moreover that would last for the coming centuries, to be challenged again only with the rise of Reform Judaism in nineteenth-century Germany, which, of course, was also the tradition that gave rise to the trope or myth of "Jewish–Muslim relations."

By the time we reach Saadya Gaon, who is often constructed as the first Jewish philosopher and the figure who sets in motion the era of medieval florescence, we witness a host of rival Judaisms, all of which are indebted in some way, shape, or form to Islam. Be it the Isawiyya in Persia, the Khazars in Central Asia, the Karaites scattered throughout the regions of Islam, but with an epicenter in the Land of Israel, and the Exilarchs. All of these Jewish groups—some powerful, some powerless; some messianic, some less so—took shape against the backdrop of Islam. It is important to remember, however, that this is not the Islam of later centuries. Instead, there existed various groups—many of which were phenomenologically identical to the Jewish groups just mentioned—that sought to define their own legitimacy by reconstituting Islamic authority. Some of these groups sought legitimacy in the House of Alī (modeled, as we saw, on the House of Aaron), as a direct descendent of the Prophet, only parts of which would later coalesce as Twelver Shiʿism; others sought it in the customs (*sunna*) and the community (*jamāʿa*), the so-called *ahl al-sunna wa'l-jamāʿa*, which would eventually emerge as Sunni Islam.

But none of this was yet clear in the period examined in the context of this chapter. The end of late antiquity signals for both Jews and Muslims—be it in the caliphal center of Baghdad or in the furthest reaches of the burgeoning Empire—a sense of flux and motion. Sectarian movements in each tradition seem to have fed off of one another as they simultaneously shared interreligious systems of meanings against a broader backdrop of political and social uncertainty. The history of Muslims and Islams, of Jews and Judaisms, in the first centuries after the death of Muhammad is covered in darkness. A paradigm that assumes two monolithic entities—"Islam" and "Judaism"—that interact occasionally with one another cannot account for the relevant data. Instead, we need a new paradigm, one that can account for the pluralism of voices and the porosity of borders between these groups.

This chapter has sought to do this by showing how Jewish sectarian movements both incorporated and thought with Muslims both positively and negatively, just as Muslim groups thought with Jews, again both positively and negatively. There is no one-size-fits-all paradigm. Rather, we witness both groups draw upon sets of decentralized messianic narratives to carve out ontic space for themselves. Phenomenologically, these Jewish and Muslim sectarian groups are very similar, using as they do a common set of terms, tropes, and vocabularies.

These groups did not disappear with the expenditure of energy on the part of what would become normative Rabbanism, Sunnism, and Shiʿism. Rather they coexisted with them, hovering around the margins, helping to define what counted as the center. But even when we get to the towering enterprise of Saadya, we will see that Judaism and Islam, even though the border that divides them is becoming less porous and more policed, still need one another.

4
The Manufacture of Orthodoxy

Are we Greeks? Are we Jews? But who, we? Are we (not a chronological, but a pre-logical question) first Jews or first Greeks? And does not that strange dialogue between the Jew and the Greek ... have the form of infinite separation and of the unthinkable, unsayable transcendence of the other? To what horizon of peace does the language which asks this question belong? From whence does it draw the energy of its question? Can it account for the coupling of Judaism and Hellenism? And what is the legitimacy, what is the meaning of the copula in this proposition from perhaps the most Hegelian of modern novelists: "Jewgreek is greekjew. Extremes meet"?[1]

THE PREVIOUS CHAPTER began the process of taxonomizing the complexities associated with the intersection of various Judaisms and Islams—and even hybrid groups of Jewmuslims and Muslimjews—in the late antique period. The focus was less on the discovery of previously undiscovered and probably nonexistent texts that might pinpoint the so-called parting of the ways between the two religions—or, better, between groups that in retrospect became signified as orthodox or heterodox in each religion—than in trying to work out a vocabulary to help account meaningfully for this complexity. This is, in other words, an attempt to return us to a period that is usually overlooked in surveys of Judaism and Islam, where the overwhelming tendency is to move directly from the role of Judaism in the rise of Islam to the medieval "golden age" in places such as Muslim Spain. This latter narrative—the abrupt shift from the late antique Arabian Peninsula to medieval al-Andalus—is predicated on a monolithic Judaism and a monolithic Islam bumping up against one another and interacting. Such interactions are often described in the secondary literature using the language of "borrowings" and "influences." Such a model works on the assumption, recall Shlomo Dov Goitein's basic symbiotic framework, that two religions (implied to be distinct species) remain largely untransformed by the other at their imagined essences. If there are changes, they are usually imagined as superficial. Jews, for example, began to write and express themselves in Arabic, but the next step, namely, that they began to think Arabically and Islamically, is rarely entertained. Jews may be "influenced," say, by the terms and categories of Islamic philosophy, but once again the next step, namely, that they began to articulate an Islamic Judaism, is never made. In none of these instances are we encouraged to think about the creation of Judaism as we would come to recognize it in subsequent centuries.

Goitein, however, was largely uninterested in the period examined in the previous chapter. His *Jews and Arabs*, for example, assumes that "Judaism was a fully developed system at the time when the Arab Muslims made their first conquests."[2] Again, though, we may ask what Judaism and where? Goitein also reasons "that Muhammad's strict monotheism must have impelled at least some of his believers to seek instruction from equally strict monotheists."[3] And, again, we might ask, what about the shared messianic frameworks witnessed in the previous chapter and why must we assume that ideas moved unidirectionally? Yet, despite his earlier self-assurance, Goitein does seem aware of a certain amount of the complexity to which I have alluded; however, he largely overlooks it in favor of normativity. He writes:

> One is led to assume that the influence of Judaism on early Islam must have been considerable, if not decisive. This question is extremely complicated, and an analysis of more technical details would be required to discuss it fully. However, the basic fact of the important rôle of Judaism in the development of post-koranic Islam cannot be denied. [Although] ... we shall learn that Islam amply repaid Judaism.[4]

Between the debt owed by Islam to the Jews of Arabia and its subsequent repayment to those Jews living under the orbit of medieval Islam, Goitein deals not with complexity, but a normativity developed in and through the law. While he acknowledges the "blackout prevailing in Jewish history during the first two centuries of Islam," he reasons that this was reflective of the lowly status of the Jews.[5] While I have argued that this "blackout" is the result of a combination of the paucity of sources and looking at the wrong sources altogether, in conjunction with the numerous ideological struggles and skirmishes that broke out over issues like authority and interpretation, Goitein reproduces the claim that in the darkness there occurred the rabbinic consolidation so that when we return to the more certain light of history we encounter a fully formed and normative Judaism. This normativity is then projected back onto the Arabian Jews with whom Muhammad would have interacted.

Mistrustful of this narrative, the present chapter once again argues that it is necessary to examine, even if it is currently impossible to describe in detail, the contents of the wide variety of Islams and Judaisms that had yet to be consolidated under their respective normative or orthodox theological programs. Instead of envisaging Saadya as the terminus of this consolidation, I prefer to see him as at or near the beginning. These varieties of Jewishmuslim or Muslimjewish groups,[6] nourished by a common set of concerns and fueled with a similar conceptual vocabulary, were often closer—as witnessed in the previous chapter—to one another than to other groups within their own so-called religious tradition. Rather than see Islam "break off" from Judaism during Muhammad's later prophetic career and in the ensuing years—something that is often symbolized in the primary and secondary literature as the nascent Muslim community's switch of its *qibla* from Jerusalem during prayer to Mecca—we need a different way of thinking about the historical development that would only much later become the partition of Judaism and Islam. Instead of positing the former as stable and the latter as instable in late antiquity, and then turning the tables in the medieval period, our paucity of sources that detail this intersection and the ubiquitous problem of later sources masquerading as earlier ones means that we need to search for different models, particularly ones that acknowledge that there existed other modes of identity formation than just a retroactively imagined religious one.[7]

My goal in the previous chapter was less to provide histories of these groups, about which we often know very little on account of later silence, than to problematize the dominant narrative that simply sees the normative Judaism and the normative Islam of later centuries interact in such a manner that there is very little or no internal transformations. This narrative, to reiterate, sees a stable Judaism give birth to Islam and then in the following centuries, as Islam became more stable, it, in turn, facilitated what Goitein calls a "bourgeois revolution" for Jews.[8] Such a narrative, however, betrays the complex struggles that course betwixt and between groups that shared a common social world, one that was defined in part by apocalypticism and messianism. Recall the Isawiyya who could combine a Jewish orthopraxy with a Muslim orthodoxy, while not quite belonging to either rabbinic Judaism or what was slowly coalescing into Twelver Shiʿism. Rather than write cartographies for such groups, we instead supply a grand narrative that invokes tropes like "midwifery" and "fructuous symbiosis"[9] that both sets the stage for and subsequently leads into the so-called golden age of Muslim Spain, the assumed high point of Jewish–Muslim relations. Such a grand narrative, however, misses out or, perhaps better, consciously avoids for various ideological reasons—most of which may stem from the reification of our own post-1948 world—the complexity of identity formation on the ground. Before we could have the construction of "Jewishness" or "Muslimness," however, we had to have the invention of both Judaism and Islam as religions that were imagined to exist independently from other cultural practices and markers of identification.[10] If these religions took centuries to develop, why should we assume that their identities preceded them?

This complexity means that a model based on "borrowing" or "influence" between stable religions with retroactively projected essences is insufficient for the task of an analytical comparison. It is why I prefer to invoke the metaphor of porous borders, across which common ideas and social forms could move to be imagined and reimagined in any number of ways. This movement would have taken place against the larger backdrop of political skirmishes and power struggles associated with a rapidly expanding and slowly consolidating Empire. Identities overlapped, clashed, and transformed as opposed to remaining static with only cosmetic changes on the surface. To quote Daniel Boyarin, in his discussion of the overlapping identities between Judaism and Christianity in antiquity:

> Once I am no longer prepared to think in terms of preexistent different entities—religions, if you will—that came (gradually or suddenly) to enact their difference in a "parting of the ways," I need to ask who it was in antiquity who desired to make such a difference, how did they accomplish (or seek to accomplish) that making, and what was it that drove them?... My proposal here is that the discourse we know of as orthodoxy and heresy provides at least one crucial site for the excavation of a genealogy of Judaism and Christianity.... Authorities on both sides tried to establish a border,

a line that, when crossed, meant that someone had definitely left one group for another.[11]

As Boyarin's work reminds us the "parting of the ways" between religions, caught up as it is in often later theological and apologetical agendas, is assumed rather than investigated. We tend to simply accept and gullibly believe all that later ideological and often highly political works tell us. In the words of John Wansbrough, if "what we know of the seventh-century Hijaz (the area of Mecca, Medina, and environs) is the product of intense literary activity, then that record has got to be interpreted in accordance with what we know of literary criticism."[12] These sources, in other words, are not history, but salvation history, a subgenre of literature, and the most appropriate way to analyze them is by means of form criticism, redaction criticism, and literary criticism—in much the same manner that they have been used in the study of early Christianity and Judaism. Wansbrough is, rightly in my opinion, opposed "to that school of sanguine historiography in which the pursuit of reconstruction is seldom if ever deflected by the doubts and scruples thrown up in recent (and not so recent) years by practitioners of form-criticism, structuralism and the like."[13]

This is the position in which we find ourselves when it comes to early Islam and the various Jewish communities situated therein. The desire to paper over blurred boundaries, however, gives us less a history of Judaism and Islam than it provides a genealogy of indeterminacy.[14] If I suggested in the previous chapter that Judaism and Islam did not become completely separate entities until much later than we are accustomed to believe, this does not mean that we cannot discern distinct social groups that are in an important sense "Jewish" or "Muslim," or at the very least in the process of becoming such. While these distinctly Jewish groups are coalescing around the notion of *halakhah* and its interpretation and the same could be said for Muslims and the concept of *sharī'a*, though it is worth noting that these legal systems (both meaning "path" incidentally) share important features in common,[15] we need to be conscious of the fact of when, where, and how these two categories—Judaism and Islam—overlap. Writing of the complexity of religious forms in the late antique period, Mary Beard, John North, and S. R. F. Price discuss the need to

> investigate the degree of religious continuity in these cults traceable across the Roman world. By and large, however, in discussing the

religions of the empire we have tried to avoid thinking in terms of uniformity, or in terms of a central core "orthodox" tradition with its peripheral "variants"; we have preferred to think rather in terms of different religions as clusters of ideas, people, and rituals, sharing some common identity across time and place, but at the same time inevitably invested with different meanings in different contexts.[16]

Although these scholars are speaking about the complexity of religion in the Roman Empire, we can apply their conceptual apparatus to the early Islamic period. In the previous chapter, we witnessed how some nominally Jewish groups related to their messianic figures in ways more similar to how some nominally Muslim groups related to theirs than they did to other Jewish groups. In like manner, some Jewish groups would have undoubtedly have related to their body of law and its interpretation in ways that were phenomenally more similar to some Muslim groups than to other Jewish ones. These, for lack of a better term, "family resemblances" might help us to further understand this complexity. There is, framed somewhat differently, no one set of features that uniquely determines a Jewish group over against a Muslim group in the years immediately after the death of Muhammad. Instead of using a model in which a stable Judaism "gives birth" to Islam and then we subsequently have the existence of two stable religions interacting with one another, it might be more profitable to imagine various Jewish and Muslim groups who inhabited a common cultural grid in which beliefs, such as the messianic implications associated with the spread of Islam, and various religio-cultural practices, such as maintaining the Sabbath, were widely distributed. Ultimate distinctions between Judaism and Islam, and here I am again invoking Boyarin's thesis, were created by later "border markers"—heresiologists, theologians, among others—eager to construct discrete identities for their fellow practitioners. In so doing, they moved individuals, groups, ideas, and behaviors to one side or another of what was then, but not later, an artificial border.[17]

One of these later individuals on the Jewish side of things was the aforementioned Saadya Gaon. In his desire to define orthodoxy and orthopraxy, it was he perhaps more than anyone in the medieval or Gaonic period who successfully created this artificial line on the "proper" side of which could reside rabbinic Judaism (though admittedly one that was Arabically defined and Islamically conceptualized) and on the "wrong" side of which resided other groups now written off as heterodox (e.g., Karaites, Isawiyya, Khazars). In the language of Boyarin:

> Therefore with respect to religious history we must add yet another factor ... to wit, the activities of certain writers/speakers who wish to transform the fuzzy category into one with absolute clear borders and the family resemblances into a checklist of features that will determine an intentional definition for who is in and who is out of the group as it defines itself and, therefore, its others.[18]

Whereas Boyarin is interested in how second- and third-century heresiologists engaged in a process of creating difference between Judaism and Christianity, my goal is slightly more modest. I certainly do not want to claim that Judaism is necessarily in as much of a flux in the eighth century as it is in the third. However, I do want to argue that certain transformations occurred in large part as a response to the political upheaval associated with Islamicization and the concomitant rise in messianic speculation leading to a crisis of leadership. While it cannot be gainsaid that the Geonim, centered as they were in the great academies of Sura and Pumbedita, constituted the supreme court of the Jewish world, it is nevertheless safe to say that the eighth and ninth centuries witnessed rapid changes in the larger Islamic world that necessarily impacted what was going on in such institutions. Primary for what follows in this chapter is the rise of *Kalām*, or rationalist dogmatic theology. This school of thought, developed in Baghdad, just down the road from Sura and Pumbedita, would enable theologians in both traditions to develop and clarify the tenets of faith, namely, to articulate who was and who was not an orthodox or orthoprax believer, and to defend the religious tradition from both internal and external polemics.

Before I examine Saadya's absorption of Kalām and his ability to utilize it in the construction of rabbinic orthodoxy, allow me to sketch, in broad strokes, some of the key features of Kalām in its Islamic context. My argument is similar to what we have seen many times in the preceding chapters, namely, that Saadya draws on a shared vocabulary, neither fully Muslim nor fully Jewish, to articulate Jewishness (just as Muslim thinkers are doing the same to define Muslimness). This shared vocabulary, in other words, is responsible for establishing borders between believers and heretics, leaders and false messiahs, nomocentric cohesion and anomic outliers. While I do not want to invoke Goitein's paradigm of "fructuous symbiosis" here, it is worth noting that it was the battle over authority, belief, and leadership "on the ground" in this period that made possible what he would subsequently take for granted.

Manufacturing Orthodoxy

Theology represents the systematic articulation of what are imagined as religious truths—the nature of God, the relationship between God and humans, providence, the existence of evil, and the problem of freewill vis-à-vis determinism, to name but a few—using human reason.[19] While theologians consider themselves to be involved in the continued attempt over time to understand their religious community, and its relationship to God, to the cosmos, and to other religions, they can also be redescribed as propagandists responsible for the manufacture of religious identity. In their quest to establish an imagined normativity, theologians create, establish, and patrol orthodoxy, deciding who or what fits and what can be proscribed as "heterodox." Through their attempt to create religious consensus, then, theologians are responsible for the definition of what subgroups can be located safely within the community of believers and which ones cannot. Prior to such activities on the part of theologians, however, heterodox groups are not surprisingly imagined as part of the community of believers.[20] It is often the case, as David Brakke argues for early Christianity—again, I think our best comparative model to understand the period of early Islam—that normativity "was the result of a complex process in which differing forms . . . competed with, influenced, borrowed from, and rejected each other."[21]

While I generally try to avoid the language of "influences" and "borrowings" here, it suffices to remark that ideas then, as now, do not know boundaries. Instead it is propagandists like theologians that seek to create the boundaries that ideas, now often embodied as discrete groups, can either cross or be held up for inspection and possible rejection. Yet, as Brakke and other scholars working on Christian origins remind us, we must be cautious of assuming the priority of orthodoxy and the concomitant assumption that so-called heretics somehow reject or distort it. The unfortunate corollary of this model, still so prevalent in scholarly circles dealing with Judaism under early Islam, is that it extracts and isolates doctrinal elements and general characteristics from complex cultural forms. The result is, as we have seen, a model or models that fail either to appreciate or understand this complexity.

Here we must remember that the birth of theological speculation is generally associated with controversy and the need to justify a belief or a practice that will subsequently emerge as normative or orthodox.[22] In Second-Temple Judaism, for example, this had to do with the debates between the Pharisees and the Sadducees over the role of freewill, the afterlife, religious authority, and the nature of biblical interpretation.[23] Similarly, in early Islam, theological speculation arose on account of the need to define correct belief in the light of a series of political controversies regarding, for example, the debate over the status of the "grave sinner" (*murtakib al-kabīra*) that broke out between two rival groups, the Khārijites and the Murji'ites.[24] This was a particularly acute issue because three of the first four successors to Muhammad were assassinated. Did the assassins, for example, remain Muslims? Or, did their acts somehow separate them from the community, both in this life and the next one? The Khārijites held the grave sinner to be an infidel (*kāfir*) and, thus, beyond the pale of the community in both this life and beyond; the Murji'ites, by contrast, argued that such an individual remains a Muslim and that it is up to God to decide his fate. Other debates involved predestination (*qadar*) between the Qadarīya and the Jabrīya, not to mention the problem of how to interpret anthropomorphic and other problematic language in the Qur'ān.

All of these early debates in both Judaism and Islam have in common the fluidity of belief and the need to define normativity. This, of course, would carry into the early medieval period, the period that I will focus on for the remaining parts of this chapter.

The Rise of Kalām

Although it is important not to reduce theological speculation in early Islam to outside influence,[25] it cannot be gainsaid that the translation movement of Greek sources into Arabic at the end of the late antique period played a major role in its subsequent articulation.[26] Within this context, the most important impetus for the rise of theology was contact with Greek sources, especially those associated with logic, which created the need to try to reconcile the terminology and categories of rationalism with those of monotheism. This reconciliation, more than anything, was responsible for the genesis of monotheism as this concept came to be subsequently understood. The initial attempt at reconciliation in Islam is known as Kalām (literally "word" or "logos"), with its practitioners known as *mutakallimūn* (sg. *mutakallim*). The *mutakallim*, literally a "speaker" is, in the words of Ignaz Goldziher, "one who made a dogma or controversial theological problem into a topic for dialectical discussion and argument, offering speculative proofs for the position he urged."[27]

It is the *mutakallimūn* who sought to establish orthodoxy in both Islam and Judaism by defining what constituted proper belief and action. This may be witnessed in their writings, which usually take the form of theological summae.[28] Such treatises begin, for example, from universal principles (e.g., creation of the world, epistemology) and move to more specific concerns (e.g., prophecy, the afterlife). In keeping with the intended desire to manufacture orthodoxy, these kalāmic texts are usually polemical, providing the believer with responses to criticism of his or her religion (e.g., "if an unbeliever should say '*x*,' one should respond to him with the claim that...").

Among the earliest practitioners of Kalām were the Muʿtazilīya, also referred to as *ahl al-ʿadl waʾl-tawḥīd* (the people of [divine] justice and unity). To reiterate, this was but one of many "schools" that arose in early Islam to deal with the fluidity examined in the previous two chapters. An attempt to establish some kind of normativity on an otherwise loose set of ideas and beliefs was shared by various Muslim-Jewish and Jewish-Muslim groups. In addition to stressing God's unity and justice—by which they meant that he could not do something that would contravene justice—they emphasized the importance of reason (*ʿaql*) in religious speculation. It was early *mutakallimūn*, for example, who emphasized the importance of four sources for ascertaining truth: the Qurʾān, agreed upon *ḥadīths* (sayings of Muhammad), rational argument, and *ijmāʿ* (i.e., consensus).[29] Theology, thus, establishes the line, fine in the early centuries but growing considerably more insoluble in the coming ones, concerning what or who is "in" and what or who is "outside" of the community of believers.

Within this context, the Muʿtazila developed a comprehensive theological framework that revolved around a number of key features: God's unity, God's justice, the intermediate state of the grave sinner (i.e., as neither an infidel nor pious Muslim), reward and punishment in the afterlife, and the ethical notion that one must avoid sin and practice virtue.[30] During the ninth and tenth centuries, the Muʿtazila enjoyed tremendous success, using their rationalist principles to develop an important and influential body of scientific and exegetical literature. Their two main epicenters were Basra and Baghdad, both of which had fairly large Jewish communities that would, as we shall see presently, absorb the general theological framework of the Muʿtazila.[31]

The Rise of "Jewish Kalām"

The development of rational theology—and thus the importation and implementation of orthodoxy and heterodoxy—in Judaism took place largely in Arabic and under Islam. Prior to this, with the possible exception of Philo of Alexandria, there was little or no systematic engagement with theology. Since Philo had very little impact on subsequent Jewish thought—his biggest influence seems to have been among the early Church Fathers[32]—and since Jews in late antiquity used other models and genres to articulate their theological concerns, the development of rational theology is intimately connected to the Jewish immersion in Arabophone culture. As Jews adopted Arabic and as they began to think in Arab-Islamic categories, it was only natural that they would begin to try to connect the themes of rationalist theology that they encountered in Islam to Judaism, thereby creating and defining Judaism along rationalist lines. If they did not, Judaism would appear to be intellectually obsolete. The result was the rise of what many call "Jewish Kalām."[33]

I have a problem with this term, however, because I am not sure what intellectual work the religio-ethnic adjective performs in this locution. By using the phrase "Jewish Kalām," for example, we imply that there was something distinct (i.e., something "Jewish") about the activity, when in fact, as we shall see, there was none. Jews who engaged in Kalām wrote the same summae, used the same arguments, and often employed the same examples to illustrate their arguments. If we are to find a new vocabulary to explain the intersection of Judaism and Islam, especially in the early period, it might be more apposite to speak of "Jews who engaged in the science of Kalām" as opposed to transforming them into a distinct branch that we can refer to as "Jewish Kalām." For Kalām, regardless of the religious or ethnic adjective we put in front of it, was engaged in the process of creating normativity, and Jewish *mutakallimūn* established precisely such a normativity in Judaism by framing the religion in terms of Islam.

We do know, however, that those Jews who engaged in the science of Kalām, according to the later rationalist Maimonides, were primarily drawn to the Muʿtazila variety. He writes in *Guide* I.71:

> As for the Kalām regarding the notion of the unity of God and regarding what depends on this notion, which you will find in the writings of some *Geonim* and in those of the Karaites, it should be noted that the subject matter of the argument was taken over by

them from the mutakallimūn of Islam and that this is very scanty indeed if compared to what Islam has compiled on the subject. Also it has happened that Islam first began to take this road owing to a certain sect, namely, the Muʿtazila, from whom our coreligionists took over certain things walking upon the road of the Muʿtazila had taken. After a certain time another sect arose in Islam, namely, the Ashʿarīya, among whom other opinions arose. You will not find any of these latter opinions among our coreligionists.[34]

Note that nowhere in this passage does Maimonides use the term "Jewish Kalām." Instead he informs us that certain Jews argued that both the unaided human intellect and sense perception form the basic sources of knowledge. Human reason, in other words, is what enables the individual to make sense of the universe, to know, for example, that it is created *ex nihilo* by an omnipotent and omniscient Creator that is fundamentally or essentially different from his creation. Human reason is also the primary means and method with which to engage in the interpretation of the Bible.

The works of those Jews who were *mutakallimūn* follow the basic structure, techniques, and topics of those found among their Muslim colleagues. These include, in part, speculation about God, divine attributes, creation, revelation, prophecy, and the importance of revelation. On many of these topics, the nature of the arguments are identical to those found in "non-Jewish" kalāmic treatises and the only thing that would seem to differ is the scripture used to supply the proof texts in support of the position. Those Jews who engaged in Kalām engaged in polemics, either with other religions or with opposing positions within one's own religion. It is worth noting, however, that certain topics prevalent among Muslim *mutakallimūn*—such as the created or eternal nature of scripture, the status of the grave sinner, or that of atomism—seemed to have been of no or marginal interest among Jews.

Dāwūd al-Muqammiṣ (d. ca. 937) is generally regarded as one of the earliest rationalists in Judaism. His place in the so-called canon of medieval Jewish rationalism,[35] however, is complicated by, among other things, his purported conversion to Christianity (and subsequent reversion to Judaism).[36] Unlike other Jews who engaged in Kalām, al-Muqammiṣ composed his major theological work—ʿIshrun al-maqāla, or, *The Twenty Chapters*—in Arabic as opposed to Judeo-Arabic (i.e., Arabic written in Hebrew characters). Even the biblical proof texts are translated into Arabic and written in Arabic characters. In its basic structure and style of argumentation, the work is certainly one of Kalām, more specifically of the Muʿtazila variety. Although Sarah Stroumsa, in her critical edition of the work, argues that it is more informed by Aristotelian philosophy and most closely resembles "Christian" Kalām, what Maimonides later labeled as *mutakallimū al-naṣārā*.[37]

The work itself is based on many of the typical themes that other *mutakallimūn* were interested in, such as the sources of knowledge, the world, God, revelation, and the refutation of other religions. In chapter 7 of the work, for example, al-Muqammiṣ, in typical fashion, argues that the created nature of the world necessarily implies the existence of a Creator:

> If someone asks, "How do we know that it is impossible for a thing to create itself?" We reply that had it created its own self, only two possibilities could have obtained at the time of its creation: either it created itself when it existed, or it created itself when it did not exist. If it created itself when it was already existing, it means that it existed before it created itself.[38]

Al-Muqammiṣ continues by arguing that the world could neither have generated itself nor have been created from pre-existent matter (*hayūlā*). Since createdness is an attribute of matter (*jawhar*), and not of the Creator, he argues that this is proof that God, who possesses eternity as an essential attribute, created the world from nothing (*lā min shayʾ*). Perhaps on account of his conversion to Christianity and subsequent reversion to Judaism, he is particularly critical of his former religion, arguing that the claim that God is "one substance, but three hypostases" (*jawhar wāḥid thalātha aqānīm*) goes against the dictates of reason.

Although I have mentioned Dāwūd al-Muqammiṣ briefly here, my interest in him is less to show how he manufactured orthodoxy—which would have been very difficult, if not impossible for him, as an apostate—than it was to show a link between Muslim and Jewish *mutakallimūn* and to provide an important precursor to Saadya Gaon, whom I shall discuss shortly. Unlike Dāwūd al-Muqammiṣ, Saadya was largely responsible for bringing the rationalist program of Arab-Islamic Kalām into Judaism, thereby imagining and defining Judaism—at its "core" and not just its "extremities"—using Arabic and Islamic categories.

Saadya

If Dāwūd al-Muqammiṣ represents the first generation of Jewish engagement with Kalām, Saadya Gaon represents the maturation witnessed in its second generation.[39] Saadya, as we have seen, was instrumental in consolidating rabbinic authority and is not infrequently held up as the harbinger of *halakhic* retrenchment in the face of numerous threats to its authority. Whereas the previous chapter examined his role in these debates and the concomitant desire to establish normativity, it is now necessary to show the means by which he was able to do this. Once again, my argument is that Islam provided him with the intellectual stability to create an Arabized or Islamicized Judaism. This was not a symbiotic relationship between two species, but something altogether different. Again our metaphorical grid must change. If anything, Islam provided the mise en scène and the script from which Jews improvised their own lines. This was not simply a Judaism that was given an Arabic patina through the adoption of terms and categories, as the dominant narrative suggests, but instead represented a fundamental rethinking that penetrated to the very heart of Judaism.

Saadya was one of the rabbinic leaders associated with the academies of Sura and Pumbedita. He also seems to have spent considerable time in Baghdad, which was a hotbed of Muʿtazila speculation in the tenth century. In terms of Kalām, Saadya's most important work is his *Kitāb al-ʾamānāt wal-iʿtiqādāt*, "The Book of Articles of Faith and Doctrines of Dogma," translated into Hebrew by Judah ibn Tibbon in the twelfth century as *Sefer Emunot ve-Deot*. It is generally considered to be the first systematic attempt to synthesize Judaism with Arabophone and Greek-inflected rationalism. In the Introduction to the work, Saadya writes:

> Blessed be God, the God of Israel, Who alone is deserving of being regarded as the Evident Truth, Who verifies with certainty unto rational beings the existence of their souls, by means of which they assess accurately what they perceive with their senses and apprehend correctly the objects of their knowledge. Uncertainties are thereby removed from them and doubts disappear, so that demonstrations become lucid for them and proofs become clear. May He be lauded, then, above the highest commendation and praise.[40]

Here Saadya informs the reader, in typical Muʿtazila fashion, that sound sense perception and sound reason are the criteria necessary to establish truth for humans. His goal in writing the book, he informs the reader, is to explain why individuals and groups in the search for such truth go astray and "to give an account of the causes by which uncertainties may beset the minds of men in their search for the truth, as well as the method by which they may resolve these uncertainties."[41] The majority of these errors, according to Saadya, stem from the fact that many individuals fail to grasp the phenomenon of sense perception. Orthodoxy is thus signified as both natural and rational. Those unable or unwilling to assent to either have an inadequate idea of the object in question or they are perfunctory in their observations. He gives us the following analogy:

> For example, if a person were to seek one Reuben, the son of Jacob, he could be in doubt about him for only one of two reasons: either (a) because he does not know him well, so that the latter might be standing before him without being recognized by him, or he might be someone else and think he is Reuben; or (b) because he takes the easiest course, abandoning thoroughness. The result [in the latter case] is that his love of ease inclines him to seek his object with the least effort and the slightest concern, wherefore, indeed, he does not discern it.[42]

Saadya informs us that the same applies to rational knowledge. Only now errors occur when the individual in question is either unfamiliar with the methods of demonstration, meaning that the individual may be unable to differentiate between a valid and an invalid proof. Or, the individual may understand proper argumentation, but still refuse to complete the work of rational investigation on account of haste.

All of this sounds remarkably similar to works of Muʿtazila *mutakallimūn*. How, then, does Saadya differ from them? For one thing, he uses biblical proof texts where a Muslim *mutakallim* would use Qurʾānic ones. But, once again, I do not think that this suffices to make someone like Saadya engaged in "Jewish Kalām" so much as simply Kalām. For example, he cites Psalm 119:18—"Open Thou mine eyes, that I may behold wondrous things out of Your Law"—as proof that the biblical text supports the type of rationalizing theology of the sort that he is engaged in. Or, again, he invokes Isaiah 48:17—"I am the Lord your God, who teaches you for your profit, who leads you by the way that you should go"—as further proof that it is incumbent upon the Jew to engage in rational speculation, despite the fact that the Bible probably had something else in mind.

More important, Saadya argues that Jews possess one feature that no other people do, an additional source of knowledge unique to them, what he calls "reliable tradition" (al-ḥabar al-ṣādiq). Again, though, this may not be so much "Jewish" as it is anti-Karaite propaganda. Thus, we witness the construction of rabbinic "orthodoxy" take place in counterpoint to both a general Islamic background and also to a group (viz., the Karaites) inspired by, among other things, Islamic rationalism (minus, of course, the Oral Torah). This tradition, not surprisingly, is the Bible as vectored through the rabbinic texts that comprise the Oral Torah—the latter being the very Torah rejected by those groups that can now be marginalized as heterodox. Whereas all people share the three basic sources of knowledge—sense perception, reason, and inferential knowledge (e.g., where there is smoke, there is fire)—only Jews, by which he means rabbinic Jews, possess a fourth. According to him:

> As for ourselves, the community of monotheists, we hold these three sources of knowledge to be genuine. To them, however, we add a fourth source, which we have derived by means of the [other] three, and which has thus become for us a further principle. That is [to say, we believe in] the validity of authentic tradition [al-ḥabar al-ṣādiq], by reason of the fact that it is based on knowledge of the senses as well as that of reason.[43]

In a subsequent chapter of the treatise, Saadya divides the commandments in Judaism into "laws of reason" and "laws of revelation." The former are ascertainable by reason (e.g., "Thou shalt not kill"), whereas the latter consist of "matters regarding which reason passes no judgment" (e.g., how ordinary days differ from festival ones). Saadya also argues that although reason can ascertain why murder or theft are wrong, humans need revelation to set the terms of punishment, and so on.

Saadya and the Manufacture of Orthodoxy

There is little to no tradition of heresiology in premodern Judaism. Jews, for the most part, and unlike their Muslim colleagues, preferred to give the "silent treatment" to those with whom they disagreed as opposed to classifying the error of their ways. In his history of Islamic heresiography, Henri Laoust argued that all Muslim thinkers were, in some way and in varying degrees, heresiographers.[44] In medieval Islam, to use the phrasing of Steven Wasserstrom, this gave way to an "Islamicate history of religions."[45] He writes:

> Muslim comparative religion began as and remained a kind of blend of science and law, and not simply a dispassionate science. That is, most of these "scientists" were also lawyers, and their law, the *shariʿa*, demanded objective information on non-Muslim communities so that those communities could be treated appropriately by law-enforcement officials. The vaunted scientific accuracy of much of the research, then, while indeed admirable, was never a plainly disinterested taxonomizing. Rather it constituted a study designed to be applied practically to living communities at hand.[46]

Into this mix, we could certainly place the *mutakallimūn*, of both the Muslim and Jewish variety, who were—as we have seen—responsible for clarifying orthodoxy and orthopraxy. Their goal was less to provide "objective" information to law-enforcement officials so much as it was to show how and why others, often other practitioners of the same religion, strayed from the "straight path." It is within this context that we must situate Saadya, whose goal becomes—in the light of rival versions of Judaism presented by groups such as the Isawiyya and the Karaites—to clarify what Jews must believe. So, while he was not a heresiologist in the strict Muslim sense of the term, he nevertheless attempted to define orthodoxy by articulating proper and improper belief and action. The heterodoxies against which he situated orthodoxy were not, as they were for Muslim heresiologists, embodied. Instead, they were often silent and nameless, defined only by their absence and what they were not, namely, the opposite of what was becoming normative despite the fact that what was normative for him drew inspiration from those groups discussed in the previous chapter.

In this, once again, Saadya represents not just an Islamicate thinker but also a fundamentally Islamic one. He is, in other words, both phenomenally and literally similar to Muslim theologians and his kalāmic treatises, also written in Arabic, employ both Muslim and Karaite terms and methods. Both Muslim and Jewish *mutakallimūn*, then, are in the business of taking the complexity of identities that they inherited from the late antique period and establishing which ones are proper ("orthodox") and which ones improper ("heterodox").

Here, again, is where the regnant paradigm begins to break down. This paradigm, as we have seen, tends to distinguish between "Muslim Kalām" and "Jewish Kalām."[47] The Muslims, according to this paradigm, develop Kalām based on their contact with Greek philosophy and the concomitant need to defend orthodox Muslim belief, and then Saadya, influenced by their writings, begins to do the same for Judaism. Rather than characterize Saadya as a "Jewish *mutukallim,*" we should envisage him simply as a *mutukallim* who was Jewish. Such a characterization avoids the religio-ethnic signifier and instead sees Saadya as but another Arab-speaking *mutukallim*, in conversation with other *mutukallimūn*, and engaged in a similar process of theological clarification. Indeed, as we have seen, Saadya's arguments are often verbatim of those used by his Muslim colleagues—the only things that is different is that he substituted biblical proof texts for their Qur'ānic ones.

Such a new paradigm has the distinct advantage of imagining Saadya as an Arab-Islamic thinker, and not just as an Islamicate thinker, to use Hodgson's terminology.[48] This is not simply the case, as the "symbiosis" model has it, that Saadya simply cashed in the debt that Islam owed Judaism two centuries earlier. On the contrary, Judaism was radically transformed by this "contact" (if this is, in fact, the operative metaphor we want to use). This was not, to be sure, a superficial contact wherein Saadya was encouraged to borrow Arabic terminology; rather, it was an encounter that represented the systematic rethinking of what Judaism was and should be. This was not so much a symbiosis as it was the creation of an Islam recast as a Judaism. Jewish orthodoxy now resembled, in more than just superficial ways, Islamic orthodoxy. This new rabbinic orthodoxy could then be further articulated in the centuries that followed.

Subsequent Developments

Much of the early centuries of rational theology in Islam and Judaism involved individuals, like those we have already encountered, articulating what they considered to be their respective tradition's theological principles. Within this context, it is often difficult to differentiate Jewish *mutakallimūn*, such as al-Muqammiṣ and Saadya, from their Muslim contemporaries. Indeed, all that seems to separate the one set from the other is the adjective in front of the activity they all engaged in—Kalām. Since the very terms "Muslim Kalām" and "Jewish Kalām" are modern terms, it is difficult to know how "Jewish" someone like Saadya regarded his thinking to be. A good example of this may be found in the theological writings of Ibn Ḥazm (d. 1064), a Muslim polymath from al-Andalus, who makes references to the writings of al-Muqammiṣ and Saadya in order to criticize them.[49] The criticism is not so important for my purposes here as is the fact that he seems to have been familiar with their writings, thereby offering us a clear insight into the fact that Jewish and Muslim *mutakallimūn* do not neatly and simply bifurcate into, as so many of our textbooks tell us, religious adjectives. The border, in other words, is not yet closed.

This lack of a clear line between Muslim and Jewish thought in the Middle Ages may also be witnessed in, for lack of a better term, Sufi-inspired works of Jewish theology, such as *Kitāb Hidāya ʿilā Farāʾid al-Qulūb* (The book of direction to the duties of the heart) by Baḥya ibn Paquda (fl. second part of the eleventh century). Although arranged and divided into the basic structure of treatises associated with Kalām, Baḥya's interest is less with ascertaining rationalist principles, though he does claim that reason is God-given, than with cultivating the inner experience of the believer.[50] While he defines reason in ways that are virtually identical to that of the Muʿtazila, he claims that the ultimate goal of the believer in ascetic and mystical terms is the reunion of the soul with its Creator, itself defined using the Arabic terms and language supplied by the Islamic mystical tradition. Baḥya's Judaism is, like Saadya's, articulated using the categories of the Muʿtazila, however he goes even further and adds to it the experiential dimension of Sufism.

Subsequent centuries, however, saw an increased differentiation between Jewish and Islamic theology, especially as the language of theological speculation in Judaism switched from Arabic to Hebrew. Perhaps, this switch is most notable in the thought of Maimonides, whom we have already encountered several times above. Although still writing his philosophical works in Judeo-Arabic, he composed his massive *Mishneh Torah*, a compendium of law and theology, in Hebrew, presumably so that Jews who did not read Arabic would be able to understand it.

In the brief space that remains in this section, however, I want to focus on two individuals who show us to just what extent the border between Jewish and Muslim theology was porous even after Maimonides. These two individuals—Ibn Kammūna (d. 1284) and David b. Joshua, the great grandson of Maimonides, who lived in Cairo in the late thirteenth and early fourteenth centuries—continue to show the filiations between Muslim and Jewish theology into the later Middle Ages.

Ibn Kammūna was, by all accounts a Jew, though some have argued that he had converted to Islam.[51] Although a Jew, he was given to making pious remarks about Muhammad, in addition to writing a detailed commentary to Suhrawardī's *al-Talwīḥāt* (Intimations), and writing glosses to his young contemporary Fakhr al-Dīn al-Rāzī's *al-Maʿālim* (Waymarks), an important work of Islamic theology. Ibn Kammūna's commentary on Suhrawardī's texts, in addition to his correspondences with Quṭb al-Dīn al-Shīrāzī and Naṣīr al-Dīn al-Ṭūsī, played a major role in both the exposition and diffusion of Suhrawardī's *Ishrāqī*, or "Eastern," philosophy in later Muslim thought. Indeed, so important is Ibn Kammūna to the understanding of Muslim theology of this period that several contemporary Iranian scholars have concentrated their efforts on Ibn Kammūna's philosophical writings and have edited several of his works, specifically his commentary on Suhrawardī's *Talwīḥāt*.[52] Individuals such as Ibn Kammūna nicely, if problematically for some, blur the boundary between Jewish theology and Muslim theology even in the later period of their interaction. Such later interaction, I submit, is based on the earlier period wherein the two theological traditions developed as one tradition. How, then, do we classify someone like Ibn Kammūna? Is he a "Jewish" theologian or a "Muslim" one? Such religious adjectives, I would suggest, are our terms, and may be unhelpful or even anachronistic.

Ibn Kammūna is also known as the author of *Tanqīḥ al-abḥāṯ li-l-milal al-thalāth* (Examination of the inquiries into the three faiths), a work, written in Arabic, that examines Judaism, Christianity, and Islam from, what he calls, an objective point of view.[53] In his introduction to the work, he writes that "I have not been swayed by mere personal inclination, nor have I ventured to show preference for one faith over the other, but have pursued the investigation of each faith to its fullest extent."[54] In his chapter on Islam, he again summarizes the theological teachings of Islam with little or no polemical intent. He writes, for example:

> The Muslims agree that Muḥammad Ibn ʿAbdallāh Ibn ʿAbd al-Muṭṭalib is the Messenger of God and Seal of the Prophets; that he was sent to all mankind, that he abrogated all the previous religions, and that his religion will remain in force to the day of resurrection; that he called upon men to believe in God and His angels, messengers, and scriptures, and to believe that God is one, has

no companion, none like or similar to Him, no mate or child, and that God is preexistent, living, all-knowing, almighty, willing, hearing, seeing, speaking; and that He sent the Torah through Moses, the Gospel through Jesus; that Muḥammad, on behalf of God, announced that He commanded the performance of prayer, payment of Zakāt, fasting during Ramaḍān, pilgrimage to the sanctuary of Mecca.[55]

My final example comes by way of David b. Joshua. If and when Maimonides's descendants are discussed, it is usually his son Abraham, a well-known *halakhist* and someone who was very much influenced by the mystical trends of Sufism. However, in the realm of theology, and the intersection of Judaism and Islam, it is Maimonides's great grandson who deserves attention. As the *nagīd* of the Jewish community there, he wrote, as many of Maimonides's descendants did, Sufi-inspired interpretations of Judaism. Most notable is his *al-Murshid ilā-l-tafarrud wa-l-murfid ilā-l-tagarrud* (The guide to loneliness and the path to detachment).[56] There are also indications in the Cairo Genizah that he wrote commentaries on the writings of al-Ḥallāj and Ibn ʿArabī. David b. Judah also commissioned many manuscripts, including a Muslim commentary on his great grandfather's *Mishneh Torah*.

Conclusions

This chapter has tried to frame the encounter, contact, or whatever other term we decide to use, between Judaism and Islam after the darkness supplied by the late antique period slowly begins to lift. Yet, rather than focus on a symbiotic relationship between two stable essences—to wit, Judaism and Islam—it tried to show how each religion defined itself in counterpoint with the other. Each did so, moreover, in such a way that the two religions changed and morphed in the process. This post-symbiotic model sees instability and the complexity of identity as an important, if not the definitive, aspect of this relationship. While this relationship may be symbiotic in the sense that each religion is interlocked with the other, defining itself in the process, neither remains unscathed by the contact.

The relationship between Islam and Judaism, as it slowly becomes illumined by the light that the early medieval period sheds on it, shows itself to be much more complex and interconnected than traditional models would have us believe. If the previous chapter charted the margins of this relationship, the present chapter has examined its center, something I have exemplified in the life and works of Saadya Gaon. He shows us how the center is not only defining itself by means of the margins, the place where the distinction between Jew and Muslim is increasingly unstable, but also how that center continues to use a shared and overlapping set of discourses. This will continue well into the medieval period as chapter 6 will show in greater detail. Before I do that, however, it is necessary to step back in order to look at how that medieval period has been imagined and constructed, and some of the uses to which it has been put.

5

Et in Arcadia Ego

"WOULD THAT I WERE not among the men of the fifth generation," writes the eighth-century BCE Greek poet Hesiod, "but either had died before or been born afterwards."[1] No one finds it easy to live in the messy present where the struggle to find meaning is obscured by political, financial, and even epistemological instability. To confront such aporia, we imagine other times and other places as exhibiting all those magnanimous traits and characteristics we so woefully perceive ourselves to lack. Great Americas or caliphates, new Reichs, to name but a few, all function in the consciousness of those who believe in them in a manner that combines nostalgia for an imagined past, fear of the present, and hope for the future.

Every age has thus functioned as a golden age . . . at least to someone or to some group. No one, however, ever lives in such a golden age, which is imagined as the inverse of the present. That is the paradox: because we do not actually have the good fortune of living in a perceived time of splendor, we often construct such a time and not infrequently in such a manner that it never could have existed in the first place. To continue using Hesiod's words,

> First of all the deathless gods who dwell on Olympus made a golden race of mortal men who lived in the time of Cronos when he was reigning in heaven. And they lived like gods without sorrow of heart, remote and free from toil and grief: miserable age rested not on them; but with legs and arms never failing they made merry with feasting beyond the reach of all evils. When they died, it was as though they were overcome with sleep, and

they had all good things; for the fruitful earth unforced bare them fruit abundantly and without stint. They dwelt in ease and peace upon their lands with many good things, rich in flocks and loved by the blessed gods.[2]

Past and future become the temporal bookends against which we must habitually dwell. Caught between the presumed beauty of the way things must have been and the hope for some vague messianic fulfillment in the future, we bide our time and look to other times and places for solace. The status of the modern ego, to use Jacques Barzun's apt metaphor, is that it walks "forward with its head turned back in fear and longing."[3] If we combine this nostalgia with the notion that ideas and methods of interpretation—the very stuff we locate in texts and the way we bring them into existence—are historically and socially conditioned, we might be closer to the truth of the matter. Perhaps, this is another way of saying, invoking Hilary Putnam, that we all think in our own present.[4] Although I expect that he might not go so far as me and claim that the assumptions brought to bear on an analysis of history are peculiar to the race, gender, and class of those doing the interpreting, and often in ways that become sublimated as universal or somehow transmuted into claims of neutrality and objectivity. Without wanting to travel fully down the path of cognitive relativism, I think it would be naïve to claim, as so many of the figures that have already and will subsequently make appearances in these pages, that we simply interpret texts from other ages neutrally or dispassionately. Time, place, training, and intellectual dispositions structure what we see (and do not see) in those texts.[5]

This chapter examines one such golden age, the one often held up as the zenith of Jewish–Muslim relations, that of al-Andalus or Muslim Spain. This arcadia, invented in the ateliers of German-Jewish intellectuals, as we witnessed in chapter 1, has performed considerable work since then. Most significantly, it forms a central ingredient in the narrative of symbiosis, the dominant paradigm that still largely structures the field. Muslim Spain now became the place of equality, emancipation, aesthetic renewal, the flight from tradition, and symbolic of the free exchange of ideas. All of these virtues, not coincidentally, were ones that these Jewish scholars lacked in the context of their own nineteenth-century German home.[6] Again, "golden ages" tell us more about ourselves and our desires than they do about anything we might label as the historical record.

Nostalgia and the Study of Religion

The academic study of religions, the larger genus under which I am here situating the species of Jewish–Muslim relations, is obsessed with origins. The intersection of modern metropolitan life and the need to find ostensibly "premodern" cultures to offset it or make it more spiritually meaningful has had a tremendous if often unacknowledged impact on the creation of the academic study of religion.[7] Nationalism and regeneration have frequently coincided in this field of study, and this has meant the need to find earlier iterations of present desires in more "primitive" forms that can then paradoxically be located and plotted on an imagined historical record.[8] This could mean "locating" an Aryan Jesus in history,[9] or it can mean, as is so common today in certain circles, of discovering primitive democracy in ancient Israel.[10] Friedrich Max Müller, one of the founding fathers of comparative religion and the first European to translate and publish the *Rig Veda*, to use another example, never traveled to India and apparently forbade his students from doing the same because the "real" India existed only in ancient texts.[11] Virtually every historian of religion from Müller to Mircea Eliade has tried to locate this primordial and presumed universal aspect of religion in the ancients, contemporary primitives (Australian aborigines or Trobriand Islanders usually fit the bill), or among rural dwellers (in, e.g., the Romanian countryside). Not infrequently such a search is bound up, as we have just seen, with nationalist sentiment.[12] As Asher Biemann notes, "the historian, of course, will know that the 'good' kind of nationalism is exceedingly rare and that the myth of regeneration belongs, more often than not, to totalitarian thought."[13] Collective memory and the creation of a homecoming to its imagined existence in the distant past not infrequently provides the hope for new beginnings and the means for national regeneration in the present.[14]

Nostalgia thus functions as the "historical" quest for essence, an attempt to make the present somehow more meaningful. Eliade's notorious revolt against the terrors of diachronic time in order to find meaning in the rebirth associated with cyclical time held out hope for an entire generation of historians of religions in the aftermath of the Second World War. In the words of Russell T. McCutcheon, however, such a position maintains that mythic narratives "are simply expressed or manifested in social and historical contexts; they do not arise from them."[15] The modern individual, newly valorized as a *homo religiosus*, might now refuse to "accept himself as a historical being."[16] Yet, as Wasserstrom has argued, Eliade's nostalgia for myth and its ability to bring cyclical wholeness is itself a return to history under the ruse of antihistoricism.[17] Or, in Biemann's apt phrasing, "while history, for Eliade, has the ability to produce only what is new, mythic time can *make new* what is old."[18] The Weimar mistrust of historicism, in other words, found the nostalgic fulfillment of longing in myth, which represented a flight from history or, at the very least, the desire to create alternate histories.[19]

And thus we return to history—that slippery and amphibolous term that can be invoked at will and for any number of national or other redemptive causes. Yet, the theory of history produced by the history of religions is also a theory of relativity. As we shall see in this chapter, we can create a fictive past for any thing or any idea so that its "history" can fulfill some function or meaning in the present. As Arthur McCalla asks, "When is history not history?"[20] His half-sarcastic answer: when it is the history of religions. Recast in vivid Technicolor, the black-and-white nature of the past can hold out a lifeline to the present or become a primer for the future. This past as presence or the present as the antonym of the past becomes a form of wish fulfillment. This imaginary world-making, however, comes with a cost.

Past as Present

If we take these insights and apply them to the field of Jewish studies, we see something remarkably similar. Again, our cast of supporting characters here is the same cast as witnessed in previous chapters. In his 1846 *Die Konstruktion der jüdischen Geschichte*, Heinrich Graetz asks, "What is Judaism?" In so doing, he sought to retrieve and unlock the "root idea of Judaism" (*judentümliche Grundidee*) that, while found in history, nevertheless transcended the very historical record in which it was located. Judaism's ahistorical essence, in other words, can only be paradoxically located in history. Such an underlying hermeneutic (one often still implicit today) is certainly not amenable to the type of complexity to which I have tried to draw attention. "The totality of Judaism is discernible only in its history," Graetz continues, "its complete nature, the sum of its powers, becomes clear only in the light of history."[21] And what is this timeless and ahistorical essence? For him,

> The highest purpose of Judaism is, therefore, the teaching of the philosophic truths about God, such as the necessity of His existence, His unity, omniscience, and omnipotence, His absolute will,

His eternity, and then, the scrupulous discarding of all the views about God that are inappropriate to the concept of God.[22]

According to Graetz, Judaism's "highest purpose" is, perhaps not surprisingly, most clearly located in Muslim Spain. In the same essay, he writes:

> From the banks of the Euphrates and Tigris both philosophic and Talmudic studies made their way to the Iberian peninsula. Kairowan in North Africa, the ancient Cyrene, formed the bridge between Babylonia and Spain. The blessed peninsula, the home of religious fanaticism and the Inquisition, became, under the tolerant scepter of the Moorish caliphs who craved both learning and comfort, the classical land of Jewish studies. It produced a long line of Jewish personalities at home in all fields of human and divine learning: Jewish mathematicians, doctors, statesmen, grammarians, philosophic exegetes, poets, and religious philosophers appeared in great numbers on the stage.[23]

The academic study of Jewish topics (outside of the Old Testament), it should be duly noted, was forbidden from being taught at German universities when Graetz was writing.[24] When Leopold Zunz approached the University of Berlin in 1848, for example, with a proposal for creating a Chair in Jewish History and Literature, the faculty disingenuously responded that it was not in the business of training Jewish clergy (training Christian clergy, of course, was okay).[25] Against this backdrop, Muslim Spain shined like a beacon in the darkness. It became the place where the study of Judaism—philosophy, grammar, exegesis—were both studied and respected by Jews and non-Jews alike. Muslim Spain, framed somewhat differently, became the mirror inverse of nineteenth-century Germany. The key figure for Graetz in all of this was the Arabophone Maimonides, who, as we shall see in the following chapter, both wrote in Arabic and translated Judaism into Muslim-inflected philosophical categories. For Graetz, Maimonides "towered over all others," and both his contemporaries and posterity paid tribute to him as a genius.[26] Maimonides was a man after Graetz's own heart. The latter, like his newly constructed medieval doppelgänger, was also drawn to the cool hand of reason, something that could confront the ignorant and pantheistic excesses of Judaism's mystical profligacy. In so doing, however, Graetz and others associated with Wissenschaft des Judentums invented the idea of medieval Jewish philosophy in their own image.[27] Graetz writes:

> Maimonides is a systematizer through and through; every block of material that his mind masters is turned by him into an organic unit. We meet the same articulate, clear mind in all the fields in which he works, in the commentaries, the halakhah, and philosophy. In every intellectual subject he extracts the principles, the starting point, which he places at the center and around which the details line up logically.[28]

If, for Graetz, the highest purpose of Judaism was to teach philosophical truths about God to the world, then the arch-rationalist Maimonides necessarily becomes the centerpiece of his analysis. He has no time for the pantheism associated with Neoplatonists or kabbalists, who risked obfuscating Judaism's rationalist essence.[29] Also interesting is the fact that Graetz, perhaps not surprisingly, does not admit that Maimonides's philosophical analysis is, for all intents and purposes, Islamic. It may have an Arabic inflection, since it was written in that language, but this inflection is in no way thought to influence or impact on the timeless and ahistorical core of Judaism. Yet, as I shall argue in the following chapter, Maimonides's Judaism—not unlike Saadya's—is also an "Islamic Judaism," one that betrays no sense of the hyphen. If anything, it was the likes of Graetz who reified the hyphen (in Jewish–Muslim) in the first place.

What is important to note for Graetz and others who imagined and invented the "golden age" of Muslim Spain is that its "discovery" facilitated the rethinking of Judaism and, of course, its relationship to Islam.[30] This relationship, in danger of being discarded in the dustbin of history, now came to take on a relevance and importance that transcended its actuality. Even though it was about Islam, it was not really. At stake was Judaism's place in the modern European nation-state. Islam now became the inverse of Christianity and Muslim leaders in Spain the opposite of Prussian leaders. In their creation of a "golden age," a young generation of German-Jewish and historically minded scholars sought to show their fellow Jews, bound by traditional and talmudic religious forms, how urbane and cultured Jews could be. In like manner, their constructions were also aimed at Prussian authorities and other critics of Judaism, by showing the dizzying heights that Jews could attain when emancipated and treated with dignity and equality.[31]

The tradition of "golden age" in al-Andalus was the product of this nostalgia and, ultimately the result of an anachronistic and historically distorted reading. This "golden age," like all golden ages, was more about the present than the actual past. Despite these problems, however, it is still invoked—as witnessed in chapter 1—for a host of scholarly and extra-scholarly ends, almost all of which are equally nostalgic. Modern assumptions about freedom and equality, tolerance and multiculturalism, have unfortunately colored our reading of al-Andalus. Such constructions may be seen in Graetz's uber-rationalist Maimonides—a figure imagined to be largely untouched by Islam and completely free of nineteenth-century intellectual vices such as mysticism, pantheism, astrology, or the like—or Goitein's nostalgia for a "Judaism [that] could draw freely and copiously from Muslim civilization and, at the same time, preserve its independence and integrity far more completely than it was able to do in the modern world or in the Hellenistic society of Alexandria."[32] Not only does such a narrative—which is now largely our narrative—ignore the social dynamic between Jews and Muslims on the Iberian Peninsula, it has contributed to the myth of "Sephardism," wherein Andalusi contributions to Jewish civilization are seen as largely secular and superior to that produced in the premodern Ashkenazi world.[33] This not only marginalizes Andalusi development in *halakhah*, it also ignores the creativity in contemporaneous non-Andalusi Jewish cultures.

Rationality: Islam between Judaism and Europe

Just as "the Orient" functioned as a discursive site as nineteenth-century European scholars engaged in the quest for self-discovery and self-definition, al-Andalus played a similar role in the German-Jewish scholarly imagination. As Ismar Schorsch has argued in his "Myth of Sephardic Supremacy":

> As constructed by Ashkenazic intellectuals, the Sephardic image facilitated a religious posture marked by cultural openness, philosophic thinking, and an appreciation of the aesthetic. Like many a historical myth, it evoked a partial glimpse of a bygone age determined and colored by social need. ... The romance with Spain offers yet another perspective on the degree to which German Jewry distanced itself from its East European origins.[34]

Medieval Jews and Arabs, in addition to the imagined intersection of premodern Judaism and Islam, function in the modern imagination as the catalyst for contemporary rebirth. This desired renaissance would create a new Jew and a new Judaism, one in sync with the modern world and ready for political and legal emancipation.[35] Within this context, medieval Spanish Jews in particular functioned as part foil and as part mirror for these German-Jewish scholars. They were a foil in the sense that they were presumed to be in possession of all the legal and aesthetic traits that contemporary German Jews lacked. Moreover, they also functioned as a mirror in which individuals like Graetz saw what they themselves hoped to be.

A generation of German-Jewish scholars romanticized Muslim Spain. Like their non-Jewish colleagues,[36] they created a grand narrative—a set of "new old stories"—that ignored or interpreted away the uncomfortable and that intertwined the rational and national. If German philhellenes saw themselves as the rediscoverers of a lost Arcadia, German-Jewish "philsephardists" envisaged themselves as unlocking the majesty of an equally vague or pliant Eden. Both sought, in other words, to recreate the present by redirecting the light of an earlier time into the present.[37]

A central feature in all of this romance and recreation was reason and the rational. If "*the* Greeks" functioned as a trope that other European cultures have invoked for a variety of purposes, "*the* medieval Jewish philosophers" associated with the "golden age" of Muslim Spain has served a similar role in Judaism since at least the nineteenth century. Philosophy, our Wissenschaft forbearers maintained, has functioned as the universal tool whereby particularistic Judaism was made compatible with the majoritarian cultures in which Jews have lived. We in the present still largely agree with our predecessors' assessment. What better way to show the compatibility between Jew and European than to show them engaged in a common project of reason, albeit one that is perceived paradoxically to derive from Muslims? While the Jews provided the monotheistic impulse locatable in the Bible, the medieval rationalists, for Graetz and others, were the ones who conflated that impulse with the rationalism supplied by the Greeks as filtered through the Arabs. Medieval Jewish philosophy, thus, represented the perfect intersection of what could be and indeed was constructed as proper reason and as proper religion.[38]

This story of Jewish rationalism is a story of intrigue, denial, transference, and the quest for acceptance. It is the story of a past that is believed to be recoverable—a past as new as it is old, and as invented as much as inherited—and one that uses history to resist history or, at the very least, to change history. This production of a past, the uncovering of a latent present, and the subsequent conflation of historiography and mythopoesis plays an important role in the story of Jewish–Muslim relations of the eleventh and twelfth centuries. It is, as we have seen, the story to which Goitein provided the script for "symbiosis," and it is the story to which a host of ecumenical types in the modern period long to return.

The Discovery and Subsequent Compartmentalization of Jewish Rationalism

In *The Greeks and the Irrational*, E. R. Dodds argued that the Greeks, those we credit as the inventors and fine purveyors of reason, were never mere rationalists. Nevertheless, the story of Greek rationalism—the story we all want to hear, and the one that we have been habitually conditioned to hear—has performed a great deal of intellectual work. All those Western cultures subsequent to the Greeks, from the Romans to the Germans, have perceived themselves to be the heirs of ancient Greece. This locus, or perhaps better trope, has functioned as a leitmotif winding its way through European history and marking a certain cultural authenticity dependent upon a variety of complex, even opposing, intellectual and artistic needs. Writing in the aftermath of Freud's pioneering research into the irrational, Dodds informs us that his goal was not simply to write a history of Greek religion, of which we already possess several books, but to open before the reader a more cautious and uncertain story. He instead presented us with

> a study of the successive interpretations which Greek minds placed on one particular type of human experience—a sort of experience in which nineteenth-century rationalism took little interest, but whose cultural significance is now widely recognized. The evidence which is here brought together illustrates an important, and relatively unfamiliar, aspect of the mental world of ancient Greece. But an aspect must not be mistaken for the whole.[39]

Since non-Jews constructed Greek rationalism in a particular way in nineteenth-century Germany—that is, in a manner that ignored, downplayed, or otherwise marginalized the irrational—it should not surprise us to learn that German Jews did the same thing for Jewish philosophy.

Missing in their constructions is all that did not fit their concerns (e.g., the non-rational, the irrational, the mystic, the pantheistic). Mysticism, astrology, astral magic, the emotions, and the body are all absent from their constructions. While this certainly does not mean that Jewish thinkers imagined as rationalist did not entertain these ideas, it does mean that those who imagined these Jewish rationalists in their own image did not.

Rationalism was so important to these earlier generations of Jewish scholars because it permitted them to read themselves and their concerns into the larger narrative of European rationalism. If reform-minded and aestheticizing German nationalists turned their gaze eastward—to Greece and, even further, to the Orient—German Jews looked westward to the Sephardic world in general and al-Andalus in particular. It was there that aesthetic-minded Jews, believed to be the freest since the loss of autonomy that occurred with the destruction of the Second Temple, produced poetry, philosophy, and took part in a larger Arabophone and cosmopolitan environment.[40] If Jews suffered persecution at the hands of Crusaders and if they lacked political emancipation in Germany, al-Andalus offered them a freedom, as imagined as it was real and as invented as it was actual.

As German Jews constructed a narrative of medieval rationalism, German scholars were similarly drawn to other civilizations with the aim of cultural renewal. Greece, according to Suzanne Marchand, became for a group of nineteenth-century German intellectuals a "powerless and almost extinct nation whose dignity and influence depended solely on its cultural legacy."[41] This was not the historical Greece, the home of philosophy and the cradle of democracy. On the contrary, it was an imagined land, an ancient trope or symbol that functioned as a testament to human freedom, artistic beauty, and scientific genius. It was a Greece that permitted a group of scholars to revolt against "religious repression, aristocratic airs, and social immobility."[42] It was, to be sure, a cultural rebellion. Greece became a mirror upon which one could see reflected all that the present lacked.

Even further, beyond Greece, a generation of German scholars looked to the Orient and developed a set of tools to imagine, construct, and taxonomize this area. Yet the study of "the Orient," as Edward Said warned us years ago, is never an innocent construction, but a more insidious method of political and intellectual domination. Europe, for Said, "gained in strength and identity by setting itself off against the Orient as a sort of surrogate and even underground self."[43] This Orient, in other words, did not exist naturally in the world, but was imagined and created through a variety of scholarly, artistic, and political acts of imagination.

The medieval Sephardic world, but especially the rationalism associated with al-Andalus, did something similar for German Jewish intellectuals. The middle of the nineteenth century, for example, witnessed a host of German translations and/or paraphrases of Andalusi and other Sephardic rationalists—Baḥya ibn Paquda (1836), Maimonides (1838, 1839), Joseph Albo (1844), Saadya Gaon (1845), and Judah Halevi (1853)—for a more general reading audience. Against the backdrop of the creation of new denominations and the entry of young Jews into universities, where many specialized in Islamic studies, al-Andalus facilitated the creation of a new model for florescence and growth.[44] It provided the aesthetic, the intellectual, and the prosodic qualities that, to this day, have had a heavy influence on research and the institutionalization of the study of Judaism in the modern university. This institutionalization, I submit, has continued to envisage Judaism and Islam as two species (or their equivalents) that interact in ways that both maintain their perceived essential qualities.

A great deal has been written on the political and ideological underpinnings of those scholars associated with Wissenschaft des Judentums.[45] Much of this work, perhaps inspired by Scholem's damning critique,[46] seeks to criticize their project, showing its investiture in a host of extracurricular activities. Although Wissenschaft des Judentums today ostensibly functions as the mirror obverse of what scholars of Jewish thought supposedly engage in, I wish to suggest that their project and the project that still maintains the "golden age" of Muslim Spain is not all that different. Our predecessors created the categories that we largely accept.[47] In this, I am often much more critical of us in the present who, while quick to point out Wissenschaft des Judentums's investment in ideology, nonetheless have taken over willy-nilly their frameworks and modes of analysis. This, of course, includes the trope of "symbiosis." We have no problems pointing out the fractures and tensions inherent to their narratives, but are largely unwilling to subject our own adaptations of these very narratives to an analogous critical scrutiny. My goal here is not so much to criticize their attempt to make Jews rational in order to make them modern; rather, it is to show how their assumptions in so doing have largely become part of our own conceptual and terminological baggage especially when it comes to speaking about Jewish–Muslim relations. While we have no qualms articulating what is wrong with past approaches to Jewish history, we are surprisingly unwilling to stop ourselves from making similar categorical mistakes. This is the case not only for the construction of medieval rationalism but also the entire analytic framework used to describe and analyze relations between Jews and Muslims since the late antique period. The privileging of medieval Jewish rationalism has traditionally functioned as the shining light in the canopy of the academic study of Judaism. Although its regnant place has now slipped considerably, much modern scholarship remains committed to the orthodoxy of Jewish rationalism.

In his *Prophets of the Past*, Michael Brenner remarked that every generation of Jewish historians has viewed its predecessors as caught up in ideological concerns, and not being objective, the purported badge of authenticity for any historian.[48] Although the early representatives of Wissenschaft des Judentums threw off the shackles of their forbearers and their religiously determined account of the past, they were soon charged by subsequent historians of using an intellectualist history in the service of emancipatory reform in Germany. Subsequent early Zionist historians criticized their predecessors in Europe and America because they thought that it was only possible to write an objective history of the Jews in a Jewish society where one did not have to worry about the judgment of non-Jews. Their revisionist students, in turn, attacked them for mixing claims to objectivity with nationalist causes.[49]

The search for a master narrative of Jewish history, then and now, has always been a major concern for Jewish historians. While this is undoubtedly the case for the writing of all nationalist histories, Jewish history is perhaps unique in the sense that it has always had to accommodate itself, and respond, to larger intellectual trends. Within this context, philosophy has functioned as one of the major discourses whereby Judaism was made compatible with larger non-Jewish cultures. This is especially true when it comes to situating the Jews of medieval Islamic culture. This desire for compatibility made a generation of German-Jewish thinkers develop a set of religious and ethical values that could enable a reconstructed or even reformed Judaism to fit into and subsequently contribute to European culture, paradoxically by stressing Judaism's filiation with Islam. As the harbinger of ethical monotheism, as we shall see in the next chapter, Judaism could be situated at the heart of all that was good in Europe. Although a large part of their story involved Islam, their primary concern however was overwhelmingly European. Rationality, thus, functioned as the yardstick to measure all forms of the tradition and select that which was deemed most authentic and what not. This has given a privileged place to a set of canonical thinkers, virtually all of whom lived in the orbit of Islam, and their textual productions that are believed to articulate Judaism using a set of universal and rationalist criteria.

This apologetical argument is still alive and well in the construction of medieval Jewish philosophy, although now it is certainly plotted differently. It has not stopped many who work in Jewish philosophy from telling us what the essence of Judaism is, and either how it is or is not compatible with certain forms of rationalism.[50] Emancipation, various forms of nationalism in the diaspora, and, of course, Zionism have functioned as lenses through which Jewish history has been constructed, examined, and organized. The story of the "golden age" of Muslim Spain, not unlike the story of Jewish–Muslim relations more generally, has always been caught up in these forces.

These forces, however, do not represent a set of objective historical facts that simply exist in the past and that await uncovering in the present. Rather they represent a set of constructions imagined in the present and then made to perform intellectual work for those who imagine them in the past. Medieval Jewish thinkers—those often held up as the purveyors of a rational aesthetic in an otherwise inhospitable era—probably had much different ideas about what constituted rationalism than did their nineteenth-century Central European heirs. Yet, for some reason, we in the present have largely bought into this nineteenth-century narrative. We still talk about the "golden age" of Muslim Spain, and we still narrate the story of a rationalism that Jewish thinkers adopted and adapted when Islam, to use Goitein's terminology, repaid its debt to Judaism.

"Golden Ages": Uses and Abuses

The "golden age" of Muslim Spain, for modern German-Jewish thinkers, as we have just seen, functioned as a locus of change, renewal, and intellectual vibrancy. My goal is less with ascertaining whether or not their assessment was historically accurate so much as it has been to show how a medieval relationship between Jews and Muslims, between Judaism and Islam, was imagined, manufactured, and disseminated. In this respect, the medieval relationship differs little from the ways in which Jewish–Muslim relations were imagined and created in the Arabian Peninsula in the late antique period. It is certainly no coincidence, I submit, that just as many of these individuals were trying to reform Jewish religious life by making it more aesthetically pleasing by, for example, introducing music into the synagogue (now renamed "temple"), creating mixed seating, and making the liturgy more congregation based, as scholars they were finding the aesthetic justification for this among the Jews of Arabia and the Jews of Muslim Spain.

In an essay entitled "Judeo-Arabic Culture," published in *The Encyclopaedia Judaica Yearbook 1977/1978*, Hava Lazarus-Yafeh writes of this "golden age." Before I examine what she says it might be worth mentioning that, in the introduction to the *Yearbook*, Teddy Kollek—the first mayor of a united Jerusalem—writes poetically about the multicultural and multiethnic makeup of the city:

> Anyone seeking the integration of peoples and religions in Jerusalem is ignoring the special nature of the city in which each ethnic group and each community maintains its own identity. This is the way Jerusalem is, and the way that it always was—a multicolored mosaic, each of its stones an ethnic group and each stone within well-defined boundaries. If you blur those boundary lines, you blur the whole picture.... I see Jerusalem in my mind's eye and behold it like its name—a city of peace in which all inhabitants live side by side in tolerance and mutual respect.[51]

The boundaries separating different religious and ethnic groups—echoing a thesis that I have consistently tried to dismantle in these pages—are, for Kollek as they are for countless others, distinct. Identity is never unstable, contested, or fraught. While Kollek and others are content to name this multiculturalism, there is rarely the desire to go further and posit a set of intricate and overlapping set of cultural and social identities. Multiculturalism is not dangerous since it is an important virtue in our contemporary world, but unstable identities are.

In her article, Lazarus-Yafeh adopts unhesitatingly Goitein's thesis of "symbiosis" and again returns us to the regnant paradigm of Jewish–Muslim relations. She writes:

> Two periods can be clearly distinguished in the interrelationship of Judaism and Islam. During the first period—the 7th and maybe also the 8th centuries—Judaism, more than any other religion and culture, left a decisive impact on Islam, a new religion in the process of consolidation. In the second period—probably from the 8th century, and in particular from the 9th century onward—Islam, which had

become a rich and variegated culture, profoundly influenced Jewish culture. Consequently, the interrelationship of these two cultures may be regarded as a closed circle, a rare phenomenon in cultural relationships.[52]

For Lazarus-Yafeh, the "extent and depth of their spiritual collaboration" is unprecedented in human history, and that "only against the special cultural background of medieval Islam could such a spiritual alliance spring up."[53] Once again, the "golden age" is repeated, not interrogated, and based on a nostalgia for another place, a place that is imagined as somehow different from a post-unification and war-torn Jerusalem.

Again, this "golden age" of al-Andalus is always held up as the opposite of the present. If for Lazarus-Yafeh this trope functioned as the mirror opposite of 1970s Israel, Graetz imagined Muslim Spain as the opposite of late nineteenth-century Germany:

> The first half of the twelfth century produced a vast number of clever men in Jewish circles, poets, philosophers, Talmudists, and almost all their labors bore the mark of perfection. The Jewish culture of this period resembled a garden, rich in odorous blossoms and luscious fruits, whose production, though varied in color and taste, have their root in the same earth.... The poets eulogized each other and cordially praised the men that devoted their powers to other intellectual work. They took the greatest interest in one another's success, consoled one another in misfortune, and regarded one another as members of one family.[54]

Here, Graetz romanticizes the spiritual and religious unity of Spanish Jewry. This unity, not surprisingly, functions as the opposite of German Jewry' increased fragmentation and polarization along ideological lines. Graetz holds up the Jewish community of Muslim Spain as an example of what a presumed unified Jewish community could attain on religious, social, and intellectual levels. Like Geiger and like many of the figures associated with Wissenschaft des Judentums, Graetz subtly excoriates the persecution complex inherent to Christocentric Europe, blaming it for a host of internal Jewish problems. He uses the Andalusi poet Shlomo ibn Gabirol (1021–1058) to show the differences between the treatment of Jews in medieval Muslim culture compared to that of medieval Christendom:

> It is true that the leading ideas of ibn Gabirol's system had been expressed by other philosophers, but he formed into one organic whole a confused mass of scattered thoughts. ... A Christian emperor destroyed the temple of philosophy in Athens, and exiled its last priests. Since that time philosophy had been outlawed in Europe. ... The Jewish thinker, ibn Gabirol, was the first to transplant it again to Europe, and he built an altar to it in Spain, where it found a permanent habitation.[55]

For Graetz, Europe needs the Jews. It needed them in the late antique period to give birth to both Christianity and Islam. It needed them in the medieval period as the conduit for the reintroduction of philosophy. And it needs them now. Ibn Gabirol, thus, becomes the symbol of Jewish integration in Europe. Deprive the Jews of their rights or deny them full emancipation, and Europe becomes—as it did in the medieval Christian period—the opposite of Muslim Spain.

Not everyone, of course, saw Muslim Spain as exemplary. However, even those who sought to denigrate its influence nonetheless had to construct other loci of authenticity. Yitzhak Baer (1888–1980),[56] for example, tended to be more critical of Jewish life under Islam and instead emphasized what he considered to be a more authentic experience under Christianity.[57] Born in Halberstadt, Germany, he left for what was then Palestine in 1930, where he was the founder of the first department of Jewish History at the Hebrew University of Jerusalem and the first editor of *Zion*, an Israeli journal devoted to historical research.[58] His most famous work is the two-volume *A History of the Jews in Christian Spain* written at the end of the Second World War when the horrors of the Holocaust were clear to all. Whereas Graetz, Geiger, Goitein, and countless others imagined the cross-pollination between Jew and Muslim in al-Andalus as, to use the word of Lazarus-Yafeh, "without parallel,"[59] Baer disagreed. For him, philosophy, poetry, and other belles-lettres amounted to an inauthentic expression created by religiously lax elites. According to him:

> The Hebrew poetry of this period reflects primarily the life of the upper classes, the bourgeoisie and courtiers, who enjoyed their life,

tasted the pleasures of wine, women, palaces, and gardens, and pursued the literary arts and sciences.... Political ambition, the passion for erotic experience, the desire for rational understanding penetrated the Jewish community, bringing disintegration and heresy.[60]

These elites, their desires and tastes, do not reflect the majority of Jews. Because of this, he reasons, they and their cultural productions cannot be reified so as to reflect accurately Jewish values or Jewish history. He writes:

> Jewish communal leadership was in the hands of a small group of men of wealth and education who were influential at court. The Jewish court officials of this period, like those who serve in a similar capacity in the courts of Christian monarchs later on, were the owners of large estates and even entire villages. But the Jewish masses derived their livelihood from the cultivation of fields and orchards, from manufacture and handicraft.[61]

Writing at a time when young Zionists were recreating a Jewish homeland in the land of Israel, Baer preferred the Jewish "masses" over "elites."[62] The former, in his view, were somehow more authentic:

> Jewish culture in Muslim Spain was guided by a line of thinking different from that of the authors of the Mishna and expressed itself in a way of life different from that of the pietists of German Jewry who died a martyr's death for their faith.... The cultural activity fostered by the couriers was allowed to flourish only through the neglect and the religious and moral laxity of the rulers, and not as a result of the definite policy of tolerance and individual freedom. In the south and in the north, both in Islam and in Christianity, nationalist and religious movements, primitive in character, were forming, which were due to make an end of the existing laxity.[63]

Baer here contrasts the Ashkenazic proclivity for martyrdom in the face of oppression with the tendency of Spanish elites to convert to Christianity in times of crisis. What these Spanish elites had that the Ashkenazic pietists did not was reason. As a result, according to Baer, philosophy and other forms of rationality impinged upon what he perceived to be the authentic Jewish identity, one that young Zionists sought to recreate in Israel after the Second World War. After writing his magnum opus, Baer increasingly turned his attention to the Second Temple period—a time, using the words of Israel Yuval, "of pre-Christian Judaism, the Judaism of the Land of Israel," the newly imagined ancient homeland—the Altneuland in Herzl's telling locution—in which he now found himself.[64]

All of the constructions witnessed in this section reveal a number of similarities. Primary is the projection of modern needs onto the past. These needs can be as diverse as the desire for Jewish emancipation or as an antidote to Jewish trauma associated with the horrors of the Second World War. It could be used to show external enemies that Judaism possessed a rich history, especially when Jews were granted freedom; and it could be used to show contemporary Jews how backward they were. Either way, these constructions of Muslim Spain are very rarely, if ever, about Muslim Spain, and even less about Arabs or Muslims.

If these scholars put their needs onto the past, our present construction of the "golden age" of Muslim Spain witnesses us putting our modern values on it. Muslim Spain, as we shall see in the following section, is all that the post-9/11 world is not. It is tolerant, multicultural, free from religious or other sectarian violence, and a place where so-called Abrahamic values carried the day.[65] Once again, though, such constructions are based on nostalgia and romance and not on any historical evidence. The "golden age" accordingly proves to be illusive, the stuff of dreams. A constructed past that leads to an imagined future. Most important for my purpose here is that such constructions actually obscure the interrelationship between these two traditions. In fact, my argument in the following chapter is that this interrelationship was much deeper and much more complex than anything the default model of symbiosis posits.

The "Golden Age" of al-Andalus Today

If German-Jewish scholars invented the trope of the "golden age" of al-Andalus, it could then take on other valences dependent upon need or utility.[66] In the aftermath of the events of September 11, 2001, for example, Muslim Spain became the cosmopolitan locus, the place where Jews, Muslims, and Christians existed in some interfaith utopia. In our new world of terrorism, occupation, and the strict patrolling and enforcement of religious boundaries, Muslim Spain stands as a beacon and sends out a light to illumine our existential darkness. Witness, for example, President Clinton's remarks with which I began chapter 1 and his hope that a cognizance of this "golden age" can help defray tensions between Israelis and Palestinians in the contemporary period.

Increasingly, then, the trope of the "golden age" of Muslim Spain has little to do with internal reform of Judaism and more to do with an imagined place—free of religious violence and terrorism—where Judaism and Islam (and, of course, also Christianity) existed in an irenic and tolerant environment which is now primarily invoked by non-Jewish scholars. New terms like "convivencia" and "Abrahamic religions" are now often used synonymously to describe this imagined social landscape. Such terms are yet another variation on the romantic, wistful, and ahistorical narrative we have seen throughout this chapter and they say more about modern agendas than historical research. Writing about an exhibition at the Jewish Museum in New York City to commemorate the 500-year anniversary of the Expulsion of Jews and Muslims from a newly unified Spain, Joan Rosenbaum, the Museum's Director, informs us:

> Remaining a Jew while participating fully as a citizen in the life of a particular country has been a continuing challenge in Jewish life for centuries. The experience of Jews living in medieval Iberia, particularly in the period of Muslim rule, provides a model of achievement for simultaneously flourishing Jewish religious and secular life.[67]

Again, the concern is as much with the present as it is with the past. And once again, while the encounter with Islam might have had important aesthetic and intellectual repercussions on Judaism's periphery, Judaism's heart or soul remained stable and unscathed. In 2008—after the attacks of 9/11, the War on Terror, and the latest round of conflict in Israel and Palestine—Bellarmine College of the Liberal Arts at Loyola Marymount University in Los Angeles put on a conference to study this "golden age." Amir Hussain and Dorian Llywelyn SJ, the conference conveners, describe this "golden age" in the following terms:

> The meeting of culture and religion in medieval Spain—a period of several centuries during which Jews, Christians, and Muslims managed to live together in comparative peace. Together, they created a bridge culture—la convivencia—which was far more than the sum of its parts. Christian architects used Islamic motifs in their buildings. Muslim and Jewish philosophers kept alive the works of Aristotle in Arabic commentaries and translations. Mosques were used as synagogues on Saturdays and churches on Sundays. Later

in history, more troubled times and places would look back on that period as a golden age of understanding and tolerance.[68]

The conference was, by an examination of its participants, an interfaith love fest as opposed to an academic conversation.[69] Another example of this usage comes by way of the Cordoba Initiative, founded in 2004, and which describes itself as "a multi-national, multi-faith organization dedicated to improving Muslim-West relations."[70] Its founder, Feisal Abdul Rauf, in a book entitled *What's Right with Islam*, contends that "many Jewish and Christian artists and intellectuals emigrated to Cordoba during this period to escape more oppressive regimes that reigned over Europe's Dark and Middle Ages. Great Jewish philosophers such as Maimonides were free to create their historic works within the pluralistic culture of Islam."[71]

This quotation is important because with it we have really come full circle. Jewish scholars invented the trope of the "golden age" of Muslim Spain for modern reasons, to show others the intellectual and artistic heights to which Jews could attain if given freedom. Abdul Rauf does the same, but with the other half of the Jewish–Muslim equation. For him, the trope of the "golden age" is a way to show others that Islam is inherently tolerant.

My concern in this chapter has been neither to investigate nor decide who was or was not more tolerant than the other. Rather, it has been to demonstrate that, with the appropriate desire and intent, ahistorical terminology and categories can be used to demonstrate the existence of modern virtues in premodern times. We then proceed to write the "histories" of such virtues. We must thus be cautious, to use the words of Barbara Johnson, of a method that "reads backwards from what seems natural, obvious, self-evident or universal, in order to show that these things have their history, their reasons for being the way they are, their effects on what follows them, and that the starting point is not a given but a construct, usually blind to itself."[72]

Conclusions

The question we must ask ourselves is: How far are we willing to go to imagine a "golden age"? What historical contortions are we prepared to undertake in the name of constructing modern narratives and contemporary virtues? If the past becomes little more than a screen on which we project our own desires and fantasies, we will never know, let alone understand, the historical record. Too much of our understanding of Jewish–Muslim relations in the premodern world either in the seventh century, the eleventh, or anything in between, I have suggested time and again in this study, is based precisely on such projections. The entire narrative has to change. The invocation of terms like "convivencia" or tropes such as "golden age" do not help us understand the complexity of places like al-Andalus let alone the relations between Jews and Muslims that we imagine to have existed therein. On the contrary, such terms problematically paper over real differences and tensions, all the while ignoring the complexity and fluidity of identity formation. Ecumenicism and the need to construct or imagine a different future unfortunately and frequently reign supreme in so much of this literature.

A new look at al-Andalus, as I shall offer in the following chapter, ought to imagine less an interfaith utopia than to demonstrate a real set of encounters in which Muslims and Jews used the other to think about themselves and, in the process, to limn and subsequently patrol their own boundaries. The anxiety with the other as witnessed in the previous chapters, then, neither suddenly nor magically lifts in the medieval period. Rather, this anxiety continues to function as an identity marker, one that seeks to overcome intellectual and social fluidity as it simultaneously reveals their porosity.

6

Re-frame

WHAT MIGHT A redescribed al-Andalus look like? If we lose the language of "golden age," and the wistful romanticism that follows in its wake, what remains? Must symbiosis—to return to Shlomo Dov Goitein and even to Steven Wasserstrom[1]—be the default metaphor that generates our narrative and defines its parameters? While the borderlines separating Muslim and Jew gradually firm up and begin to stabilize somewhat in the eleventh century, each remains in the imagination of the other, often providing the raw material for the other's world-making. "Jew" and "Muslim" now increasingly become reinscribed as textual strategies to limn the contours of group belonging. This feature—a form of mythopoeic cartography, for lack of a better word—has functioned, as witnessed in previous chapters, as a constant in Jewish–Muslim relations since the time of Muhammad. It is a feature, moreover, that certainly shows no sign of slowing down into the present. The history of the one, in many ways, becomes bound up as a function of the history of the other.[2]

Once again, and perhaps surprisingly given the fact that we would seem to be on more solid terrain than in the late antique period, we run up against a paucity of sources, especially on the Muslim side of the spectrum. As David Wasserstein observed close to twenty years ago, the fact remains that most Muslims barely noticed the literary and intellectual production of Andalusi Jews.[3] In the words of Jacob Lassner, "at best the Jews are shadowy figures in the pages of the Muslim chronicles, geographical writings and belletristic texts."[4] This led Ross Brann to argue that when Jews are mentioned in Arab literature it is often on account of "a real or perceived but geographically and temporarily localized problem involving [the Jewish] community or one of its members."[5] I wish to go further in the present chapter and argue that the concern in many Muslim texts from this period is less about real Jews than about fictive ones. Not infrequently Jews function as literary stand-ins for other, often heterodox, Muslims. Jews thus become tropes that reveal further the instability of the cultural boundaries created by and in a set of textual representations. "The Jew in the Muslim text" and the "Muslim in the Jewish text" function then as discursive sites wherein each community could think about itself by means of thinking about the other, and, of course, vice versa.

Despite the increased stabilization of boundaries, however, we should not assume a modern wall that prevents transgression. The question we have to ask, though, is: What does this transgression look like? For Goitein, our default "theorist" of symbiosis, there was never any doubt about either the stability or the superiority of Judaism, and the ability of Jewish thinkers to maintain the differential qualities between their own religion and Islam. For him:

> Most of the Jewish authors of the Middle Ages who wrote in Arabic never had the slightest doubt about the absolute superiority of Judaism. I emphasize this fact not because I believe such an attitude should be adopted in our times, but simply as an indication that Judaism inside Islam was an autonomous culture sure of itself despite, and possibly because of, its intimate connection with its environment.[6]

A natural environment, and here it is worth underscoring again Goitein's use of a metaphoric grid imported from the domain of biology to that of comparative religion, is one wherein there exists presumed and clear boundaries between species, boundaries that for Goitein and for others permit autonomy. Such metaphors, according to George Lakoff and Mark Johnson, are not mere poetic indulgences, but actually structure perceptions and understanding of reality.[7] Our metaphors, framed somewhat differently, construct our objects of study as opposed to vice versa. The symbiotic relationship, to return briefly to chapter 1, is a relationship that is predicated on an ontological distinction between two or more groups. Once invoked, distinct and exclusive essences are imagined and/or created as opposed to, say, the existence of overlapping and/or mutually inclusive identities. I am not sure, however, whence Goitein and others derive the evidence to support a claim of exclusivity. Perhaps the arrogance of "absolute superiority" instead masks an insecurity, an awareness on the part of Andalusi authors that the distinction between

Muslim and Jew is not nearly as great as we assume it is today. Indeed, I wish to suggest that the "absolute superiority" that Goitein located in the Middle Ages was less an arrogance than an anxiety derived from using Muslim categories to show the imagined superiority of the Bible over the Qur'ān.[8] Note the irony as Jewish thinkers attempted to show the superiority of a Judaism that they had largely fitted into Arabic and Islamic categories.

The present chapter seeks to show further the creation of a boundary that could be used or invoked to define certain beliefs as "Jewish" or "Muslim" by situating them on one side of this artificial line. I wish to suggest here that, once again, "Jewish–Muslim" functions as a cultural map wherein alterity can be located neatly, if imprecisely. Upon this map, each could plot the other in a way that they could imagine and, if not actual, create discrete identities for themselves. For medieval Muslims, "the Jew" often functions as trope against which Sunni orthodoxy, for example, could be defined and maintained. "Jews" and "Jewish" thus could be used as a sort of code to designate the inverse or opposite of normative belief. In this regard, it is not uncommon to find "Jew" used alongside the cognate *al-Rāfiḍa*, literally "rejectors," a pejorative and catch-all term used to denote all those who reject legitimate Islamic authority and leadership, and which Sunnis often used to refer to the Shīʿa.[9] Indeed, as Wasserstrom has pointed out, "Sunni anti-Shiʿite propagandists could eventually develop lengthy lists of Shiʿite-Jewish equations."[10] These could take the form, for example, of "The Jews say sovereignty is only valid when in the House of David, the Rafida say: The Imamate rightly belongs to the descendants of Ali."[11] This Jewish-Shīʿa equivalence, of course, is but one way that Sunni thinkers defined themselves. Indeed, according to such Sunni sources, even the founder of the Shīʿa, ʿAbd Allah ibn Sabāʾ, was a Jew.[12] To use the theoretical language of Jonathan Z. Smith:

> While the "other" may be perceived as being either LIKE-US or NOT-LIKE-US, he is in fact, most problematic when he is TOO-MUCH-LIKE-US, or when he claims to BE-US. It is here that the real urgency of a "theory of the self" emerges. This urgency is called forth not by the requirement to place the "other," but rather to situate ourselves. ... The problem is not alterity, but similarity—at times, even identity. A "theory of the other" is but another way of phrasing a "theory of the self."[13]

If the history of religions tells us anything, it is that such stability, often projected onto the past to save us from the complexity of the present, never actually existed. Because other groups are "too much like us" they need to be theorized and taxonomically placed within metaphysical cartographies. If "golden ages," to return us to the theme of the previous chapter, are mere poetic fictions, they nevertheless function in our collective imaginations as providing intellectual and categorical security. Symbiosis provides the luxury of imagining strong Jews who could maintain their own essential identities while rejecting the destructive elements of the secularizing forces of Islam. This ostensibly enabled Jews to be attracted to the positive and secular elements of the Islamic world all the while remaining steadfast to the religion of their ancestors. The core of Jewish identity, to reiterate, remains untouched by and from the encounter with Islam. This is why Norman Stillman can write that Muslim Spain offered Jews "a brighter, more humane side" of Islam.[14] He continues:

> It is not mere coincidence that the flowering of Jewish culture in the Arab world should occur at the very time that Islamic civilization was at its apogee. Classical Islamic civilization was not Islam the religion, although the latter was an essential component. Islamic civilization was an amalgam of cultural elements that included Islamic religion, Arabic culture with its strong pre-Islamic roots, Greek humanism, and subtle remnants of the ancient heritage of the Near East. For a few brief centuries, Greek humanism and Islam's own universal tendencies combined with a dynamic mercantile economy to produce a relatively open society in which more often than not Muslims and non-Muslims could participate.[15]

Once again, we witness the assumption of stable borders, not to mention the assumption that religions "ebb and flow," have "apogees and nadirs," and/or "peaks and valleys." A cosmopolitan, universal, and humanistic Islam is imagined as giving Judaism the wherewithal to create distinctly Jewish ideas in an Arabic environment. The Arabic or Arabophone nature of this environment is always emphasized, but rarely the Islamic. The mirror inverse, so that master narrative goes, of what happened in seventh-century Arabia.[16] Yet, such narratives, as I have argued throughout this study, mask and blur that which was simmering just below the surface. Both Muslim and Jewish grammarians, for example, were imagining and manufacturing national languages; Muslim and Jewish philosophers were forcing a set of filiations between received Greek ideals and monotheism. This was an overlapping as opposed to symbiotic activity. The textual and hermeneutical processes that Jewish and Muslim thinkers engaged in were identical. So, why should we assume that these thinkers even recognized the ethnic and religious boundaries that the modern model of symbiosis ascribes to them?

Remove the frame of symbiosis and a more accurate narrative or frame may well be one wherein two (or more) overlapping and unstable social groups think about themselves using similar hermeneutics while simultaneously invoking select elements of the other as tropes or metaphors to better understand themselves. Thinking with and about others becomes an effective way of, in Stanley Tambiah's language, "embodying highly emotional charged ideas in respect to which intellectuality and affectivity cannot be rigidly separated."[17] In this thinking, we witness how the fear of porosity, the aporia of fluidity, work in the service of a retroactively projected and subsequently manufactured normativity.

It is worth noting that this dialectic does not necessarily mirror the late antique period so much as it represents a historical development, if we can call it that, reflective of the increased stability of social borders. This, of course, was the product of what was going on at the center. My argument now is that despite the increased existence of these borders, there still remains a real porosity that witnesses the migration of ideas and concepts. Again, it is not so much who had what first as it is about social groups on both sides of this border sharing a common set of categories and vocabulary. Such migration continues to destabilize centers even as it firms up the margins. Once more, we find that our regnant model or models used to account for Jewish–Muslim relations—whether in the late antique period, the medieval period, or even today—are unable to either account for or appreciate this migration on account of their desire to posit a stability based on imagined essences.

For medieval Jews, the subject matter of the present chapter, Islam becomes a way of creating orthodoxy. This is not an equivalent transaction to what we just witnessed with Muslim thinkers, however. In the hands of medieval Arabophone framers of Judaism, an imagined "Islam" becomes the paradigm of what a religion should be. It becomes the model into which Judaism must be fitted and in the process created anew.[18] This Islam, then, is not the inverse of orthodoxy, but becomes the very ideal of orthodoxy. While anisomorphic, the result is similar: to imagine, create, and maintain the semblance of normativity. If in Judaism, Islam creates orthodoxy in the sense of establishing an "Islamic Judaism," in Islam, Judaism is imagined as the opposite of orthodoxy that is perhaps owing to the increased hegemonic status of Islam. This imaginative reconstitution and reconciliation of symbolic structures simultaneously permit and facilitate group cohesion; or, in the words of Benedict Anderson, they are responsible for the creation of "imagined communities."[19]

The primary focus of the present chapter will be on how Jewish intellectuals adopted the interpretive strategies of various gnostic-inspired Muslim subcultures to think both about themselves and about Judaism more generally. These included selectively adopting teachings and techniques associated with: (1) the Ismaʿīlis, a minority Shīʿī group whose teachings pivoted around a *ẓāhir/bāṭin*, "exoteric/esoteric," dialectic;[20] (2) Sūfī sources that utilized mystical and other meditative techniques;[21] and (3) the absorption of new literary genres, inspired by Arab poets and intellectuals, to reconfigure the biblical narrative.[22] The individuals to be discussed were all luminaries, scholars and artists that forever changed the shape of Judaism. That they did so using the language, terms, categories, and genres of Muslims is no coincidence. Although Goitein, as indeed an entire generation of scholars committed to symbiosis, would go so far as to agree with this assessment, they nevertheless want to retain an untampered and untamperable "Jewish" essence that exists behind all of this. I am not convinced we can do this, however. If Judaism is articulated Islamically and not just Arabically, then surely we have, for lack of a better term, an Islamic Judaism.

As in chapter 4, I wish to suggest that Islam functions as the catalyst for the construction of an "Islamic Judaism." Islam, in other words, provided the intellectual and religious context for the florescence of Judaism at a formative moment in its development. In that chapter, we witnessed how Islam provided a stability that facilitated the intellectual context of what would emerge as the normative rabbinic Judaism. Now, however, I wish to go a step further and argue that the border separating Jew from Muslim even in the medieval period may well be more retrofitted from the present than real.

The Muslim as Text

In what remains of this chapter, I would like to look at a series of strategies that permitted Jewish thinkers to deal with Islam. Again, this was not necessarily the Islam of history so much as the Islam that they imagined as an antidote to a problem or set of problems they located in the Judaism of their own day. In this, they were paradoxically similar to a much later generation of German Jewish thinkers, examined in previous chapters, the ones who created our model of symbiosis in the first place.

Unlike the late antique period where the border was virtually nonexistent between the two, we now have a minority thinking with and about a majority and in such a manner that the minority is actively trying to define itself both with and against that majority. The figures that are doing this are certainly the usual suspects that are invoked in the "golden age" narrative. I do not doubt that they are luminaries of medieval Judaism. However, I am less interested in that narrative in which they are habitually and customarily located than I am in showing how these thinkers further destabilize the line between Judaism and Islam. I do this, to reiterate, to show how Muslim figures of speech, tropes, and ideas became absorbed into Judaism in such a manner that the "Islamic Judaism" originally articulated by Saadya became even further inscribed. Rather than imagine a kernel or essence of Judaism that remains untouched by contact with Islam, and a stable border that prevents the free flow of unsavory ideas or concepts, my goal is to demonstrate that neither in fact exist.

What follows is less the desire to engage a technical description of this transparency and fluidity than it is to begin the process of redescribing the narrative. The examples that follow provide, I trust, a set of overlapping vignettes wherein Jewish elites thought with and about Islam. Once we begin to appreciate this overlap, we may well be able to get a glimpse of how the so-called golden age was less about symbiosis between two species than about a porous border across which ideas could be easily moved.

Halevi's Spark

Judah Halevi (1075–1141) represents, on one level, a quintessential Jewish thinker from Muslim Spain.[23] Secular and religious poet, philosopher, rabbi, he is perhaps best known for writing one of the most articulate pleas for Jewish particularity and chosenness. His *Kitāb al-radd wa'l-dalīl fī'l-dīn al-dhalīl*, "The Book of Refutation and Proof in Defense of the Despised Religion," also known as the *Kitāb al-khazarī* was, as should be clear from its title, written in Arabic.[24] Note the paradox that a plea for Jewish particularity would be written in Arabic as opposed to Hebrew, especially when we know that Halevi wrote also in Hebrew. Significantly, Halevi wrote the book in the form of a dialogue, a genre largely unused in earlier Jewish thought, but one that was common among Muslim esoteric groups such as the Ismāʿīlis.[25] Moreover, the very terms that govern his articulation of Judaism in the work are technical ones derived from them.[26] These include *amal/niyya* (actions/intentions),[27] *ẓāhir/ bāṭin* (exoteric/esoteric),[28] and *ṣafwa* (chosenness/election).[29]

Since I have devoted an entire study to this topic in Halevi's work,[30] let me give a few brief examples to show how Halevi recycled these topics. In his monumental study from the 1980s, the Israeli intellectual historian Shlomo Pines demonstrated how Halevi adopted and adapted several terms from the Ismāʿīlis. One such term is *ṣafwa*, which the Ismāʿīlis used to denote an elite line of prophets.[31] Halevi, however, uses this term not to refer to a line of prophets, but to the entire Jewish people. In *Khuzari* I:44–47, the *ḥaver*, the representative of normative Judaism, informs the proselyte, who has just asked him what the date is:

> Four thousand and nine hundred years. The details can be demonstrated from the lives of Adam, Seth, Enoch to Noah, then Shem and Eber to Abraham, then Isaac and Jacob to Moses. These [individuals] possess a connection [*ittiṣālahum*] to Adam on account of his election [*ṣafwa*]. Each of them had children who were like empty vessels when compared to their fathers because the divine influence did not unite with them [*lam yittaṣalu bi-hum amr ilāhī*]. This account occurs through sainted persons [*al-ilāhūn*] who were individuals and not a group until Jacob gave birth to the twelve tribes who all united with the divine influence [*kullahum yaṣilun li-l-amr al-ilāhī*].[32]

All of Israel, according to Halevi in this passage, share in and inherit the divine influence (*amr ilāhī*) on account of their descent from their ancestors. In like manner, Halevi takes the technical terms *amal/niyya*, which the Ismāʿīlis had used to elevate the former term at the expense of the latter, and inverts them. In his deft hands, religious actions—inscribed on and by the body—are as important, if not more so, than spiritual intention. In the dramatic opening to the *Khuzari*, an angel appears to the king in his dream and informs him:

> "Your intention [*niyya*; pl. *niyyāt*] is pleasing to God, but your action [ʿ*amal*; pl. *aʿmāl*] is not." Yet he was so zealous in the cult of the Khazar religion, and with a pure and sincere *niyya* he devoted himself to the *aʿmāl* of the temple and the offering of sacrifices. Yet the

angel came again at night and said to him: " Your *niyya* is pleasing, but your *'amal* is not.³³

Halevi's use of these two technical terms is the opposite of that found in Ismāʿīlī texts. In these latter texts, the *a'māl* are meant for all Muslims, but only a select few properly understand the *niyyāt* behind them.

What Halevi has done, then, is taken an Ismāʿīlī genre (e.g., the dialogue), Ismāʿīlī terminology, and a similar narrative structure (one wherein a potential disciple asks a potential teacher for help), but gives them a radically different interpretation. In so doing, Halevi defines Judaism using Islamic concepts and terms of reference, even if by negating them. That he uses such terms and genres shows how Islam powers his understanding of Judaism. The result is, once again, a Judaism whose essence is by no means fixed and the terminology used to bring it into existence or at the very least give it definition is Islamic, and, again, not just Arabic. While the latter applies to linguistic articulation, the former implies a systematic rethinking of what Judaism is or should be.

The very genre, terms, and structure that Halevi used argue for Jewish superiority (recall Goitein's argument), but in a way that is derivative of minority Shīʿī groups who had used them to define their own presumed superiority in light of Sunni majorities. On a fundamental level, then, Halevi did as other minorities had done under Islam. We ought to understand his Ismāʿīlī-inspired Judaism as another minority's religious struggle for self-definition under majoritarian Sunnism. Halevi, thus, uses an Islamic narrative in the exact same way that other Muslim subgroups did. Like these groups, he reimagines his religious and social worldview in a manner that is ultimately defined by the terms and categories that normative Islam has supplied. Such terms and categories remain, even in their subversion.

Abraham Ibn Ezra's Intellect

Abraham ibn Ezra (1089–1167) was a contemporary and friend of Judah Halevi.³⁴ He was an eclectic thinker, what one study calls a medieval "polymath,"³⁵ but his primary interests resided in astrology, mathematics, and biblical exegesis. He was, then, a classic "Neoplatonist."³⁶ I wrote my dissertation close to twenty years ago on Ibn Ezra's *Ḥay Ben Meqitz*, a Hebrew and Jewish version of Avicenna's (980–1037), one of the most important of the medieval the Islamic philosophers, *Ḥayy ibn Yaqẓān*.³⁷ Both texts are quasi-mystical, quasi-philosophical, and quasi-literary compositions that describe a novice's journey from relative ignorance to enlightenment.[38] At that time, I argued that Ibn Ezra tried to write a better version of Avicenna's text based on contemporaneous rules governing literary production. Discussions of medieval plagiarism focused less on who said what first, but who said what best.[39] It is, to be sure, a relative argument. I now wish to revisit my earlier argument and see if I can make better sense of it by also using the analytical framework I am developing here.

If we work on the assumption that Jewish thinkers articulated an Islamicized Judaism, this means that the individuals discussed in this chapter are quite literally manufacturing a Judaism that is meant to conform on fundamental levels to that which they imagine Islam to be. Rather than assume that there exists some spiritualized and ahistorical essence to Judaism that remains separate from and untouched by this Islamic frame as it were, I maintain that the perceived essence can only be imagined through the frame. There is, in other words, nothing behind the frame that brings its objects into existence. The latter, quite literally, cannot exist without the former. This means that Jewish thinkers imagined a Judaism that was much more similar in structure, form, and contents to Islam than we in the present may be willing to admit for a host of extra-intellectual reasons.

In terms of *Ḥay ben Meqitz*, then, Ibn Ezra's goal, as I maintained close to twenty years ago and as I still maintain today, was to rewrite the biblical narrative by putting it into the categories of medieval Islamic Neoplatonism. For example, at the beginning of the poem,[40] Ibn Ezra describes the protagonist in the following terms:

> *An old man was walking in the field*[41]
> *Praising God giving thanks.*
> *His appearance was like that of kings*
> *An Aura surrounded him, shining like the angels.*
> *Seasons had not changed him*
> *Years seemed not to pass him.*
> *His eyes shined like those of a dove*[42]
> *His brow gleamed as a slice of pomegranate.*[43]
> *Neither distortion in his height*
> *Nor weakness in his strength.*
> *Neither darkness in his eyes*
> *Nor was his vigor unabated.*[44]

The poem continues, but it should suffice to note here that Ibn Ezra has taken biblical verses and provided them with a new context—the context supplied by Avicenna's *Ḥayy ibn Yaqẓān*.[45] What is interesting here, though, and this is unique among my examples, is that Ibn Ezra's work is written in Hebrew. However, that his model was Avicenna's Arabic version clearly demonstrates that behind the Hebrew and Jewish production is an Arabic and Islamic model. His goal was not just to make Judaism intellectually respectable by showing the correspondence between biblical verses and contemporaneous scientific theory, nor was it simply to show his readers that the Bible—and, by extension, Judaism—was superior to Islam.[46] Instead, I would now go so far as to claim that Ibn Ezra was actively producing a Judaism that conformed to the intellectual and aesthetic sensibilities of Arab-Islamic culture. This could only be done, I maintain, if Judaism was a lot more unstable than the likes of Goitein would have us believe.

Baḥya's Asceticism

In medieval Islam and Judaism, it is often difficult to separate neatly what constitutes mysticism and what constitutes philosophy.[47] This may well be on account of the fact that these two terms are ours as opposed to those whom we are too easily willing to label as "philosophers" or "mystics." Indeed, just as the symbiotic model is one of modern provenance and, as I have argued, actual hinders more than helps our ability to examine the data, so too does an equally modern model that posits sharp distinctions between philosophy and mysticism. The result is that philosophy is signified as good and mysticism, including its analogues (magic, astrology, for example), is imagined as obscurantist. The fact of the matter, however, is that the majority of medieval thinkers straddled the border between philosophy and mysticism, often seeing the latter as a continuation of the former.[48] In the secondary literature this is often referred to using the anachronistic and often pejorative term "Neoplatonism." However we frame it or whatever term we decide to call it, this intersection, especially in the eleventh and twelfth centuries, witnesses a tremendous cross-pollination between Jewish and Muslim thinkers by again providing them with a common vocabulary and set of shared categories.

We witness this intersection in Baḥya ibn Paqūda (b. 1050), and his *Kitāb al-Hidāya ilā Farāʾiḍ al-Qulūb* (The book of directions to the duties of the heart), which represents one of the earliest attempts to introduce the terminology of Islamic mysticism, especially Sufism, into Judaism. Like his Muslim counterparts, Bahya sought to create a rupture in the mundane order of things—reality, religious performance, Scripture—in order to get at what he considered to be the true reality (Ar. *ḥaqīqa*) behind it. Once the veil of the exoteric world (Ar. *ẓāhir*) has been pierced, the mystic is able to experience the hidden and esoteric world (Ar. *bāṭin*) that supports it.[49]

Bahya, as Diana Lobel has shown, was a very synthetic thinker.[50] He absorbed many of the premises of Kalām, such as arguments for the creation of this world out of nothing, in addition to adopting the general kalāmic method of argumentation. Bahya is also customarily identified as a "Jewish philosopher" in the sense that he employs philosophical arguments to clarify religious belief by eradicating misconceptions about God and the divine world, and philosophy also serves as a reminder to the pious one when he becomes distracted by the needs of the body. However, for Bahya, philosophy and theology are but steps on the path, a path that he describes in the Introduction to his magnum opus as differentiating the duties of the body from those of the heart. Whereas the former are external and concern the body, the latter are internal and involve "secret duties." In the opening section to his *Kitāb al-Hidāya ilā Faraʾiḍ al-Qulūb*, Bahya writes:

> Thus I have come to know for certain that the duties of the members are of no avail to us unless our hearts choose to do them and our soul desires their performance. Since, then our members cannot perform an act unless our souls have chosen it first, our members could free themselves from all duties and obligations if it should occur to us that our hearts were not obliged to choose obedience to God. Since it is clear that our Creator commanded the members to perform their duties, it is improbable that He overlooked our hearts and souls, our noblest parts, and did not command them to share in His worship, for they constitute the crown of obedience and the very perfection of worship.[51]

Bodily actions, framed somewhat differently, are meaningless unless they are buttressed by the proper duties of the heart. It is only the latter, according to Bahya, that make the former possible. Despite this, Bahya is quick to criticize the majority of Jews who simply perform their religious duties and obligations externally. True worship (Ar. *al-ʿibāda*; Heb. *ha-ʿavoda*), according to Bahya, involves a wholehearted devotion (*al-ikhlāṣ*) to God, something that can only occur when the individual has purified oneself from spiritual blemish. The Sufi overtones of such a claim should be apparent, and indeed *ikhlāṣ* is a technical term (in addition to being a chapter of the Qur'ān) that Bahya has again introduced into Judaism.

Like many Sufi manuals, Bahya's *Kitāb al-Hidāya ilā Farāʾiḍ al-Qulūb* is divided into gates, each of which describes a particular state or awareness that the seeker needs to embody. Bahya does not, however, present the various stages that the mystic must go through in the way that systematic Sufis like al-Qushayrī do. This may well be on account of the fact that Bahya presents an intellectual journey as much as a spiritual one, and in fact does not see, as was typical in medieval Neoplatonism, the two modes as unconnected from one another. Since space does not permit a full-scale analysis of each gate, allow me to focus briefly on the final gate, that of the true love (*ṣidq fī'l-maḥabba*) of God. Bahya ends this gate with an account of the signs of those who truly love God. This description, as Georges Vajda has shown, has parallels in Abū Nuʿaym al-Iṣfahānī's *Ḥilyat al-Awliyāʾ* (The adornment of the saints).[52] Vajda is quick to point out, however, that Bahya never goes as far as the Sufis and declares that there is a union between the lover and God. Vajda here, like many commentators on Jewish thinkers inspired by Sufis, does not want to see a complete mystical union as there is in Sufism. I am not convinced by this argument that Jewish mystics denied such a union, as one can certainly find numerous examples to the contrary.[53] At any rate, Bahya here argues that the ultimate state of love culminates in reliance (*tawakkul*) on the divine. In part seven of the final gate, he writes:

> This way of worship is included in the duties of the heart. This is the inner knowledge (*ʿilm al-bāṭin*) hidden in the hearts of those who know and contained in their inner being. When they speak of it, its truth becomes apparent to all, for every person of sound mind and intelligence will attest to its truthfulness and justice. This is the way they attain to the highest stage of God's obedience and reach the noblest rank of devotion [*ikhlāṣ*] to God and truthfulness in love of him [*ṣidq fī'l-maḥabba*] in heart and soul, body and property, as stressed by the prophet, "And you shall love the Lord your God with all your heart, soul, and might." Those who have reached this stage are closest to the rank of the virtuous prophets [*al-anbiyāʾ al-abrār*] and God's chosen favorites [*al-aṣfiyāʾ al-akhyār*]. The Scriptures describe them as "lovers of God" and "lovers of His name," and it is

said "That I may cause those that love me to inherit substance, and that I may fill their treasuries."[54]

Again, we face the question. What do we do with Baḥya? Is he a Muslim, a Jew, a Jewmuslim or a Muslimjew? Is he a Jewish-Sufi? We can do what we usually do and call him a "synthetic thinker" who, like other Jewish thinkers of the "golden age" of Muslim Spain, bathed in the civilizational stream of Islam. Yet, I worry that such an assessment—which functions as the regnant discourse—papers over the complexity of self-definition. Baḥya is, for all intents and purposes, an Arab-Islamic thinker, one who takes ideas from that tradition in order to imagine or re-imagine Judaism. If Baḥya were singular, he could be written off as idiosyncratic. But as we have seen throughout this chapter, he represents but one iteration of how Jews used the dominant narrative of Islam to actively create Judaism. Symbiosis, the default metaphor for this creation, does not do the complex structure justice.

The Maimonides Family

Maimonides (1136–1204), the individual who, as we have seen several times in this study, is generally held up as the arch-rationalist of premodern Jewish thought, picks up a number of these Islamic pietistic themes, especially in the so-called Sufi chapter (III:51) of his philosophical magnum opus, *The Guide of the Perplexed*. Therein he, like Baḥya, employs numerous terms and phrases in vogue among Sufis. In this chapter, one which some believe he originally intended to conclude his *Guide*,[55] Maimonides provides his famous parable of the palace.[56] He describes a king in his palace with six different levels of citizens, from those who are completely outside of the country to those who sit in the palace but do not actually meet the king. After explaining each group, Maimonides comes to those few individuals who possess the ability to comprehend—"to see him from afar or nearby"—this king, who is quite clearly a metaphor for God. His description is once again, like that found in the work of Baḥya, based on a fundamental and ontological distinction between the soul and the body. As such, it certainly appears to be more mystically inspired than it is philosophical:

> And there may be a human individual who, through his apprehension of the true realities and his joy in what he has apprehended,

achieves a state in which he talks with people and is occupied with his bodily necessities while his intellect is wholly turned toward Him, may he be exalted, so that in his heart he is always in His presence, may He be exalted, while outwardly he is with people.[57]

Here, Maimonides—like Baḥya, Abraham ibn Ezra, and Judah Halevi before him—imports Sufic terminology and categories in order to push elite Jews like himself to a deeper understanding of the commandments and, through them, of God. While Maimonides is often described as the "arch-rationalist" in Judaism, such a moniker, as others have suggested, only goes so far.[58] His intention, and this will become even clearer among his descendants, is to use the language of Islam, especially Islamic mysticism, as a way to imagine anew Jewish worship. His elite Judaism is, once again, an Islamic or Islamized Judaism. Maimonides concludes the same chapter by invoking Moses, Aaron, and Miriam, all of whom, according to rabbinic tradition, died by a kiss. The rabbis' purpose in using this phrase, according to Maimonides, "was to indicate that the three of them died in the pleasure of the apprehension due to the intensity of passionate love [*ishq*].[59] *Ishq*, more akin to the Greek *erōs* than *agapē*, was used, for example, in certain Sufi circles to denote the passionate love that the individual has for God, the love the created has for its Creator.

Like so many of the medieval Jewish philosophers, Maimonides shared the same worldview that we can locate among various Muslim subcultures, such as the Sufis and the Ismāʿīlis. Like the other thinkers already discussed, Maimonides framed Judaism Islamically. Whereas many are content to appreciate the Islamic frame yet assume that the image that it holds is uniquely Jewish, I argue that all we have is the frame. Judaism, in other words, proves to be indistinct from the language by which it is constructed and subsequently articulated. As for Sufis and other Islamic thinkers, Maimonides conceives of reason and the rational faculty as only taking the individual so far. Beyond the corporeal world, there was imagined to exist a world without matter, and the only way to access this other world was through the imaginative faculty,[60] working in close harmony with the intellect. Here their deployment of esotericism (*al-bāṭin*) and initiation, such as that provided by the Ismāʿīlis, is omnipresent.[61]

If the influence of Islamic mysticism and esotericism is evident in Maimonides, it would find even further articulation and expression in the work of his son Abraham Maimonides (1186–1237).[62] Abraham succeeded his father as the *nagīd* of the Jewish community of Egypt, which meant that he was the highest legal authority in the country. He was also an accomplished physician, philosopher, and *halakhist*.[63] Abraham so admired the Islamic mystics that he called them the direct descendants of the prophets, and regretted that his contemporary Jews did not follow their example.[64] To try to rectify this he took many of their practices and surrounded himself with disciples with the aim of creating a path (*ṭarīqa*) toward spiritual perfection.[65] Like many Sufis, his enemies criticized him for holding heretical beliefs and doctrines. For Abraham, however, the path to God, and here he invokes the technical discussion of Sufi stations (*maqamāt*), involved mercy, gentleness, humility, trust in God, contentedness, abstinence, fighting against one's nature, the control of faculties to serve spiritual ends, and solitude.[66] As with Bahya, this fulfillment cannot occur simply through external or esoteric performance, but only through the "duties of the heart." The novice needs a teacher and the end can only be reached once the individual has passed all the stages and attained perfection in each.

In his *Kifāyat al-ʿĀbidīn* (The guide for the pious), Abraham Maimonides distinguishes between two types of fulfilling the law: a common way and a special way. He describes them as follows:

> As for the common way it is a way of [consisting] in the performance of the explicit commandments—i.e., the carrying out of what is commanded to be done and the avoidance of what is commanded not to be done—by every person in Israel according to his requirements thereof ... as for the special way it is the way [that takes account] of the purposes of the commandments and their secrets and of what can be understood of the intentions of the Law and the lives of the prophets and the saints and their ilk. ... the best name for him is a *ḥasīd* because it is derived from *ḥesed*, the meaning of which is benevolence for he goes beyond what is required of him according to the explicit sense of the Law.[67]

Here Abraham, in typical mystical fashion, distinguishes between two modalities of fulfilling the commandments. In a distinction that goes back in Jewish pietism at least to Bahya, but in Sufism back much earlier, he argues that those who go over and above the mere performance of religious duties and obligations are the true people of faith. But it is a path that is open only to the initiated: "The reason we say it is a special way is because it is not explicitly obligatory, and therefore no secular punishment by human hands applies to him who is remiss in it."⁶⁸ The *ḥasīd*, then, is the one who engages in superogatory acts of faith and is someone, to use the language of Sufism, who tries to understand the *ṭarīqa* (order or path) behind the *sharīʿa* (the law), or the *bāṭin* (esoteric) behind the *ẓāhir* (exoteric).

This movement from the revealed to concealed and from the manifest to the hidden represents the essence of Sufism and the teachings of those Jews who sought to introduce it into Jewish thought and practice. It was not, to reiterate, the adoption of Islam at the expense of Judaism, it was, on the contrary, the adaptation of a certain mystically inspired language to mine the deeper truths of Judaism. We see this at work in Abraham's son Obadya Maimonides (1228–1265) and his *al-Maqāla al-Ḥawḍiyya* (Treatise of the pool). In this treatise, we see again the uses to which the language and categories of the Islamic mystical tradition were put not only in the family of Maimonides, but in a certain elite cross-section of the Jewish community of Cairo. Obadyah, like his father and like other Jewish pietists, is extremely critical of what passes for contemporary belief. He writes, for example:

> It has been repeatedly said that true devotion (*al-ʿibāda al-ḥaqīqiyya*) stems from the heart. As it is said, "And to serve Him with all your heart and all your soul" (Dt. 11:13). This is indeed the goal of the exoteric law. If an individual turns toward Him, it needs to be with the totality of his heart. Few, however, accomplish such a thing, whether it be in prayer or in studying and listening to the reading of the Torah. Indeed, they occupy themselves with serving that which distracts them from proper worship and with knowing that which distracts them from this knowledge. Even the sole concern of those renowned for their science is to hear the interpretation of a biblical verse or a pleasant expression, such as a line of poetry, with which they can embellish their prayers, in short, something that will charm their listeners.⁶⁹

Once again we see the intersection of Sufi-inspired language, the medieval Neoplatonic tradition to which Obadyah was an heir, and a deep-seated criticism of contemporary Jewish practice. Many of these Jewish pietists were critical of prevailing forms of religious worship that, as we have already seen, they considered to be too exoteric and too focused on the body at the expense of the heart. As a result, they sought to create new forms of worship that they borrowed from the Sufis, but that they often claimed had previously existed in Judaism. In this, they certainly prefigure what later Kabbalists would do. Such practices included ablution before prayer, prostration during prayer, and kneeling in parts of the daily ritual. All of these practices were certainly inspired by Islamic worship.[70] Abraham Maimonides, for instance, had also recommended weeping as a part of prayer.

Opponents to the Maimonides family frequently criticized such practices on both political and religious grounds. In terms of the former, it is important to remember that the Maimonides family was among the most important in Cairo, and had many critics who desired their power and, as a result, tried to undermine them on account of their adoption of Sufi religious expressions. Pietists, like their Muslim colleagues, were accused of innovation (Ar. *bid'a*) and of introducing heterodox views into the liturgy. The opponents of Abraham Maimonides, for example, accused him of this to the Muslim authorities of Cairo, who did not take lightly to the charge of innovation either among Muslims or non-Muslims.[71] Abraham responded that the practices were confined to his own private synagogue and were not meant to be an imposition on other Jews.[72] In his conclusion to *al-Maqāla al-Ḥawḍiyya*, Obadya writes:

> In the presence [of the elect] exercise humility, modesty, and submission, both externally and internally. Clasp your head and let your tears fall, allow purity to follow in your wake and spend your days by fasting. Delight not in the joys of the vulgar and the sorrow that grieves them. Do not be sad with their sadness and do not rejoice in what they rejoice. Despise frivolity and laughter, rather observe silence and speak only when necessary. Do not eat unless you must or sleep unless absolutely exhausted. All the while your heart should contemplate its true pursuit and your thoughts should be preoccupied by it, as it is said, "I am asleep, but my heart is awake" (Song 5:2). ... Know that the discipline that you undertake is boundless and requires much spiritual predisposition and preparation, as it is said, "And let the priests also that come near to the Lord, sanctify themselves" (Ex. 19:22).[73]

The fifth and final Maimonidean *nagīd* of the Jewish community in Egypt was David ben Joshua Maimonides (d. 1415).[74] Like his predecessors, he was greatly influenced by Sufism. Like many other Jews influenced by

Sufi ideas, he translated Arabic technical terms designating mystics with the more autochthonous sounding *ḥasīd*, and in passages lifted directly from Sufi manuals he replaced Quranic verses with biblical ones. This presumably had the effect of making his ideas seem less radical to a Jewish readership. The very title of his *al-Mursid ila al-Tafarrud* (The guide to detachment), for example, clearly reveals his Sufi sympathies. Paul Fenton notes that each stage of the spiritual journey equates with a station (*maqām*) on the Sufi path.[75] Fenton also notes that numerous extracts of *Kalimāt al-Taṣawwuf* (Sayings of Sufism) by Shihāb al-Dīn Suhrawardi (d. 1191) are found in this treatise.

Conclusions

The Maimonides family reveals fully the complexity and ambiguity of the relationship between Judaism and Islam in the medieval period. We should not assume, as pretty much all interpreters of this material do, that this is a simple case of Jews adopting Muslim categories to help them understand their own religion. This model works on the assumption that the essence of Judaism remains untouched and/or protected from externally supplied frameworks. On the contrary, as I have suggested throughout this chapter, such external frameworks rather than showcase a timeless and ahistorical essence actually facilitate its creation. This dialectic is what powers identity formation. Unfortunately, however, it is now the identity formation of our post-1948 world wherein we are determined to know with clarity who or what is "Jewish" and who or what is "Muslim." The figures examined in this chapter, I submit, are not simply "golden age" Jewish thinkers enthralled by Islamic esotericism and pietism. They are something more, and their ideas of what Judaism is or should be are much more Islamic than we are often willing to admit.[76]

This chapter has focused on several exemplary figures and a set of interrelated texts that provide paradigmatic reflections on the encounter between Jews and Muslims, Judaism and Islam, at the height of medieval Jewish creativity. The texts examined do not so much show historical encounters between two groups as they do a set of imagined and literary constructions. These constructions reveal not so much an arrogance on the part of Jewish intellectuals, in Goitein's formulation, as they do an anxiety about instability and permeability of cultural, religious, and intellectual boundaries between two religions at a formative moment for both.

Even six centuries after the initial encounter between Muhammad and the so-called Jewish community of the Arabian Peninsula we still witness a shared grid upon which can be plotted any number of ideas that can simultaneously be defined, by whichever group in question, as "Jews" or "Muslim." This model, so paramount for the first six hundred years of Jewish–Muslim interaction, shows less a symbiotic relationship, I wish to suggest, than it does a set of shared identities—dependent upon the era, the locale, and thinker or group—that overlap, intersect, and even skirmish at certain moments.

The Islam that all of these individuals were attracted to was less the Islam of history and more an idealized version of what each imagined to represent some sort of authentic religious expression. In framing Judaism in this manner, "Islamically" if you will, they did as Jews had done since the first encounter with Muhammad five centuries earlier. They used Islam—though admittedly much more inchoate in the seventh century than in the twelfth—to give definition to Judaism, again one more choate in the twelfth century than in the seventh. If previous chapters have played on the center–margins dialectic, showing how what happened at the margins often helped to provide doctrinal and other theological content at the center, the present chapter has tried to show something of what took place in the center and how, in coming centuries, it would reverse the earlier course and move out to the margins.

Conclusion

Two Solitudes

On April 14, 2002, then-Prime Minister Ariel Sharon ordered the construction of a physical barrier to separate the occupied Arab West Bank from Israel proper. Alternately called a separation wall (Heb. *ḥomat ha-hafrada*), a security fence (Heb. *geder ha-bitaḥon*), or an apartheid wall (Ar. *jidār al-faṣl al-'unṣurī*), the pretense for its construction was to protect Israelis from Palestinian attacks. Most of this contested structure is comprised of a two meter-high, electrified barbed-wire fence complete with trenches and a sixty meter-wide exclusion zone on the Palestinian side. In more densely populated urban areas, however, like those around East Jerusalem, space limitations have forced the Israelis to instead build a much higher concrete wall. Largely ignoring the so-called Green Line, that marks the pre-1967 boundary between Israel, on the one side, and the West Bank and East Jerusalem, on the other, the barrier divides villages, cuts farmers off from their fields, and prevents many Arabs from regular access to businesses, hospitals, and religious centers.

A hawkish Israeli government has thus tried to do what history could not: to control the flow of ideas and people across an artificially constructed border. One can only anticipate the results. Writing in an op-ed in the *Los Angeles Times*, Israeli author and peace activist, Amos Oz, perhaps says it best, "Once divorced, let us experience coexistence and leave notions of possible cohabitation to future generations. Ours is not a Hollywood western of good vs. evil. It is a real life tragedy of two just causes. We can continue to clash, inflicting further pain. Or we can be reconciled via separation and compromise."[1] Coexistence and separation, cohabitation and divorce, take us to the heart of the story I have here tried to tell.

We have now come 180 degrees. What began as a porous border has, for all intents and purposes, become fixed in cement and protected by barbed wire. A common and continually fragile social world, an intertwined intellectual and literary heritage, would seem to have reached its tipping point. The signs were certainly there much earlier, perhaps even as early as the thirteenth century when elite Jews increasingly began to use other languages than classical Arabic to express themselves and chronicle their intricate vision of what Judaism was or should be. What the future holds in store is anyone's guess. The model of an interfaith utopia or some supposed "golden age" of Muslim Spain holds out hope for some that this past can come to be again. Perhaps this is why it is continually invoked in numerous political, religious, and even intellectual contexts.

In his "Swiss Mountain View: A Story," another Israeli author, David Grossman, creates a protagonist, Gidi, a young idealistic officer in charge of administering an Arab village. By the end of the story, he comes to the realization that "his Arabs," not unlike himself, are broken from the occupation. They humor him because they have no choice and they inform on one another to secure safe passage if they have to visit family in other areas. The result is moral decay both within and between Jews and Arabs. At the end of the story, as Gidi stands alone, he reflects on his predicament. In Grossman's prose:

> Then [Gidi] thought that he did not want to be there, in the twilight area created when two peoples turn their dark, corrupt sides towards each other, and the thought startled him, because he loved his work and believed in it, and felt it gave him the necessary rules to navigate through his life. But he also knew clearly that when two apples touch one another at a single point of decay, the mold spreads over them both.[2]

It is difficult not to be pessimistic. I refuse to engage in the nostalgia of so many, namely, that the very genre of historical Jewish–Muslim relations dictates that one should be optimistic about a past that can be future again. I will leave it for others to prognosticate. What I will point out, however, is that any attempt at fixity, as we have seen continually in the pages of this book, betrays an anxiety with and for the other. This other—constructed either as Jew, Muslim, Israeli, or Palestinian—still functions as the pretext for self-definition and thus for the maintenance of some imagined order. The new heresiologists, however, have become the politicians, populists, and other demagogues, those who, with a confidence and self-assurance that either reinforces or belies their elected office or self-importance, know who goes where and what gets to count as authentic.

In his 1984 *Jews of Islam*, the historian Bernard Lewis could boldly entitle his final chapter "The End of the Tradition." He concludes that chapter, and the work as a whole, on a note of pessimism with the rise of Arab–Jewish revolts in Mandate Palestine. According to him:

> There have been many chapters in the long history of the Jewish people. Greek Alexandria was the home of Philo, Babylon of the Talmud, medieval Spain of a rich Hebrew literature; the Jews of Germany and Poland wrote major chapters in modern Jewish history. They have all gone, and only their monuments and memories remain. The Judaeo-Islamic symbiosis was another great period of Jewish life and creativity, a long, rich, and vital chapter in Jewish history. It has now come to an end.[3]

Lewis bases his assessment on the rise of anti-Semitism in Arab lands and the gradual diminution of tolerance on the part of Arab leaders, while largely overlooking Zionist transgression.[4] Pain for him, as it is for so many fixated on the modern iteration of this relationship, is once again unidirectional. Lewis's assessment, however, returns us full force to the messy present where each side points its finger and cloaks itself in the mantle of righteous victimhood.[5] Beyond the finger-pointing, the name-calling, and the violence however resides a deep-seated connection that the present study has sought to uncover. This uncovering, I trust, has not been of the typical variety, the one supplied by the model of symbiosis, that sees Judaism help form Islam in the late sixth century and then a return of the same favor a couple of centuries later.

This model, as I have argued throughout this study, only takes us so far. Certainly the fate of Jews and Muslims have been intertwined and interrelated since the late antique period. I doubt anyone would disagree with such a statement. However, the symbiotic model obscures the extent of the relationship, thereby diminishing our view, because it focuses on centers rather than margins, on reified religions (often imagined as species) as opposed to localized skirmishes between various social actors, and works on the model of borrowing and influence. In its desire to isolate what is "Jewish" and what is "Muslim," symbiosis overlooks the complexity as various groups—nether Muslim nor Jew, both Muslim and Jew, and what I have occasionally called Jewmuslim or Muslimjew—sought to make sense of their chaotic social worlds by appealing to a shared vocabulary and conceptual framework.

The result is that, *pace* Lewis, the relationship does not come to an end precisely because it cannot. This relationship continues into the uncertain present as Jews and Muslims mistrust one another and, while they may appeal simplistically to previous "golden ages" to expiate the hatred, they simultaneously ignore the sheer messiness and utter complexity of their real historical interactions. I certainly would not be so naïve as to claim that the study of this past will solve any let alone all of the problems of the present. I will go so far, however, as to declare that an ignorance of that past further reifies contemporary borders. I will also go so far as to proclaim that each side of the Jewish–Muslim dyad has been using the other since at least the seventh century to define itself. The difference between then and now is that identity is today largely defined by conflict that is the direct result of occupation and oppression. Identity is now constructed along national lines and reinforced using the language of hate. This is the current tragedy and I would hope that it is not a journey to the end of the land.

This study has instead opted to move beyond headlines and romantic wistfulness in order to get at some of the complexities that are the inevitable outcome of various social groups engaged in the collective activity of world-making in the context of the sixth to twelfth centuries. This activity saw Jewmuslims and Muslimjews, and subsequently Jews and Muslims, think from, with, and about the other. It has argued that we need to reimagine the paradigm we use to look at Jews and Muslims in the early centuries of Islam. Changing the paradigm, I hope, will result in the discovery of new data and new narratives to account for this data.

While not wanting to posit an "end" to the story between Judaism and Islam, Jews and Muslims, in the same manner that Lewis does, it is perhaps fitting or at least symbolic that the porous should become impervious and the transparent opaque. This is certainly not to insert a teleology into the relationship, that things could or should have been otherwise, but the history of their relations is in many ways the history, as we have seen, of those who want to stop free exchange and movement.

In this larger context of Jewish–Muslim relations, the first chapters of this *longue durée*, reveal a complexity that is unfortunately obscured or papered over in the quest for normativity and the desire to see discrete essences that survive unscathed from contact with others. As an attempt to write a post-symbiotic narrative of Jewish–Muslim relations, I have focused on undermining traditional claims and instead sought to organize some of the wide range of complexity that we find. My results here are certainly not meant to be definitive, but suggestive. They represent but an initial foray into a rich and multi-textured, but unfortunately little understood, period of history.

Much of this study has been about trying on different frames and utilizing an appropriate vocabulary for comparison. As Jonathan Z. Smith has remarked for the study of Christian origins, "the use of comparison as a hermeneutic device, or as a principle of discovery for the construction of theories plays no role. What rules, instead, is an overwhelming concern for assigning value, rather than intellectual significance, to the results of comparison."[6] This need to assign value to data, often anachronistically, is endemic to the academic study of religion in general and of the comparative enterprise in particular. This is no less true for the comparison of Judaisms and Islams in the early Islamic period than it is for the comparison, so expertly performed by the likes of Smith and others, between Christianities, Judaisms, and other religions of late antiquity.

Both comparative enterprises are saturated in the problematic construction of orthodoxy and heterodoxy and in the need to apportion the unique at the expense of the shared. In this regard, as I suggested numerous times, and here I echo the voices of others, it is important to situate Jewish and Islamic religious expressions in this early period against the backdrop of late antique apocalypticism. Even as this apocalyptic retreated into the background, however, the free exchange of ideas never stopped. This exchange, I suggested, was not just superficial but pierced to the very core of each tradition.

Too much comparative work on Judaism and Islam wants to recycle what I hope readers will now realize is an outmoded narrative. In its place it is surely time—among scholars of religion and also among interested readers in the historical interactions between these two religions—to appreciate just how complex the interactions between Judaism and Islam were, are, and will no doubt continue to be. The history of Judaism and Islam is thus one of mutual world-making and self-definition. No wall—textual or cement—will be able to stop that.

Notes

PREFACE

1. See the comments in Sandra Wallman, "Introduction: The Scope for Ethnicity," in *Ethnicity at Work*, ed. Sandra Wallman (London: MacMillan, 1979), 1–14.
2. E.g., Bain Attwood, *The Making of Aboriginees* (Sydney: Allen and Unwin, 1989), 135–138; John Hutchison and Anthony Smith, *Ethnicity* (Oxford: Oxford University Press, 1996); Richard Jenkins, *Rethinking Ethnicity* (London, Sage, 2008), 22–24.
3. See, e.g., Jonathan Z. Smith, *Drudgery Divine: On the Comparison of Early Christianities and the Religions of Late Antiquity* (Chicago: University of Chicago Press, 1990); David Chidester, *Savage Systems: Colonialism and Comparative Religion in Southern Africa* (Charlottesville: University of Virginia Press, 1996); Chidester, *Empire of Religion: Imperialism and Comparative Religion* (Chicago: University of Chicago Press, 2014). Such studies, in addition to related ones, will make regular appearances in the pages that follow. Unfortunately, however, such studies—to use language that I wish to dismantle in the coming pages—tend not to be seen as normative in the academic study of religion, but as heterodox.

    Two problems follow from this lack of critical posture—one general to the field of religious studies and the other specific to the ways in which Jewish–Muslim relations are situated within it. When it comes to the latter, there is an overwhelming tendency simply to reproduce what later, often medieval, sources say about the late antique period. In terms of the former, an irenic orientation may well encourage us to think about "Judaism" or "Islam" in monolithic terms and in such a manner that avoids historical or contextual nuance. As Arnal and McCutcheon argue, for example, it is now customary to speak of religions as opposed to religion or Judaisms instead of Judaism (i.e., using the plural as opposed to the singular form of these nouns). But, as they write, "the erstwhile singular family identity in each case is just deferred to the level of genus; identity of some sort remains intact, unspoken, and thus untheorized." See William E. Arnal and Russell T. McCutcheon, *The Sacred is the Profane: The Political Nature of "Religion"* (New York: Oxford University Press, 2013), 11–12.

INTRODUCTION

1. "We cannot take terminology for granted, nor can we impose our own conceptions of value-laden words such as 'Arabia' onto early Arabic terms, nor even assume that early Muslims divided space and ethnicity in the ways we presume today." See Peter Webb, *Imagining the Arabs: Arab Identity and the Rise of Islam* (Edinburgh: Edinburgh University Press, 2016), 137.
2. Steven M. Wasserstrom, *Between Muslim and Jew: The Problem of Symbiosis under Early Islam* (Princeton, NJ: Princeton University Press, 1995), 6.
3. Such works include, but are certainly not limited to Mark R. Cohen, *Poverty and Charity in the Jewish Community of Medieval Egypt* (Princeton, NJ: Princeton University Press, 2005); Marina Rustow, *Heresy and the Politics of Community: The Jews of the Fatimid Caliphate* (Ithaca, NY: Cornell University Press, 2008); David M. Freidenreich, *Foreigners and their Food: Constructing Otherness in Jewish, Christian, and Islamic Law* (Berkeley: University of California Press, 2011); Jessica Goldberg, *Trade and Institutions in the Medieval Mediterranean: The Geniza Merchants and the Business World* (Cambridge: Cambridge University Press, 2011); Arnold E. Franklin, *This Noble House: Jewish Descendants of King David in the Medieval East* (Philadelphia: University of Pennsylvania Press, 2013); Shai Secunda, *The Iranian Talmud: Reading the Bavli in Its Sasanian Context* (Philadelphia: University of Pennsylvania Press, 2014); and Phillip Ackerman-Lieberman, *The Business of Identity: Jews, Muslims, and Economic Life in Medieval Egypt* (Stanford, CA: Stanford University Press, 2014). I note, however, that all of these books are devoted to understanding commonalities and intersections between Judaism and Islam in the medieval period. Very few, however, are interested in the period prior to this. None of them, moreover, are interested in larger questions supplied by the study of religion.
4. There is no need to rehearse the history of this field here. I do so and situate myself therein in *Islam and the Tyranny of Authenticity: An Inquiry in Disciplinary Apologetics and Self-Deception* (Sheffield: Equinox, 2015), 115–127.
5. Wasserstrom, *Between Muslim and Jew*, 10.
6. See, for example, Wasserstrom, *Between Muslim and Jew*, 224.
7. This, of course, has not stopped many from making normative pronouncements. See, for example, Gordon D. Newby, *A History of the Jews of Arabia: From Ancient Times to Their Eclipse under Early Islam* (Columbia: University of South Carolina Press, 1988); and more recently, Haggai Mazuz, *The Religious and Spiritual Life of the Jews of Medina* (Leiden: Brill, 2014). These and other works will be analyzed in greater detail in chapter 2.
8. Daniel Boyarin, *Border Lines: The Partition of Judaeo-Christianity* (Philadelphia: University of Pennsylvania Press, 2014), 13–16.
9. Aaron W. Hughes, *Abrahamic Religions: On the Uses and Abuses of History* (New York: Oxford University Press, 2012).

10. Aaron W. Hughes *Rethinking Jewish Philosophy: Beyond Particularism and Universalism* (New York: Oxford University Press, 2014).
11. As recounted, for example, in Genesis 16. On Muslim accounts of this story, see Reuven Firestone, *Journeys in Holy Lands : The Evolution of the Abraham-Ishmael Legends in Islamic Exegesis* (Albany: State University of New York Press, 2000).
12. Beginning with works such as Michel Foucault, *The Order of Things: An Archaeology of the Human Sciences* (New York: Random House, 1970); Jean-François Lyotard, *The Postmodern Condition: A Report on Knowledge*, trans. Geoff Bennington and Brian Massumi (Minneapolis: University of Minnesota Press, 1984); Jean Baudrillard, *Simulacra and Simulation*, trans. Sheila Faria Glaser (Ann Arbor: University of Michigan Press, 1995).
13. See, for example, David Brakke, *The Gnostics: Myth, Ritual, and Diversity in Early Christianity* (Cambridge, MA: Harvard University Press, 2011), 5–8.
14. Richard W. Bulliet, *Islam: The View from the Edge* (New York: Columbia University Press, 1994), 8.
15. Bulliet, *Islam: The View from the Edge*, 8.
16. Bulliet, *Islam: The View from the Edge*, 9.
17. D. S. Margoliouth, *Relations between Arabs and Israelites Prior to the Rise of Islam* (London: Oxford University Press for the British Academy, 1924), 59–60.
18. The most recent example of this may be found in Mazuz, *The Religious and Spiritual Life of the Jews of Medina*. I will discuss this and other such works in greater detail in chapter 2.
19. Webb, *Imagining the Arabs*, 78–79.
20. See, for example, Fred Donner, *Muhammad and the Believers: At the Origins of Islam* (Cambridge, MA: Harvard University Press, 2010).
21. Donner, *Muhammad and the Believers*, 56–89. Although I remain unconvinced by Donner's comments that Islam began as a "religious" movement as opposed to a social or political one. Not only do we not possess the sources to make such a claim, how is it possible to separate between the religious and the political in the sixth century? See the comments in Brent Nongbri, *Religion before Religion: A History of a Modern Concept* (New Haven, CT: Yale University Press, 2013), 60–62.
22. To name but one recent example, Catherine Hezser, *The Social Structure of the Rabbinic Movement in Roman Palestine* (Tübingen: Mohr Siebeck, 1997); Hezser, "Roman Law and Rabbinic Legal Composition," in *The Cambridge Companion to the Talmud and Rabbinic Literature*, ed. Charlotte E. Fonrobert and Martin S. Jaffee (Cambridge: Cambridge University Press, 2007), 144–164.
23. Natalie Dohrmann and A. Yoshiko Reed, "Introduction," in *Jews, Christians, and the Roman Empire: The Poetics of Power in Late Antiquity*, ed. N. Dohrmann, and A. Y. Reed (Philadelphia: University of Pennsylvania Press, 2013), 2.
24. Erich S. Gruen, *Rethinking the Other in Late Antiquity* (Princeton, NJ: Princeton University Press, 2011), 5.

25. Gruen, *Rethinking the Other in Late Antiquity*, 4.
26. See Nongbri, *Religion before Religion*, 15–24.
27. Andrew S. Jacobs, *Christ Circumcised: A Study in Early Christian History and Difference* (Philadelphia: University of Pennsylvania Press, 2012), 5.
28. Jacobs, *Christ Circumcised*, 5.
29. Alon Idan, "By Banning Book, Israel Maintains Purity of Blood." Online at http://www.haaretz.com/misc/iphone-article/.premium-1.694673.

CHAPTER 1

1. The transcript of the speech may be found at http://millercenter.org/scripps/archive/speeches/detail/3925.
2. This is, for example, the general hermeneutic that informs much crossover literature including, but not limited to, María Rosa Menocal, *The Ornament of the World: How Muslims, Jews, and Christians Created a Culture of Tolerance in Medieval Spain* (New York: Back Bay Books, 2002); *Convivencia: Jews, Muslims, and Christians in Medieval Spain*, ed. Vivian Mann, Thomas Glick, and Jerrilyn Dodds (New York: George Braziller, 1992); Chris Lowney, *A Vanished World: Muslims, Christians, and Jews in Medieval Spain* (New York: Oxford University Press, 2005).

    Such books show that Christianity is often thrown into the mix. My interest, as I have already explained in the Preface, is less in the triptych than it is in the cultural *imaginaire* that links Judaism and Islam to one another. I have, however, tried to write about all three in my *Abrahamic Religions*.
3. Made famous by Shlomo Dov Goitein, *Jews and Arabs: Their Contact through the Ages*, 3d rev. ed. (New York: Schocken, 1955); and subsequently recycled by the likes of Bernard Lewis, *The Jews of Islam* (Princeton, NJ: Princeton University Press, 1984), e.g., xi, 191; Sarah Stroumsa, *Maimonides in His World: Portrait of a Mediterranean Thinker* (Princeton, NJ: Princeton University Press, 2011), 3–6.
4. Michael M. Laskier and Yaacov Lev, "Introduction," in *The Convergence of Judaism and Islam: Religious, Scientific, and Cultural Dimensions*, ed. Michael M. Laskier and Yaacov Lev (Gainesville: University Press of Florida, 2011), 2–3.
5. E.g., Norman Stillman, "Judaism and Islam: Fourteen Hundred Years of Intertwined Destiny?," in *The Convergence of Judaism and Islam*, 10–21.
6. In addition to the citations in ch. 1, n. 2, see Dominique-D. Junod (Arbell), *Convivencia and Its French and English Equivalents: The Word and the Concept*, trans. Martin Hemmings (n.p.: Editions Florent HUET, 2012).
7. One does not have to invoke one metaphorical grid to describe the interface. So while Goitein uses "symbiosis" in *Jews and Arabs*, the overarching goal of his *magnum opus*, the 6-volume *A Mediterranean Society: The Jewish Communities of the Arab World as Portrayed in the Documents of the Cairo Geniza* (Berkeley: University

of California Press, 1967–1993) is to show the common "Mediterranean" culture of Jews and Arabs in the world of the Cairo Geniza. "Mediterranean" is also employed by Stroumsa in *Maimonides in His World*, including in the very subtitle *Portrait of a Mediterranean Thinker*.

8. It is certainly also worth noting that some want to define the relations between Jews and Muslims in the premodern period negatively, as a long history of persecution, prejudice, and so on. Perhaps one of the most famous iterations of this approach may be found in Bat Yeor, *The Dhimmis: Jews and Christians under Islam* (East Rutherford, NJ: Fairleigh Dickinson University Press, 1985). And, of course, given the recent political climate, many neo-conservative commentators are also interested in showing how Islam has always been "intolerant" of other religions. See, in this regard, *The Myth of Islamic Tolerance: How Islamic Law Treats Non-Muslims*, ed. Robert Spencer (Amherst, NY: Prometheus Books, 2005). And, more recently, Dario Fernandez-Morera, *The Myth of Andalusian Paradise: Muslims, Christians, and Jews under Islamic Rule in Muslim Spain* (Wilmington, DE: ISI Books, 2016).

9. I have in mind here the work of Jonathan Z. Smith who reminds us that it is part of our job as scholars to "expose the set of tacit understandings which inform, but are rarely the objects of, our corporate discourse about religion." See his "Connections," *Journal of the American Academy of Religion* 58.1 (1990): 1–15, at 5.

10. Two important studies that, in their own ways, have sought to do this, are Wasserstrom, *Between Muslim and Jew*, and Mark R. Cohen, "Myth and Countermyth," which functions as chapter 1 of his *Under Crescent and Cross: The Jews in the Middle Ages* (Princeton, NJ: Princeton University Press, 1994), 3–14. Wasserstrom is a religionist, whereas Cohen is a historian. Both of these works are close to twenty-years-old, and the present study is an attempt to revisit their work and carry it forward. Given my own interest in "theory and method" in the study of religion, my concerns are more akin to those of Wasserstrom, who unfortunately no longer works in this area of study.

11. Oliver Leaman once published an intellectual biography of Maimonides entitled *Moses Maimonides* (London: Routledge, 1990). It appeared in a series called "Arabic Thought and Culture," and Alfred Ivry, in a subsequent review in the *AJS Review*, called this "amusing" and even "embarrassing." See Alfred L. Ivry, "Review of *Moses Maimonides* by Oliver Leaman," *AJS Review* 18.2 (1993): 306–308, at 306. I should be clear that although I do see Maimonides, as will be clear in chapter 6, as an Arab-Islamic thinker, I do not necessarily disagree with Ivry's overall intellectual assessment of the book, nor do I think Leaman finesses the problematic border between Judaism and Islam.

12. Here I am influenced by the path-breaking work of Daniel Boyarin, especially his *Border Lines*, 1–10.

13. See my comments in chapter 2.

14. See the comments in Ignaz Goldziher, "Le Dénombrement des sects mohamétanes," *Revue de l'histoire des religions* 26 (1892): 129–137. See further Wasserstrom, *Between Muslim and Jew*, 156–163.
15. Wasserstrom, *Between Muslim and Jew*, 156.
16. See Israel Friedlander, "Abdallah b. Saba, der Begründer der Shi`a, und sein jüdischer Ursprung," *Zeitschrift für Assyriologie* 23 (1909): 296–327; 24 (1910): 1–46.
17. Vladimir Ivanow, *Ibn al-Qaddah: The Alleged Founder of Ismailism*, 2d ed. (Bombay: Ismaili Society Press, 1957).
18. Salo W. Baron, *A Social and Religious History of the Jews* (New York: Columbia University Press, 1952–1983), 6:484n104.
19. See, for example, Timothy Fitzgerald, *The Ideology of Religious Studies* (New York: Oxford University Press, 2000), 3–32.
20. Chidester, *Savage Systems*, xiii.
21. Relevant secondary literature on the formation of Wissenschaft des Judentums include Ismar Schorsch, *From Text to Context: The Turn to History in Modern Judaism* (Hanover, NH: University Press of New England, 1994); Shmuel Feiner, *The Jewish Enlightenment*, trans. Chaya Naor (Philadelphia: University of Pennsylvania Press, 2002); Christian Wiese, *Challenging Colonial Discourse: Jewish Studies and Protestant Theology in Wilhelmine Germany*, trans. Barbara Harshav and Christian Wiese (Leiden: Brill, 2005); Michael Brenner, *Prophets of the Past: Interpreters of Jewish History*, trans. Steven Rendall (Princeton, NJ: Princeton University Press, 2010).
22. Franz Delitzsch, *Zur Geschichte der jüdischen Poesie* (Leipzig: Tauchnitz, 1836), 44–45. For relevant context, see Israel Davidson, "The Study of Medieval Hebrew Poetry in the Nineteenth Century," *Proceedings of the American Academy for Jewish Research* 1 (1928): 33–48. On Delitzsch's anti-Semitism, see Susannah Heschel, *Abraham Geiger and the Jewish Jesus* (Chicago: University of Chicago Press, 1998), 194–198.
23. In addition to the bibliography cited in the previous two notes, see Yosef Hayim Yerushalmi, *Zakhor: Jewish History and Jewish Memory* (Seattle: University of Washington Press, 1982), 77–104; and David N. Myers, *Re-inventing the Jewish Past: European Jewish Intellectuals and the Zionist Return to History* (New York: Oxford University Press, 1995), 1–12.
24. See the comments in Ivan G. Marcus, "Beyond the Sephardic Mystic," *Orim: A Jewish Journal at Yale* 1 (1985): 35–53; see also my "The 'Golden Age' of Muslim Spain: Religious Identity and the Invention of a Tradition in Modern Jewish Studies," in *Historicizing "Tradition" in the Study of Religion*, ed. Steven Engler and Gregory P. Grieve (Berlin: Walter de Gruyter, 2005), 51–74.
25. See, for example, the essay by Leopold Zunz, "Die Zukunft der jüdischen Wissenschaft," *Hebraische Bibliographie* 9 (1869): 76–78. An English translation may be found as "Scholarship and Emancipation," in *The Jew in the Modern*

> *World: A Documentary History*, 3d ed., ed. Paul Mendes-Flohr and Jehuda Reinharz (New York: Oxford University Press 2011), 256–258.

26. The classic study remains Schorsch, "Scholarship in the Service of Reform" in his *From Text to Context*, 303–333. He writes:

    > [Wissenschaft des Judentums'] primary practitioners were to be found among the first generation of university-trained school teachers and rabbis who pressed for internal accommodations dictated by the change in external conditions. The new Jewish learning offered a powerful challenge to the hegemony of an entrenched rabbinate rooted in an older universe of discourse. . . . Recovery of the past became the means of reconstituting the present. (303)

27. Heinrich Graetz, *History of the Jews* (Philadelphia: Jewish Publication Society of America, 1956), 3:53.
28. Graetz, *History of the Jews*, 3:235–236.
29. Samuel Bäck, *Die Geschichte des jüdischen Volkes und seiner Literatur vom babylonischen Exil bis auf die Gegenwart*, 3d ed. (Frankfurt am Main: J. Kauffmann, 1906), 264.
30. There were certainly variations on this trope of peaceful and fruitful coexistence. Abraham Geiger (1810–1874), for example, one of the founders of Reform Judaism and an important scholar on Judaism and Islam, and someone that we will encounter several times in the pages that follow, could write:

    > Islam rendered great service to Judaism by leaving to it room; it did not go in advance of it in everything and could not offer everything to it, but it gave it room for the development of its powers. And thus we look back upon that illustrious time as a brilliant period.

    See Abraham Geiger, *Das Judentum und seine Geschichte*, 2 vols., 2d ed. (Breslau: Schletter, 1871). English translation: *Judaism and Its History in Two Parts* (Hanover, NH: University Press of America, 1985), 352. We can then compare this with someone like Graetz, someone critical of Geiger and who himself was associated with the historical positivist school of Judaism, later to be rebranded as the Conservative movement. He writes:

    > Judaism ever strove towards the light while monastic Christianity remained in the darkness. Thus in the tenth century there was only one country that offered sustainable soil for the development of Judaism where it could blossom and flourish—it was Mahometan Spain. (*History of the Jews*, 3: 214)

    Regardless of how they constructed the essence of Judaism or their own denominational commitments, many of these German-Jewish historians sought to create a new national consciousness for German-Jews based on a common identity. This national history would not be a pariah history—as Christian German scholars tended to describe it—but a history that flourished, to recycle Graetz's agricultural metaphor, when planted in the right soil, to wit, the soil of Islam.

31. See Suzanne L. Marchand, *Down from Olympus: Archaeology and Philhellenism in Germany, 1750–1970* (Princeton, NJ: Princeton University Press, 1996), 1–16;

Ursula Wokoeck, *German Orientalism: The Study of the Middle East and Islam from 1800–1945* (London: Routledge, 2009), 86–116.

32. Schorsch, "The Myth of Sephardic Supremacy," in his *From Text to Context*, 71–92.
33. On the creation of the "medieval" in modern Jewish thought, see my "'Medieval' and the Politics of Nostalgia: Ideology, Scholarship, and the Creation of the Rational Jew," in *Encountering the Medieval in Modern Jewish Thought*, ed. James A. Diamond and Aaron W. Hughes (Leiden: Brill, 2012), 17–40.
34. Although we still wait a book-length study devoted to the transference of Wissenschaft des Judentums to America, in the meantime see my *The Study of Judaism: Identity, Authenticity, Scholarship* (Albany: State University of New York Press, 2013), 57–76. On the migration of German-Jewish scholars to Israel, see the important study in Myers, *Re-inventing the Jewish Past*.
35. On his biography, see Mark R. Cohen, "Eulogy: Shelomo Dov Goitein," *American Philosophical Society Yearbook 1987*; and Jacob Lassner's foreword to Shlomo Dov Goitein, *A Mediterranean Society: An Abridgment in One Volume* (Berkeley: University of California Press, 1999), xi–xxii.
36. Goitein, *Jews and Arabs*, vii. See further his *Temanim: Historyah, sidre hevrah, haye ha-ruah: Mivhar mehkarim*, ed. Menahem Ben-Sason (Jerusalem: Mekhon Ben-Tsevi le-heker kehilot Yisra'el bamizrah, 1983).
37. Requisite biographical material may be found in Lassner, "Foreword," in Goitein, *A Mediterranean Society: A Abridgement in One Volume*, xi–xxii.
38. Lewis, *The Jews of Islam*, 77–78.
39. See Wasserstrom, *Between Muslim and Jew*, 8.
40. On "Islamicate," see Marshall G. S. Hodgson, *The Venture of Islam: Conscience and History in a World Civilization* (Chicago: University of Chicago Press, 1974), 1:57–60.
41. "The most eloquent testimony to the Greek-Jewish symbiosis is the Greek New Testament, large parts of which must be regarded as a product of the Jewish genius and intrinsically Jewish in every respect" (Goitein, *Jews and Arabs*, 128).
42. "The Science of Judaism, i.e., the creation of a full and coherent picture of the history and spiritual life of the Jews as a whole, came into being through the efforts of scholars like Zunz, Graetz and countless others, who write in German, and certainly contributed much to the rise of the self-respect of the Jewish people and to a better understanding of its fate among non-Jews. It paved the way for world-embracing Jewish philanthropy and even for the nationalist movement which led to the creation of the State of Israel" (Goitein, *Jews and Arabs*, 129).
43. Goitein, *Jews and Arabs*, 130.
44. Goitein, *Jews and Arabs*, 130.
45. Goitein, *Jews and Arabs*, 130.
46. Goitein, *Jews and Arabs*, 10.
47. Abraham Geiger, *Was hat Mohammed aus dem Judenthume aufgenommen?* (Bonn: F. Baaden, 1833). English translation: *Judaism and Islam*, trans. F. M.

Young (Madras: MDCSPK Press, 1835; repr. New York: Ktav 1970), 3. See my comments in *The Study of Judaism*, 129–132.
48. Goitein, *Jews and Arabs*, 11.
49. I discuss this in greater detail in my *Muslim Identities: An Introduction to Islam* (New York: Columbia University Press, 2013), 17–40.
50. Goitein, *Jews and Arabs*, 127.
51. Goitein, *Jews and Arabs*, 32.
52. Goitein, *Jews and Arabs*, 140.
53. Goitein, *Jews and Arabs*, 155.
54. Goitein, *Jews and Arabs*, 167.
55. Goitein, *A Mediterranean Society*, 5:424.
56. Michael M. Laskier and Yaakov Lev, "Introduction," in *The Convergence of Judaism and Islam*, 1–3.
57. See, for example, Herbert A. Davidson, *Alfarabi, Avicenna, and Averroes, on Intellect: Their Cosmologies, Theories of the Active Intellect, and Theories of Human Intellect* (New York: Oxford University Press, 1992); see also my *The Texture of the Divine: Imagination in Medieval Islamic and Jewish Thought* (Bloomington: Indiana University Press, 2004), 82–114.
58. Michael M. Laskier and Yaakov Lev, "Introduction," in *The Divergence of Judaism and Islam: Interdependence, Modernity, and Political Turmoil* (Gainesville: University Press of Florida, 2011), 1–2.
59. Laskier and Lev, "Introduction," in *The Divergence of Judaism and Islam*, 1.
60. Laskier and Lev, "Introduction," in *The Convergence of Judaism and Islam*, 3.
61. Américo Castro, *The Spaniards*, trans. Williard F. King and Selma Margaretten (Berkeley: University of California Press, 1971), 584. See Junod, *Convivencia and Its French and English Equivalents*, 21–27.
62. Junod, *Convivencia and Its French and English Equivalents*, 23.
63. Menocal, *The Ornament of the World*. See further Jerrilynn D. Dodds, María Rosa Menocal, and Abigail Krasner Balbale, *The Arts of Intimacy: Christians, Jews, and Muslims in the Making of Castilian Culture* (New Haven, CT: Yale University Press, 2008).
64. Lewis, *The Jews of Islam*, 3.
65. Menocal, *The Ornament of the World*, 11.
66. This seems to be the basic rationale behind two recent reference works devoted to Jewish–Muslim relations. While I briefly examine the rationales here, I wish to make clear that I have no intention of either denigrating the tremendous contributions that both works make to our understanding of specific interactions, nor do I assume that all the contributors share the general vision of the editors. In his very short introduction to the massive and unprecedented 5-volume *Encyclopedia of Jews in the Islamic World*, Norman Stillman, its executive editor, once again invokes the trope of "Judeo-Arabic symbiosis." See Norman Stillman, "Why an Encyclopedia of Jews in the Islamic World?," in *Encyclopedia of Jews in*

the Islamic World, vol. 1 (Leiden: Brill, 2010), vii. It was this symbiosis, he continues, in which:

> Jewish philosophy was created, and Jews took part in the economic and intellectual life of the medieval Islamic oikoumene on a scale unprecedented until the modern era. Hebrew language and literature underwent its most important revival prior to the Haskala (Jewish Enlightenment) and the emergence of Modern Hebrew as the only example of a revived vernacular. The Islamic Middle Ages also gave birth to the most important sectarian movement since Late Antiquity—Karaism which, despite its relatively small number of adherents, had a profound impact as a catalyst upon majoritarian Rabbinic Judaism. (vii)

Based on this description and the re-invocation of symbiosis, we seem to be back where we started. But none of what Stillman goes on to list here is necessarily mutually beneficial; rather it is, at best, and in keeping with the metaphors discussed above, based on commensalism (in which only the symbiont benefits with little or no effect on the host) or perhaps one could even go so far as to say (while certainly aware of the potentially anti-Semitic stereotype) of parasitism.

The next example comes from the 1,200-plus page *A History of Jewish–Muslim Relations: From the Origins to the Present Day*, published simultaneously in French by Albin Michel and in English by Princeton University Press in 2013. Hailed as "the first encyclopedic guide to the history of the relations between Jews and Muslims around the world from the birth of Islam to today," the general editors—the late Abdelwahab Meddeb and Benjamin Stora, an Arab and a Jew—introduce the volume through the theme of memory. Meddeb, who was a professor of Comparative Literature at the Université Paris-X (Nanterre) reminisces of his childhood in Tunis, where, walking among its streets as a young boy, "the murmur of Jewish prayers sent shivers through me. That recitation, barely chanted, heads swaying to its rhythm, reminded me of Qur'anic readings I heard at home or at al-Zaytuna Mosque. . . . These Jews, whom I saw on a daily basis, bore within themselves what made them similar to me and also what made them different. It was that difference in resemblance that confused me" (13). Benjamin Stora recollects his own childhood in Constantine, Algeria, likewise gravitating to the theme of the rhythm of the other: "The Jewish quarter overlapped with the Arab quarter, so that we knew the rhythm of their lives, and they the rhythm of ours. You heard prayers when you passed the mosques, and these prayers had the same resonance as those at our synagogue" (14).

After these initial memories, the wistful remembrances of youth, the two editors write the remainder of their Introduction together. "This book," they now speak in unison, "has the humble ambition of making contemporary research available to readers in order to propose a synthesis of the memories on both sides. It will serve as a preamble. The intention is that it will be continued, that it will prompt exchanges and dialogue" (16). They seek "to *restore* a relationship between Jews and Muslims" (16; my italics), to work toward a "reconciliation" (16), "a *reunion*, a *restoration* of the ancient historical bonds established between Jews and Muslims for more than fourteen centuries ... of passions and oppressions, of sometimes tragic, sometimes auspicious relations" (17–18).

67. See, for example, the criticism in Fitzgerald, *The Ideology of Religious Studies*, 33–53. See also Tomoko Masuzawa, *The Invention of World Religions; or, How European Universalism Was Preserved in the Language of Pluralism* (Chicago: University of Chicago Press, 2005), 37–45.

68. Smith, *Drudgery Divine*, 51.

69. See, for example, the romantic portrayal in Eliyahu Ashtor's 3-volume work, *The Jews of Moslem Spain*, trans. Aaron Klein and Jenny Machlowitz Klein (Philadelphia: Jewish Publication Society of America, 1973–1984).

70. It also ignores the systematic use of violence that maintained majority–minority relations in places such as al-Andalus. See, for example, David Nirenberg, *Communities of Violence: Persecution of Minorities in the Middle Ages* (Princeton, NJ: Princeton University Press, 1996), e.g., 8–10.

71. For a corrective, see Mark D. Meyerson, *A Jewish Renaissance in Fifteenth-Century Spain* (Princeton, NJ: Princeton University Press, 2004), 22–64.

72. Graetz, *History of the Jews*, 3:187.

73. Lewis, *The Jews of Islam*, 32–33.

74. His term as used on p. xi. Lewis, of course, would subsequently recycle this phrase in his "The Roots of Muslim Rage," *Atlantic Monthly* (September 1990), which would, in turn, be picked up, further recycled, and made famous by Samuel Huntington.

75. This is also the opinion of Cohen, *Under Crescent and Cross*, 195–200.

76. Lewis, *The Jews of Islam*, 67. Lewis himself translated some of the poetry associated with al-Andalus. See, for example, his translation of Shlomo ibn Gabirol's *Keter Malkhut* as *The Kingly Crown* (South Bend, IN: University of Notre Dame Press, 2002).

77. Susan L. Einbinder, *Beautiful Death: Jewish Poetry and Martyrdom in Medieval France* (Princeton, NJ: Princeton University Press, 2002), 8. See, more recently, Kirsten A. Fudeman, *Vernacular Voices: Language and Identity in Medieval French Jewish Communities* (Philadelphia: University of Pennsylvania Press, 2010), 26–40.

78. See my *Rethinking Jewish Philosophy*, 58–61.

79. See my "Epigone, Innovator, or Apologist?: The Case of Judah Abravanel," in *Epigonism and The Dynamics of Jewish Culture*, ed. Shlomo Berger and Irene Zweip (Louvain: Peeters, 2007), 109–125; and, more recently, my *Rethinking Jewish Philosophy*.

80. Lewis, *The Jews of Islam*, 190–191.

81. Others, however, have argued that what Israel must do to survive in this environment is to return to some sort of "symbiotic" relationship with its Arab

neighbors by forming a common "Levantine" culture or the like. See, for example, Ammiel Alcalay, *After Jews and Arabs: Remaking Levantine Culture* (Minneapolis: University of Minnesota Press, 1992).
82. Cohen, *Under Crescent and Cross*, 9–11.
83. AIPAC subsequently folded *Myths and Facts* into a separate publication, with the subtitle "*A Concise Record of the Arab–Israeli Conflict*," which received massive distribution. See Cohen, *Under Crescent and Cross*, 208–209n36.
84. "Obituary: Saul S. Friedman," *Holocaust and Genocide Studies* 27.2 (2013): 384.
85. Saul S. Friedman, "The Myth of Arab Toleration," *Midstream* 16.1 (1970): 56–59, at 56, qtd. in Cohen, *Under Crescent and Cross*, 10. See also Martin Gilbert, "The Jews of Islam: Golden Age or Ghetto?" *Jewish Chronicle Colour Magazine*, November 23, 1979, 56–60.
86. Qtd. in Cohen, *Under Crescent and Cross*, 9.
87. Cecil Roth, *The Jews in the Renaissance* (Philadelphia: Jewish Publication Society of America, 1977).
88. Wasserstrom, *Between Muslim and Jew*, 6.

CHAPTER 2

1. The theme of the dialectic between history and ahistory plays a large role in modern Jewish thought. Here I rely on the important works of David N. Myers, *Resisting History: Historicism and Its Discontents in German-Jewish Thought* (Princeton, NJ: Princeton University Press, 2003), 13–34; Asher D. Biemann, *Inventing New Beginnings: On the Idea of Renaissance in Modern Judaism* (Stanford, CA: Stanford University Press, 2009), 23–62; Elliot R. Wolfson, *Language, Eros Being: Kabbalistic Hermeneutics and Poetic Imagination* (New York: Fordham University Press, 2005), 1–45.
2. Masuzawa, *In Search of Dreamtime*, 13–15.
3. I am critical of this in my *Abrahamic Religions*, 77–98.
4. Teofilo F. Ruiz, *The Terror of History: On the Uncertainties of Life in Western Civilization* (Princeton, NJ: Princeton University Press, 2011), 1–34.
5. See the suggestive language in Wolfson, *Language Eros Being*, xv–xxxi. He poetically captures this in the following statement:

> The presence of the present yields the present of the presence remembering the past that is future and anticipating the future that is past, a presence, that is, enfolded in a double absence that renders the timeline irreversibly reversible. From that standpoint we set out on the path to uncover that what may be recovered. (xxxi)

6. I list here a set of requisite titles. Mention herein does not preclude the fact that some authors within these collections might not subscribe to such an early dating. *Israel and Ishmael: Studies in Muslim–Jewish Relations*, ed. Tudor Parfitt

(New York: St. Martins Press, 2000); *Hagar, Sarah, and Their Children: Jewish, Christian, and Muslim Perspectives*, ed. Phyllis Trible and Letty M. Russell (Louisville, KY: Westminster John Knox Press, 2006). Increasingly, these volumes are part of the "Abrahamic religions" discourse, of which I have been critical. A particularly good study that focuses on the legends surrounding Abraham and Ishmael in later Islamic and Jewish exegetical literature is Firestone, *Journeys in Holy Lands*.

7. The essay was written in response to a competition put on by the Faculty of Philosophy at the University of Bonn and announced as follows: Inquiratur in fontis Alcorani seu legis Mohammediciae eos, qui ex Judaismo derivandi sunt ("The subject to be investigated is those sources of the Qur'ān or Law of Muhammad that is derived from Judaism").

8. On the adoption and use of Orientalist discourse by Jewish intellectuals, see John M. Efron, "Orientalism and the Jewish Historical Gaze," in *Orientalism and the Jews*, ed. Ivan Davidson Kalmar and Derek J. Penslar (Stanford, CA: Stanford University Press, 2005), 80–93. Also see the studies in *The Jewish Discovery of Islam: Studies in Honor of Bernard Lewis*, ed. Martin S. Kramer (Tel Aviv: Moshe Dayan Center, 1999).

9. James L. Kugle, for example, is guilty of this in his otherwise excellent and entertaining *In Potiphar's House: The Interpretive Life of Biblical Texts* (Cambridge, MA: Harvard University Press, 1990).

10. This model is all too common in the history of religions, which puts pride of place on the putative "oldest." In this model, Judaism gives birth to Christianity, Hinduism to Buddhism, and so on. It is precisely this model—who has what first? And who borrowed from or influenced whom?—that needs to be queried not just in terms of Judaism and Islam, but more generally.

11. On the invention and genealogy of this term, see my *Abrahamic Religions*, 34–56.

12. Most of these have a decidedly feel-good tenor to them. E.g., Azyumardi Azra, "Trialogue of Abrahamic Faiths: Toward an Alliance of Civilizations," in *The Meeting of Civilizations: Muslim, Christian, and Jewish*, ed. Moshe Maoz (Eastbourne, UK: Sussex Academic Press, 2009), 220–229; Joan Chittester OSB, Murshod Saadi Shakur Christi, and Rabbi Arthur Waskow, *The Tent of Abraham: Stories of Hope and Peace for Jews, Christians, and Muslims*, foreword by Karen Armstrong (Boston: Beacon Press, 2006); Bruce Feiler, *Abraham: A Journey to the Heart of Three Faiths* (New York: HarperCollins, 2002); Karl-Josef Kuschel, *Abraham: Sign of Hope for Jews, Christians, and Muslims*, trans. John Dowden (New York: Continuum, 1995).

13. On the connection between Muhammad, Abraham, and the ideology of prophetic transference, see David S. Powers, *Muhammad Is Not the Father of Any of Your Men: The Making of the Last Prophet* (Philadelphia: University of Pennsylvania Press, 2009), 3–10. On the role of Abraham in the early spread of Islam, see Stephen J. Shoemaker, *The Death of a Prophet: The End of Muhammad's Life*

and the Beginnings of Islam (Philadelphia: University of Pennsylvania Press, 2012), 15–17.
14. Though some Muslim narratives claim that it was in fact Adam who built the structure.
15. See Firestone, *Journeys in Holy Lands*, 76–79.
16. Firestone, *Journeys in Holy Lands*, 135–152.
17. See the comments in F. E. Peters, *The Children of Abraham: Judaism, Christianity, Islam*, new ed. (Princeton, NJ: Princeton University Press, 2006), 9. See further his *The Monotheists: Jews, Christians, and Muslims in Conflict and Competition*, 2 vols. (Princeton, NJ: Princeton University Press, 2006), 1:6–7.
18. Webb, *Imagining the Arabs*, 95.
19. Josephus, *The Antiquities of the Jews*, Book One, chapter 12, section 4 (i.e., I.12.4).
20. In addition to the example of S. D. Goitein to be discussed presently, consider even more recent formulations such as those found in, e.g., *Hagar, Sarah, and Their Children*, ed. Trible and Russell; and, more recently, *The Oxford Handbook to the Abrahamic Religions*, ed. Adam J. Silverstein and Guy G. Stroumsa (New York: Oxford University Press, 2015). While the latter volume certainly includes some voices that are critical of the category "Abrahamic religions," it cannot be gainsaid that the very volume seeks to create or at least reify what it names. See, for example, my *Abrahamic Religions*, 1–6.
21. Goitein, *Jews and Arabs*, 25.
22. This is a variation on what J. Z. Smith would call the "encyclopaedic" type of comparison. See his "Adde Parvum Parvo Magnus Acervus Erit," in his *Map Is Not Territory: Studies in the History of Religions* (Chicago: University of Chicago Press, 1978), 240–264. He writes: "The encyclopaedic style offered a topical arrangement of cross-cultural material (arranged either by subject matter or alphabetically) culled from reading. It is the style of the 'armchair' anthropologist rather than the fieldworker" (250).
23. Goitein, *Jews and Arabs*, 38.
24. Goitein, *Jews and Arabs*, 27 (his italics).
25. Goitein, *Jews and Arabs*, 27.
26. There is an interesting parallel in recent works that seek to read political science into the Hebrew Bible. Only these scholars are less interested in showing connections between ancient Israel and the Arabs than they are in establishing precursors to the modern State of Israel. For example, Joshua A. Berman, *Created Equal: How the Bible Broke with Ancient Political Thought* (New York: Oxford University Press, 2008); Yoram Hazony, *The Philosophy of Hebrew Scripture* (Cambridge: Cambridge University Press, 2012). On my criticisms of their work, see my "The Politics of Biblical Interpretation: A Review Essay," *Critical Research on Religion* 3.3 (2015): 282–296.
27. Goitein, *Jews and Arabs*, 27.

28. See, for example, Mazuz, *The Religious and Spiritual Life of the Jews of Medina*. He wants to posit—though he has not a shred of evidence—a continual Jewish identity that stretches out from the ashes of the destruction of the Second Temple and moves directly through to the codifiers of the Babylonian Talmud (and beyond). Arabian Jews, for him as for others, form a missing piece of this continuity.
29. On the Jews of ancient South Arabia, see G. W. Bowersock, *The Throne of Adulis: Red Sea Wars on the Eve of Islam* (New York: Oxford University Press, 2013), 78–91. For a more technical study, see Christopher Julien Robin, "Himyar et Israël," in *Comptes-Rendus de l'Académie des Inscriptions et Belles-Lettres* (2004): 831–908. Although, of course, neither the fate nor migration of this community is anything but clear. On the Island of Elephantine, see, for example, *The Elephantine Papyri in English: Three Millennia of Cross-Cultural Continuity and Change*, rev. ed., ed. Bezlalel Porton et al. (Leiden: Brill, 1996); Yochanan Muffs, *Studies in the Aramaic Legal Papyri from Elephantine*, prolegomena by Baruch Levine (Leiden: Brill, 2013).
30. This is the problem with the otherwise impressive *The Jews of Islam* by Bernard Lewis. He assumes, like so many do, a stable Jewish essence in this period with the result that these Arabian Jews take on a level of "orthodoxy" for which we have absolutely no evidence. See, for example, *The Jews of Islam*, 10–12. To what could they have converted, however?
31. E.g., Lewis, *The Jews of Islam*, 10; Francis E. Peters, *Muhammad and the Origins of Islam* (Albany: State University of New York Press, 1994), 222–224.
32. These events, of course, have been used by some (neo-)conservative interpreters and websites to argue for the inherent "anti-Semitism" of Islam.
33. This is, for example, part of the argument supplied by Donner, *Muhammad and the Believers*, 39–49.
34. To quote David S. Powers, "many of the early Muslims had been exposed to one or another form of Judaism or Christianity; and Islam developed in a sectarian milieu that was characterized by dialogue and debate among the children of Abraham." See his *Muhammad is Not the Father of Any of Your Men*, 10. On the sectarian milieu, see John Wansbrough, *The Sectarian Milieu: Content and Composition of Islamic Salvation History* (Oxford: Oxford University Press, 1978), 1–49.
35. This is why early Muslims came up with the concept of the *ḥanīf* ("primordial monotheist") that enabled them to transform Muhammad into a monotheist without actually being either a Jew or a Christian, and presumably uninfluenced by their respective scriptures and scriptural traditions.
36. Geiger was a traditionally trained Jew who went on to receive a secular doctorate in Islamic studies. Since his ethnicity prevented him from getting an academic job, he entered the rabbinate. Within this context, he was one of the founding fathers of Reform Judaism. For requisite bibliography, see Ken Koltun-Fromm, *Abraham Geiger's Liberal Judaism: Personal Meaning and Religious Authority*

(Bloomington: Indiana University Press, 2006). See also my *Situating Islam: The Past and Future of an Academic Discipline* (London: Equinox, 2007), 12–24.

37. Abraham Geiger, *Was hat Mohammed aus dem Judenthume aufgenommen?* (Bonn: F. Baaden, 1833). English translation: *Judaism and Islam*, trans. F. M. Young (Madras: MDCSPK Press, 1835; repr. New York: Ktav 1970), xxix. Young, "a member of the Ladies' League in Aid of the Delhi Mission" translated the book to aid in the proselytization of Indian Muslims. She informs us in her Translator's Preface that:

> I undertook to translate this Prize Essay by the Rabbi Geiger at the request of the Rev. G. A. Lefroy, the Head of the Cambridge Mission in Delhi, who thought that an English translation of the book would be of use to him in his dealings with the Muhammadans. The Rev. H. D. Griswold of the American Presbyterian Mission at Lahore has very kindly put in all the Hebrew and Arabic citations for me, and has also revised my translation. (xxvii)

38. Geiger, *Judaism and Islam*, 4–5.
39. See, for example, Geiger, *Judaism and Its History*.
40. Geiger, *Judaism and Islam*, 6.
41. See the comments in Michael Pregill, "The Hebrew Bible and the Quran: The Problem of the Jewish 'Influence' on Islam," *Religion Compass* 1.6 (2007): 643–659.
42. Again, this is the basic narrative that we work with in the study of religion and governs the discourse of so-called Western or Abrahamic religions. For an idiosyncratic account that simultaneously endorses and debunks this narrative, see Rodney Stark, *One True God : Historical Consequences of Monotheism* (Princeton, NJ: Princeton University Press, 2003).
43. See, for example, the discussion in Talya Fishman, *Becoming the People of the Talmud: Oral Torah as Written Tradition in Medieval Jewish Cultures* (Philadelphia: University of Pennsylvania Press, 2001), 20–64; also see Robert Brody, *The Geonim of Babylonia and the Shaping of Medieval Jewish Culture* (New Haven, CT: Yale University Press, 1998), 1–18.
44. I. Gastfreund, *Mohammed nach Talmud und Midrasch* (Berlin: L. Gerschel, 1875).
45. R. B. Smith, *Mohammed and Mohammedanism* (London: Smith, Elder, and Co., 1889).
46. M. Grünbaum, *Neue Beiträge zur semitischen Sagenkunde* (Leiden: Brill, 1893).
47. J. Barth, *Midraschische Elemente in der muslimischen Tradition* (Berlin: Druck von H. Itzkowski, 1903) and *Studien zur Kritik und Exegese des Qorans* (Strassberg: Trübner, 1915).
48. H. Speyer, "Von den biblischen Erzählungen im Koran," *Korrespondenzblatt* (1923–1924): 7–26.
49. I. Ben-Zeev, *Ha-yehudim be-ʿArav* (Jerusalem, 1931).
50. J. J. Rivlin, *Gesetz im Koran: Kultus und Ritus* (Jerusalem: Bamberger und Wahrmann, 1934).
51. J. Oberman, "Islamic Origins," in *The Arab Heritage*, ed. N. A. Faris (Princeton, NJ: Princeton University Press, 1944), 58–120.

52. H. Z. Hirschberg, *Yisra'el be-ʿArav* (Tel Aviv: Bialik Foundation, 1946).
53. Abraham I. Katsh, *Judaism in Islam: Biblical and Talmudic Backgrounds of the Koran and Its Commentaries* (New York: Sepher-Hermon Press, 1954).
54. Newby, *A History of the Jews of Arabia*.
55. Mazuz, *The Religious and Spiritual Life of the Jews of Medina*.
56. J. Wellhausen, *Reste arabischen Heidentums* (Berlin: G. Reimer, 1897).
57. H. P. Smith, *The Bible and Islam, or, the Influence of the Old and New Testaments on the Religion of Mohammed* (New York: Scribner's, 1897).
58. C. H. Becker, *Christentum und Islam* (Tübingen: Mohr, 1907).
59. A. Moberg, *Über eine christliche Legende in der islamischen Tradition* (Lund: H. Ohlssons Buchdruckerei, 1930).
60. K. Ahrens, "Christliches im Koran," *ZDMG* 60 (1930): 15–16, 148–190.
61. C. Brockelmann, *History of the Islamic Peoples* (London: G. P. Putnam's Sons, 1950), 16–17.
62. In specialized circles this is known as the so-called authenticity debate. This debate concerns how we are to treat the earliest textual sources of Islam. There are at least three different perspectives in this debate. The first maintains that even though the earliest sources of Islam may come from a later period, they nonetheless represent reasonably reliable accounts concerning the matters upon which they comment or describe. A representation of such scholars and their work includes W. Montgomery Watt, *Muhammad at Mecca* (Oxford: Clarendon Press, 1953); Fred Donner, *Narratives of Islamic Origins: The Beginnings of Islamic Historical Writing* (Princeton, NJ: Darwin Press, 1998), and *Muhammad and the Believers*; Wael Hallaq, *The Origins and Evolution of Islamic Law* (Cambridge: Cambridge University Press, 2005).

Another point of view argues that the Muslim historical record of the first two centuries is problematic on account of the social and political upheavals associated with the rapid spread of Islam. Competing political claims, for such scholars, fatally compromise the earliest sources. These sources, according to this position, are written so much after the fact and with distinct ideological or political agendas that they provide us with very little that is reliable with which to re-create the period they purport to describe. A representative sample of scholars who take this position includes John E. Wansbrough, *The Sectarian Milieu*, and *Quranic Studies: Sources and Methods of Scriptural Interpretation* (Oxford: Oxford University Press, 1977); Patricia Crone, *Meccan Trade and the Rise of Islam* (Princeton, NJ: Princeton University Press, 1987); Patricia Crone and Michael Cook, *Hagarism: The Making of the Islamic World* (Cambridge: Cambridge University Press, 1979); Gerald R. Hawting, *The Idea of Idolatry and the Rise of Islam: From Polemic to History* (Cambridge: Cambridge University Press, 1999); and Yehuda D. Nevo and Judith Koren, *Crossroads to Islam: The Origins of the Arab Religion and the Arab State* (Amherst, NY: Prometheus, 2003).

The third perspective acknowledges the problems involved with the early sources but tries to solve them using form and source criticism, both of which seek to determine the original form and historical context of a particular text. For example, scholars employing such methods might try to show how early texts may exist embedded in later edited and compounded materials. Examples of works with this perspective include Harald Motzki, ed., *The Biography of Muhammad: The Issue of the Sources* (Leiden: Brill, 2000); Powers, *Muhammad Is Not the Father of Any of Your Men*.

63. Michael Lecker has done the most work on the Jews of early Islam. However and unfortunately, he is largely uninterested in establishing whether or not these Jews were normative or rabbinic and instead seems to assume that they are. See his comments in *Muslims, Jews, and Pagans: Studies in Early Islamic Medina* (Leiden: Brill, 1995), 21–28; see also his "Were the Jewish Tribes in Arabia Clients of Arab Tribes?," in *Patronate and Patronage in Early and Classical Islam*, ed. Monique Bernards and John Nawas (Leiden: Brill, 2005), 50–69.
64. Graetz, *History of the Jews*, 3:48.
65. Graetz, *History of the Jews*, 3:54.
66. Graetz, *History of the Jews*, 3:56.
67. Graetz, *History of the Jews*, 3:58.
68. Graetz, *History of the Jews*, 3:59.
69. Margoliouth, *Relations between Arabs and Israelites*, 59–60.
70. Margoliouth, *Relations between Arabs and Israelites*, 61.
71. D. S. Margoliouth, *Mohammed* (London: Blackie, 1939; repr. Westport, CT: Hyperion Press, 1982), 54.
72. Margoliouth, *Relations between Arabs and Israelites*, 61–62. He is relying on H. Winckler, "Arabisch-semitisch-orientalisch: Kulturgeschichtlich-mythologische Untersuchung," *Mitteilungen der vorderasiatischen Gesellschaft* 6 (1901): 222–25.
73. Margoliouth, *Relations between Arabs and Israelites*, 62.
74. Margoliouth, *Relations between Arabs and Israelites*, 71.
75. Newby, *A History of the Jews of Arabia*, xi.
76. Newby, *A History of the Jews of Arabia*, xi.
77. Newby, *A History of the Jews of Arabia*, 4. The main difference between his study and previous ones is his desire to nuance the language of "borrowing" or "influence" of the early Arabs from Judaism.
78. In another context I refer to this literature as belonging to the genre of "Muhammad and Me." See my *Theorizing Islam: Disciplinary Deconstruction and Reconstruction* (London: Routledge, 2012), 10–33.
79. Newby, *A History of the Jews of Arabia*, 54.
80. Newby, *A History of the Jews of Arabia*, 54.
81. See, for example, his comments in Newby, *A History of the Jews of Arabia*, 59.
82. Jonathan Brockopp, "Islamic Origins and Incidental Normativity," *Journal of the American Academy of Religion* 84.1 (2016): 28–43.
83. On the use of tropes in early Islamic salvation history, see Wansbrough, *The Sectarian Milieu*, 141–148.

84. Wansbrough, *The Sectarian Milieu*, 143.
85. Newby's response to such criticism is to fall back on the explanation that he will use "more critical tools to investigate the past that the text purports to describe" (121). However, it is still unclear to me as to what these "critical tools" are.
86. It may be telling of the paucity and general unhelpfulness of sources that despite the fact that Newby and Mazuz attempt to rewrite the history of the Jews of Arabia, Newby's book (not including appendix) clocks in at 108 pages and Mazuz's (again minus appendices and diagrams) is under 100 pages.
87. The rest of this section is based on my review of Mazuz's book that appeared in the *Journal of the American Academy of Religion* 83.2 (2015): 580–582.
88. Mazuz, *The Religious and Spiritual Life of the Jews of Medina*, 1.
89. Mazuz, *The Religious and Spiritual Life of the Jews of Medina*, 99.
90. E.g., Mazuz, *The Religious and Spiritual Life of the Jews of Medina*, 12–13.
91. Indeed, according to later tradition, the Qur'ān did not reach its final iteration until the caliphate of Uthmān (d. 656). Though, again, this is but later conjecture. It may well have been much later.
92. Mazuz, *The Religious and Spiritual Life of the Jews of Medina*, 25–26.
93. Mazuz, *The Religious and Spiritual Life of the Jews of Medina*, 26.
94. He concludes rather optimistically:

    The foregoing study of Islamic sources, inferentially confirmed by Jewish sources, lends itself to three conclusions: the Islamic sources presented above are in fact authentic, their reports about the religious and spiritual lives of the Jews of Medina pass the historicity test—meaning *ipso facto* that the hypotheses concerning the existence of the Medinan Jewish community pass this test as well—and the Jews at issue were Talmudic-Rabbinic. (102)

    —Compare with Newby, *A History of the Jews of Arabia*, 122.

95. Robert Hoyland, *Arabia and the Arabs: From the Bronze Age to the Coming of Islam* (London: Routledge, 2001), 243.
96. See Robert G. Hoyland, intro. and trans., *Theophilus of Edessa's Chronicle and the Circulation of Historical Knowledge in Late Antiquity and Early Islam* (Liverpool: Liverpool University Press, 2011), 63–64; Michael Philip Penn, *Envisioning Islam: Syriac Christians and the Early Muslim World* (Philadelphia: University of Pennsylvania Press, 2015), 20–25.
97. See the comments in Crone and Cook, *Hagarism*, 152nn5 and 6.
98. Crone and Cook, *Hagarism*, 24. Shoemaker argues that only in later sources did Arabia, especially Mecca and Medina, come to take on the designation of the Muslim "Holy Land." The result is that later compilers tended not to pass on those traditions that did not fit with what was by then becoming normative Islamic beliefs. See, for example, Shoemaker, *The Death of a Prophet*, 260–265.
99. Shoemaker, *The Death of a Prophet*, 28
100. Shoemaker, *The Death of a Prophet*, 29.

101. This is, for example, what Aziz al-Azmeh does in his recent *The Emergence of Islam in Late Antiquity: Allāh and His People* (Cambridge: Cambridge University Press, 2014).
102. Recall here the comments of Gruen to which I referred in the Preface.
103. Muhammad Hamidullah, *The First Written Constitution in the World: An Important Document of the Time of the Holy Prophet*, 3d rev. ed. (Lahore, Pakistan: Sh. Muhammad Ashraf, [1394] 1975).
104. Julius Wellhausen, "Muhammads Gemeindeordnung von Medina," in *Skizzen und Vorarbeiten*, vol. 4, ed. Julius Wellhausen (Berlin: G. Reimer, 1889), 65–83.
105. Michael Lecker, *The Constitution of Medina: Muḥammad's First Legal Document* (Princeton, NJ: Darwin, 2004), 77.
106. Lecker, *The Constitution of Medina*, 48. See also his "Did Muhammad Conclude Treaties with the Jewish Tribes Naḍir, Qurayẓa, and Qaynuqāʿ?," *Israel Oriental Society* 17 (1997): 29–36.
107. In this context, see Moshe Gil who goes so far as to claim that the treaty reflects Muhammad's anti-Jewish policy, which was coming into effect at this point. See his "The Constitution of Medina: A Reconsideration," *Israel Oriental Studies* 4 (1974): 44–66. There is, of course, no evidence for this.
108. See Uri Rubin, "The 'Constitution of Medina': Some Notes," *Studia Islamica* 62 (1985): 5–23.

CHAPTER 3

1. Goitein, *Jews and Arabs*, 60.
2. We, again, confront the problem that comparison is less a natural act than it is, to invoke J. Z. Smith, a political one based on the idiosyncratic choice or choices of the one doing the comparison. See, for example, J. Z. Smith, "In Comparison a Magic Dwells," in his *Imagining Religion: From Babylon to Jonestown* (Chicago: University of Chicago Press, 1982), 19–35; see further his *Drudgery Divine*, 36–53. I think Smith's analysis still holds despite the overconfidence of many who insist that comparison is somehow natural or even illustrative. On the latter account, see David M. Freidenreich, "Comparisons Compared: A Methodological Survey from "'A Magic Dwells' to *A Magic Still Dwells*," *Method and Theory in the Study of Religion* 16 (2004): 80–101.
3. See Susannah Heschel, "How the Jews Invented Jesus and Muhammad: Christianity and Islam in the Work of Abraham Geiger," in *Ethical Monotheism, Past and Present: Essays in Honor of Wendell S. Dietrich*, ed. Theodore M. Vial and Mark A. Hadley (Providence, RI: Brown Judaic Studies, 2001), 49–73.
4. Ismar Schorsch, "Scholarship in the Service of Reform," in his *From Text to Context*, 303–333; more specifically, see Heschel, *Abraham Geiger and the Jewish Jesus*, 50–75; Wiese, *Challenging Colonial Discourse*, 166–181.

5. I think, for example, of the pioneering work of Daniel Boyarin. See, for example, his *Border Lines*; Boyarin, *The Jewish Gospels: The Story of the Jewish Christ* (New York: New Press, 2012). More recently, see, for example, John G. Gager, *Who Made Early Christianity?: The Jewish Lives of the Apostle Paul* (New York: Columbia University Press, 2015).
6. E.g., the works of Crone and Cook, Wansbrough, Powers, Shoemaker, and Webb discussed in the previous chapter.
7. Important work on Islamic origins, in addition to that cited in the previous chapter, include Pregill, "The Hebrew Bible and the Quran," 643–659; Pregill, "Isra'iliyyat, Myth, and Pseudepigraphy: Wahb b. Munabbih and the Early Islamic Versions of the Fall of Adam and Eve," *Jerusalem Studies in Arabic and Islam* 34 (2008): 215–284.
8. Goitein, *Jews and Arabs*, 60–61.
9. Goitein, *Jews and Arabs*, 95.
10. Solomon Katz, *The Jews in the Visigothic and Frankish Kingdoms of Spain and Gaul* (Cambridge, MA: Monographs of the Medieval Academy of America, 1937).
11. Yitzhak Baer, *A History of the Jews in Christian Spain*, vol. 1: *From the Age of the Reconquest to the Fourteenth Century* (Philadelphia: Jewish Publication Society of America, 1961–1966).
12. Richard D. Barnett, ed., *The Sephardi Heritage*, vol. 1 (London: Vallentine and Mitchell, 1971).
13. Ashtor, *The Jews of Moslem Spain*.
14. Bernard S. Bachrach, *Early Medieval Jewish Policy in Western Europe* (Minneapolis: University of Minnesota Press, 1977).
15. Norman A. Stillman, *The Jews of Arab Lands: A History and a Sourcebook* (Philadelphia: Jewish Publication Society of America, 1979).
16. Lewis, *The Jews of Islam*.
17. Haim Beinart, *The Expulsion of the Jews from Spain*, trans. Jeffrey M. Green (London: Littman Library of Jewish Civilization, 2005).
18. Jane S. Gerber, *The Jews of Spain: A History of the Sephardic Experience* (Philadelphia: Jewish Publication Society of America, 1992).
19. Cohen, *Under Crescent and Cross*.
20. Gerber, *The Jews of Spain*, 2.
21. Wasserstrom, *Between Muslim and Jew*, 18. He bases the percentage on Jane S. Gerber, "Judaism in the Middle East and North Africa since 1492," *Encyclopedia of Religion*, ed. Mircea Eliade (New York: Macmillan, 1987), 8:157–164, at 158.
22. See, for example, the comments in Avraham Grossman, *The Babylonian Exilarchate in the Gaonic Period* (in Hebrew) (Jerusalem: Zalman Shazar Center, 1984), 15–44; also his "Aliya in the Seventh and Eighth Centuries," *Jerusalem Cathedra* 3 (1988): 65–94.

23. Louis H. Feldman, *Jew and Gentile in the Ancient World: Attitudes and Interactions from Alexander to Justinian* (Princeton, NJ: Princeton University Press, 1993), 35–38.
24. See, for example, *Asceticism, Eschatology, Opposition to Philosophy: The Arabic Translation and Commentary of Salmon b. Yeroham on Qohelet (Ecclesiastes)*, ed. and trans. James T. Robinson (Leiden: Brill, 2012); and *The Arabic Translation and Commentary of Yefet b. 'Eli the Karaite on the Book of Joshua*, ed. and trans. James T. Robinson (Leiden: Brill, 2014).
25. The main exception being the pioneering work of Wasserstrom, *Between Muslim and Jew*, 47–89. See further his "The Isawiyya Revisited," *Studia Islamica* 75 (1992): 57–80.
26. More generally, see the work of Averil Cameron, e.g., her *The Mediterranean World in Late Antiquity: A.D. 395–700*, 2d ed. (London: Routledge, 2012), 168–190; al-Azmeh, *The Emergence of Islam in Late Antiquity*, 1–46.
27. Wasserstrom, *Between Muslim and Jew*, 17–18.
28. On the attempt to tell this story from the text themselves, if not their immediate historical contexts, see Jacob Neusner, *Judaism: The Classical Statement. The Evidence of the Bavli* (Chicago: University of Chicago Press, 1986); Neusner, *Judaism States Its Theology: The Talmudic Re-Presentation* (Atlanta, GA: Scholars Press, 1993). On the rise of Jewish philosophical and other sciences, especially their interconnectedness to Islamic philosophy, see Julius Guttmann, *Philosophies of Judaism: A History of Jewish Philosophy from Biblical Times to Franz Rosenzweig*, trans. David W. Silverman (New York: Schocken, 1964), 53–69; Colette Sirat, *A History of Jewish Philosophy in the Middle Ages* (Cambridge and Paris: Cambridge University Press and Editions de la Maison de l'Homme, 1985), 15–56; Raphael Jospe, *Jewish Philosophy: Foundations and Extensions*, vol. 1: *General Questions and Considerations* (Lanham, MD: University Press of America, 2008), 5–54.
29. On the rise of rabbinic Judaism, see, inter alia, Jacob Neusner, "The History of Earlier Rabbinic Judaism: Some New Approaches," *History of Religions* 16.3 (1977): 216–236; Shaye J. D. Cohen, *The Beginnings of Jewishness: Boundaries, Varieties, Uncertainties* (Berkeley: University of California Press, 2001), 198–237; Gabriele Boccaccini, *Roots of Rabbinic Judaism: An Intellectual History, from Ezekiel to Daniel* (Grand Rapids, MI: Eerdmans, 2002), 1–40; Alexei M. Sivertsev, *Households, Sects, and the Origins of Rabbinic Judaism* (Leiden: Brill, 2005).
30. Wasserstrom, *Between Muslim and Jew*, 11.
31. On the Mu'tazilites more generally, see Ignaz Goldziher, *Introduction to Islamic Theology and Law*, trans. Andras and Ruth Hamori (Princeton, NJ: Princeton University Press, 1981), 67–115; Binyamin Abrahamov, *Islamic Theology: Traditionalism and Rationalism* (Edinburgh: Edinburgh University Press, 1998); Joseph van Ess, *The Flowering of Muslim Theology*, trans. Jane Marie Todd (Cambridge, MA: Harvard University Press, 2006), 79–116.

32. As a corrective see, for example, J. Z. Smith, "Fences and Neighbors: Some Contours of Early Judaism," in his *Imagining Religion*, 1–18.
33. For an attempt to theorize the "hyphen" from the perspective of Judaism and Christianity, see Jean-François Lyotard and Eberhard Gruber, *The Hyphen: Between Judaism and Christianity*, trans. Pascal-Anne Brault and Michael Naas (Amherst, NY: Humanity Books, 1999).
34. E.g., Henry Malter, *Saadia Gaon: His Life and Works* (Philadelphia: Jewish Publication Society of America, 1921), 89–134; Salo Wittmayer Baron, "Saadia's Communal Activities," *Saadia Anniversary Volume* (1943): 9–74; and more recently Robert Brody, *Sa'adiyah Gaon*, trans. Betsy Rosenberg (Oxford: Littman Library of Jewish Civilization, 2013), ch. 2.
35. On the historiographic problems associated with this period, see Gerson Cohen, "The Reconstruction of Gaonic History," in *Texts in Jewish History and Literature*, vol. 1, ed. Jacob Mann (New York: Ktav, 1972), xiii–xcvii; see also Simha Assaf, *Tekufat ha-geonim ve-sifrutah* (Jerusalem: Mossad ha-Rav Kook, 1955). More recently, see Brody, *The Geonim of Babylonia and the Shaping of Medieval Jewish Culture*.
36. See, for example, Harry Austryn Wolfson, *Repercussions of the Kalam in Jewish Philosophy* (Cambridge, MA: Harvard University Press, 1979); Sarah Stroumsa, *Dāwūd Ibn Marwān al-Muqammiṣ's Twenty Chapters ('Ishrun al-Maqāla)* (Leiden: Brill, 1989), 15–23; Haggai Ben Shammai, "Kalām in Medieval Jewish Philosophy," in *History of Jewish Philosophy*, ed. Daniel H. Frank and Oliver Leaman (London: Routledge, 1997), 115–148.
37. Requisite biographical materials may be found in works mentioned in n. 34.
38. On Ibn Ezra as a polymath, see *Rabbi Abraham Ibn Ezra: Studies in the Writings of a Twelfth-Century Jewish Polymath*, ed. Isadore Twersky and Jay M. Harris (Cambridge, MA: Harvard University Press, 1994).
39. Malter, *Saadia Gaon*, 16.
40. Malter, *Saadia Gaon*, 16.
41. A selection of his exegetical work is conveniently collected in *Mpirushei Rav Saadya Gaon la-mikra* (Jerusalem: Mossad ha-Rav Kook, 2004); see also his *tafsīr kitāb al-mabādī*, or commentary to the Sefer Yetsirah, in Saadya Gaon, *Sefer Yezirah 'im perush Rabbeinu Saadya ben Yosef Fayyumi*, Arabic text and Hebrew translation by Yosef Kafiḥ (Jerusalem: Mossad ha-Rav Kook, 1972).
42. E.g., *Or rishon bi-ḥokhmah ha-lashon: Sefer siḥot lashon ha-ivrim le-rav saadya gaon*, ed. A. Dotan (Jerusalem: World Union of Jewish Studies, 1997).
43. E.g., *Kitāb amānāt wa'l-i'tiqādāt*, ed. S. Landauer (Leiden: Brill, 1880). Translated into English as *The Book of Beliefs and Opinions* (New Haven, CT: Yale University Press, 1976).
44. *Ha-Egron: Kitāb 'usūl al-sh'ir al-'ibrānī*, critical edition with introduction and commentary by Nehemya Allony (Jerusalem: Academy of the Hebrew Language, 1969).

45. A convenient list of his polemical works on the Karaites and others may be found in Malter, *Saadia Gaon: His Life and Works*, 260–271.
46. See the comments in Daniel Frank, *Search Scripture Well: Karaite Exegesis and the Origins of the Jewish Bible Commentary in the Islamic East* (Leiden: Brill, 2004), 248–257.
47. Graetz, *History of the Jews*, 3:188.
48. Goitein, *Jews and Arabs*, 134.
49. On Saadya as one of the first Jewish philosophers, consult any introductory textbook on Jewish philosophy. See, for example, Isaac Husik, *A History of Mediaeval Jewish Philosophy* (Philadelphia: Jewish Publication Society of America, 1941), 23–47; Guttmann, *Philosophies of Judaism*, 69–94; Sirat, *A History of Jewish Philosophy in the Middle Ages*, 15–47.
50. See the study in Grossman, *The Babylonian Exilarchate in the Gaonic Period*. I still remained impressed with Israel Friedlander, "The Jews of Arabia and the Gaonate," *Jewish Quarterly Review* 1 (1910–1911): 249–252; and his "Jewish-Arabic Studies," *Jewish Quarterly Review* 1 (1910–1911): 183–215; 2 (1911–1912): 481–517; 3 (1912–1913): 235–300.
51. Wasserstrom, *Between Muslim and Jew*, 30.
52. Daniel Jeremy Silver, *Maimonidean Criticism and the Maimonidean Controversy, 1180–1240* (Leiden: Brill, 1965), 61.
53. For an account of the story, see Leon Nemoy, "Anan ben David: A Re-appraisal of the Historical Data," in *Karaite Studies*, ed. Philip Birnbaum (New York: Hermon Press, 1971), 309–318.
54. See, for example, Haggai Ben-Shammai, "Between Ananites and Karaties: Observations on Early Muslim–Jewish Sectarianism," *Studies in Medieval Jewish–Islamic Relations* 1 (1993): 19–31; see also his "The Attitude of Some Early Karaites Towards Islam," in *Studies in Medieval Jewish History*, vol. 2, ed. Isadore Twersky (Cambridge, MA: Harvard University Press, 1984), 3–40 and "A Note on Some Karaite Copies of Muʿtazilite Writings," *Bulletin of the School of Oriental and African Studies* 37 (1974): 295–304. Also, Frank, *Search Scripture Well*, 1–32.
55. Wasserstrom, *Between Muslim and Jew*, 31.
56. In terms of late antique Christianity, consult the sources found in James Howard-Johnston, *Witnesses to a World Crisis: Historians and Histories of the Middle East in the Seventh Century* (Oxford: Oxford University Press, 2011). On the social context behind this, see Glen Warren Bowersock, *Empires in Collision in Late Antiquity* (Waltham, MA: Brandeis University Press, 2012). For general overlay, see Guy G. Stroumsa, *The Making of Abrahamic Religions in Late Antiquity* (New York: Oxford University Press, 2015), 59–100.
57. Although, as Stroumsa has duly noted, we must not forget the messianism associated with Manichaean texts, which also date to this period. This, of course,

adds another layer to the puzzle and further attests to the need to avoid easy typologies. See his "Gnostics and Manichaeans in Byzantine Palestine," in *Studia Patristica* 18, ed. Elizabeth A. Livingston (Kalamazoo, MI: Cistercian Press, 1985), 273–278.

58. Friedlander, "Jewish-Arabic Studies"; Wasserstrom, *Between Muslim and Jew*, 47–48.
59. Shlomo Pines, "Notes on Islam and on Arabic Christianity and Judaeo-Christianity," *Jerusalem Studies in Arabic and Islam* 4 (1985): 135–152.
60. Averil Cameron, "The Eastern Provinces in the Seventh Century: Hellenism and the Emergence of Islam," in *Hellēnismos: Quelques jalons pour une histoire de l'identité grecque: Actes du Colloque de Strasbourg. 25–27 octobre, 1989*, ed. Suzanne Saïd (Leiden: Brill, 1991), 287–313.
61. I say "proto-Shī'ī" because, although Shī'ism had yet to be worked out doctrinally at this point, there was certainly an impetus in certain groups—some of which would later be declared as *ghulāt* ("extremist") and "heterodox"—to elevate the "House of Ali" over what was slowly coalescing as more "normative" Sunni paradigms of authority.
62. See, e.g., Moshes Sharon, *Black Banners from the East: The Establishment of the Abbasid State: Incubation of a Revolt* (Jerusalem and Leiden: Magnes Press and Brill, 1983).
63. Most recently, see the important study in Mushegh Asatryan, *Cosmology and Community in Early Shi'i Islam: The Ghulat and their Literature* (London: I. B. Tauris, 2016).
64. See Shlomo Pines, "The Jewish Christians of the Early Centuries of Christianity according to a New Source," in *Proceedings of the Israel Academy of Sciences and Humanities* (Jerusalem: Academy of Sciences and Humanities, 1966), 2(13):237–310. On the Jewish-Christian context of early Islam, see more recently Patricia Crone, "Jewish Christianity and the Qur'ān," *Journal of Near Eastern Studies* 74 (2015): 225–253; Guy G. Stroumsa, "Jewish Christianity and Islamic Origins," in *Islamic Cultures, Islamic Contexts: Essays in Honor of Patricia Crone*, ed. Behnam Sadeghi, Asad Q. Ahmed, Adam Silverstein, and Robert Hoyland (Leiden: Brill, 2015), 72–96; Holger Zellentin, *The Qur'ān's Legal Culture: The Didascalia Apostolorum as a Point of Departure* (Tübingen: Mohr Siebeck, 2013), 150–153; Emran El-Badawi, *The Qur'an and the Aramaic Gospel Traditions* (London: Routledge, 2013), 138.
65. Wasserstrom, *Between Muslim and Jew*, 71–72.
66. Friedlander, "Jewish-Arabic Studies."
67. Wasserstrom, *Between Muslim and Jew*, 71.
68. Wasserstrom, *Between Muslim and Jew*, 57.
69. Qtd. in Wasserstrom, *Between Muslim and Jew*, 68.
70. Wasserstrom, *Between Muslim and Jew*, 79.

71. Pines, "The Jewish Christians of the Early Centuries of Christianity according to a New Source," 237–250; Wasserstrom, *Between Muslim and Jew*, 84–88; Stroumsa, *The Making of Abrahamic Religions in Late Antiquity*, 76–77.
72. See the studies of Pines and Wasserstrom examined in the previous note.
73. Wasserstrom, *Between Muslim and Jew*, 85.
74. Wasserstrom, *Between Muslim and Jew*, 89.
75. See, e.g., the comments in Gerson Cohen, "Rabbinic Judaism (2nd–18th Centuries)," *Encyclopedia Britannica*, 15th ed. (Chicago: Encyclopedia Britannica, 1974), 22:416–422.
76. Maimonides, "Epistle to Yemen," in *Epistles of Maimonides: Crisis and Leadership*, trans. Abraham Halkin (Philadelphia: Jewish Publication Society of America, 1985), 127.
77. Maimonides, "Epistle to Yemen," 128.
78. Maimonides, "Epistle to Yemen," 128.
79. Sharon, *Black Banners from the East*, 73–100; Moojan Momen, *An Introduction to Shiʿi Islam* (New Haven, CT: Yale University Press, 1985), 61–85; Said Amir Arjomand, "Abd Allah Ibn al-Muqaffaʾ and the Abbasid Revolution," *Religion and Society in Islamic Iran during the Pre-Modern Era* 27.1 (1994): 9–36.
80. On the work, see Moritz Steinschneider, "Apocalypsen mit polemischer Tendenz," *ZDMG* 28 (1874): 627–659; a translation may be found in Bernard Lewis, "An Apocalyptic Vision of Islamic History," *BSOAS* 13 (1950): 308–338; Shoemaker, *The Death of a Prophet*, 28–31. On the role of Jerusalem in early Islam, see Ofer Livne-Kafri, "The Early Shiʿa and Jerusalem," *Arabica* 48 (2001): 112–120; Livne-Kafri, "Jerusalem in Early Islam: The Eschatological Aspect," *Arabica* 53 (2006): 382–403.
81. See Wasserstrom, *Between Muslim and Jew*, 181–205.
82. Lewis, "An Apocalyptic Vision of Islamic History," 313.
83. Lewis, "An Apocalyptic Vision of Islamic History," 314.
84. Wasserstrom, *Between Muslim and Jew*, 89.
85. Shoemaker, *The Death of a Prophet*, 248–258.
86. See, for example, Suliman Bashear, "Apocalyptic and Other Materials in Early Muslim–Byzantine Wars: A Review of Arabic Sources,' *Journal of the Royal Asiatic Society*, n.s., 1–2 (1991): 173–207; David Cook, *Studies in Muslim Apocalyptic* (Princeton, NJ: Darwin Press, 2002), 92–122; see also Cook, *Contemporary Muslim Apocalyptic Literature* (Syracuse: Syracuse University Press, 2005), 1–12.
87. On the latter, see Wasserstrom, *Between Muslim and Jew*, 57.
88. Relevant literature on the Karaites include Leon Nemoy, *Karaite Anthology: Excerpts from the Early Literature* (New Haven, CT: Yale University Press, 1980); Meira Polliack, *The Karaite Tradition of Arabic Bible Translation: A Linguistic and Exegetical Study of Karaite Translations of the Pentateuch from the Tenth and Eleventh Centuries CE* (Leiden: Brill, 1997); Meira Polliack, ed., *Karaite Judaism: A Guide to Its History and Literary Sources* (Leiden: Brill, 2003); Fred Astren, *Karaite Judaism*

and *Historical Understanding* (Columbia: University of South Carolina Press, 2004); Frank, *Search Scripture Well*.

89. It is important, however, not to ignore the messianic impulse of the Karaites who referred to themselves as the "mourners of Zion." In this regard, see Astren, *Karaite Judaism and Historical Understanding*, 65–100; Yoram Erder, "The Negation of the Exile in the Messianic Doctrine of the Karaite Mourners of Zion," *Hebrew Union College Annual* 68 (1997): 109–40; Daniel Frank, "The *Shoshanim* of Tenth-Century Jerusalem: Karaite Exegesis, Prayer, and Communal Identity," in *The Jews of Medieval Islam: Community, Society, and Identity*, ed. Daniel Frank (Leiden: Brill, 1995), 199–245.

90. Haggai Ben-Shammai, "The Karaite Controversy: Scripture and Tradition in Early Karaism," in *Religionsgespräche im Mittelalter*, ed. Bernard Lewis and Friedrich Niewöhner (Wiesbaden: Otto Harrassowitz, 1992), 11–26, at 20.

91. See Christopher Melchert, *The Formation of Sunni Schools of Law, 9th–10th Centuries CE* (Leiden: Brill, 1997).

92. Frank, *Search Scripture Well*, 2.

93. Qtd. in Frank, *Search Scripture Well*, 3.

94. Baron, *A Social and Religious History of the Jews*, 5:275.

95. Baron, *A Social and Religious History of the Jews*, 5:275.

96. Rina Drory, "The Function of Karaite Literature in the Evolution of Tenth-Century Jewish Literature (Hebrew)," *Dappim le Mehqar be-Sifrut* 9 (1994): 101–110.

97. Frank, *Search Scripture Well*, 257.

98. While I will examine this in greater detail when it comes to Saadya Gaon in the next chapter, it suffices here to say that much of this absorption was the result of the rationalist agenda as set by the Muʿtazilites. This school of dogmatic rationalist theologians in early Islam went a long way to defining "orthodoxy" in emerging Sunni circles.

CHAPTER 4

1. Jacques Derrida, "Violence and Metaphysics: An Essay on the Thought of Emmanuel Levinas," in his *Writing and Difference*, trans. Alan Bass (Chicago: University of Chicago Press, 1978), 153.

2. Goitein, *Jews and Arabs*, 60.

3. Goitein, *Jews and Arabs*, 60.

4. Goitein, *Jews and Arabs*, 60–61.

5. Goitein, *Jews and Arabs*, 98. This is echoed in Wasserstrom in *Between Muslim and Jew*, 17–46.

6. This term plays on "Greekjew as Jewgreek" as witnessed by the passage from Derrida's "Violence and Metaphysics" that opens this chapter.

7. Susana Elm, for example, has argued that as early as the fourth century, early Christians were aware of the distinction between religion and other modes

of identification. See her "Orthodoxy and the True Philosophical Life: Julian and Gregory of Nazianus," *Studia Patristica* 37 (2001): 69–85. See also Vasiliki Limberis, "'Religion' as the Cipher for Identity: The Case of Emperor Julian, Libianius, and Gregory Nazianzus," *Harvard Theological Review* 93.4 (2000): 373–400.

8. Shlomo Dov Goitein, "The Rise of the Near Eastern Bourgeoisie in Early Islamic Times," *Journal of World History* 32 (1956–1957): 583–604. This sentiment is echoed in, among others, Lewis, *The Jews of Islam*, 74–80. Cohen, *Under Crescent and Cross*, 88–102. Wasserstrom, in contrast, has done a good job in showing the complexity that this statement masks in his *Between Muslim and Jew*, 20–27.
9. Goitein, *Jews and Arabs*, 130.
10. See, for example, the comments in Seth Schwartz, *Imperialism and Jewish Society from 200 BCE to 640 CE* (Princeton, NJ: Princeton University Press, 2001), 1–22.
11. Boyarin, *Border Lines*, 2.
12. John Wansbrough, *Res Ipsa Loquitur: History and Mimesis* (Jerusalem: Israel Academy of Sciences and Humanities, 1987), 14–15.
13. John Wansbrough, "Review of Josef van Ess, *Anfänge muslimischer Theologie: Zwei antiqadaritische Traktate aus dem ersten Jahrhundert der Higra*," in *Bulletin of the School of Oriental and African Studies* 43 (1980): 361–363, at 361.
14. See, in this regard, Gil Anidjar, *The Jew, the Arab: The History of the Enemy* (Stanford, CA: Stanford University Press, 2003), 3–39.
15. Though more sanguine than I would like, see Jacob Neusner and Tamara Sonn, *Comparing Religions Through Law: Judaism and Islam* (London: Routledge, 1999).
16. Mary Beard, John A. North, and S. R. F. Price, *Religions of Rome* (Cambridge: Cambridge University Press, 1998), 249.
17. Boyarin, *Border Lines*, 13–17.
18. Boyarin, *Border Lines*, 26. Boyarin, using the language laid out in George Lakoff, further defines this type of categorization as the "prototype theory of categorization." On the latter, see George Lakoff, *Women, Fire, and Dangerous Things: What Categories Reveal about the Mind* (Chicago: University of Chicago Press, 1987), 12–58.
19. See, for example, Michael Cook, *Commanding Right and Forbidding Wrong in Islamic Thought* (Cambridge: Cambridge University Press, 2000); van Ess, *The Flowering of Muslim Theology*.
20. See the comments in Brakke, *The Gnostics*, 5–8.
21. Brakke, *The Gnostics*, 3.
22. See my discussion in the previous chapter.
23. See, for example, Shaye J. D. Cohen, *From the Maccabees to the Mishnah*, 2d ed. (Louisville, KY: Westminster John Knox Press, 2006), 119–165; Boccaccini, *Roots of Rabbinic Judaism*, 73–110.
24. See Racha el-Omari, "The *Muʿtazilite* Movement: The Origins of the *Muʿtazila*," in *The Oxford Handbook of Islamic Theology*, ed. Sabine Schmidtke (New York: Oxford University Press, 2016), 130–141.

25. This influence as we shall see shortly is usually Greek or even Syriac. On the latter, see Michael Cook, "The Origins of the *Kalām*," *Bulletin of the School of Oriental and African Studies* 43 (1980): 32–43.
26. E.g., Dimitri Gutas, *Greek Thought, Arabic Culture: The Graeco-Arabic Translation Movement in Baghdad and Early 'Abbasaid Society (2nd–4th/5th–10th c)* (London: Routledge, 1998), 11–27; and Franz Rosenthal, *The Classical Heritage in Islam* (London: Routledge, [1975] 1992), 1–15.
27. Goldziher, *Introduction to Islamic Theology and Law*, 85.
28. See Gyonghi Hegedus, "Theological Summae," in *The Literary Forms of Medieval Jewish Philosophy*, ed. Aaron W. Hughes and James T. Robinson (Bloomington: Indiana University Press, forthcoming).
29. See, for example, Abd al-Jabbār, *A Critique of Christian Origins*, ed., trans., and ann. Gabriel Said Reynolds and Samir Khalil Samir (Provo, UT: Brigham Young University Press, 2010).
30. See the exhaustive study in Cook, *Commanding Right and Forbidding Wrong in Islamic Thought*, 32–45.
31. Parts of this section and the following one rework my "Theology: The Articulation of Orthodoxy," in *The Routledge Companion of Muslim–Jewish Relations*, ed. Josef Meri (New York: Routledge, 2016), 77–94.
32. See Harry A. Wolfson, *Philo: Foundations of Religious Philosophy in Judaism, Christianity, and Islam* (Cambridge, MA: Harvard University Press, 1948).
33. Harry A. Wolfson, *Repercussions of the Kalam in Jewish Philosophy*. More recently, see Haggai Ben-Shammai, "Kalām in Medieval Jewish Philosophy," 124–127.
34. Maimonides, *Guide*, I.71.
35. On the construction of this canon, and who gets to be included therein, see Hughes, *Rethinking Jewish Philosophy*, 61–65.
36. On his biography, see Stroumsa, *Dāwūd Ibn Marwān al-Muqammiṣ's Twenty Chapters*, 15–23. See also Pines, "Jewish Christians of the Early Centuries of Christianity according to a New Source," at 47–48.
37. Stroumsa, *Dāwūd Ibn Marwān al-Muqammiṣ's Twenty Chapters*, 19–20. On Maimonides' reference, see *Guide* I.71.
38. Stroumsa, *Dāwūd Ibn Marwān al-Muqammiṣ's Twenty Chapters*, 126–127.
39. Although Judah ben Barzillai, a twelfth-century Catalan Talmudist, reports that Saadia actually studied with al-Muqammiṣ, there is no independent evidence that he did.
40. Saadya, *The Book of Doctrines and Beliefs*, trans. Samuel Rosenblatt (New Haven, CT: Yale University Press, 1948), 3.
41. Saadya, *The Book of Doctrines and Beliefs*, 3.
42. Saadya, *The Book of Doctrines and Beliefs*, 4.
43. Saadia, *The Book of Doctrines and Beliefs*, 18.
44. Henri Laoust, "L'Hérésiographie musulmane sous les Abbassides," *Cahiers de civilization medieval* 19 (1967): 157–178, at 157. More recently, see Wasserstrom, *Between Muslim and Jew*, 136–165.

45. Steven M. Wasserstrom, "Islamicate History of Religions?" *History of Religions* 27 (1988): 405–411; see also Gustav E. von Grunebaum, "Medieval Islam" (in conversation with Norman Cantor), *Perspectives on the European Past*, ed. N. Cantor (New York: Collier Macmillan, 1971), 168–186.
46. Wasserstrom, *Between Muslim and Jews*, 154.
47. For a representative set of examples that buy into this bifurcation see: Guttmann, *Philosophies of Judaism*, 69–94; Sirat, *A History of the Jewish Philosophy in the Middle Ages*, 17–37; Ben-Shammai, "Kalām in Medieval Jewish Philosophy," 115–148; Oliver Leaman, *Jewish Thought: An Introduction* (London: Routledge, 2006), 12, 18; Charles Manekin, "Introduction," *Medieval Jewish Philosophical Writings*, ed. Charles Manekin (Cambridge: Cambridge University Press, 2007), x–xiii; Jospe, *Jewish Philosophy*, 44–45.
48. Hodgson, *The Venture of Islam*, 1:57–60.
49. For further on Ibn Ḥazm, see Camilla Adang, *Muslim Writers on Judaism and the Hebrew Bible: From Ibn Rabban to Ibn Hazm* (Leiden: Brill, 1996), 59–69.
50. See the study in Diana Lobel, *A Sufi–Jewish Dialogue: Philosophy and Mysticism in Baḥya Ibn Paquda's Duties of the Heart* (Philadelphia: University of Pennsylvania Press, 2007), 2–10.
51. On the evidence, see Reza Pourjavady and Sabine Schmidtke, *A Jewish Philosopher of Baghdad: ʿIzz al-Dawla Ibn Kammūna (d. 683/1284) and His Writings* (Leiden: Brill, 2009), 8–23.
52. See, for example, Hossein Ziai and Ahmed Alwishah (eds.), *Ibn Kammūna: Al-Tanqīḥāt fī sharḥ al-talwīḥāt. Refinement and Commentary on Suhrawardī's Intimations. A Thirteenth Century Text on Natural Philosophy and Psychology* (Costa Mesa, CA: Mazda Publishers, 2003).
53. An English translation may be found in *Ibn Kammūna's Examination of the Three Faiths: A Thirteenth-Century Essay in the Comparative Study of Religion*, trans. Moshe Perlmann (Berkeley: University of California Press, 1971).
54. Perlmann, *Ibn Kammūna's Examination of the Three Faiths*, 1.
55. Perlmann, *Ibn Kammūna's Examination of the Three Faiths*, 67. This sounds very similar to the speech of the Christian that may be found in the opening paragraphs of Judah Halevi's (d. 1141) *Kuzari*.
56. *Al-Murshid ilā-l-tafarrud wa-l-murfid ilā-l-tagarrud*, ed. and trans. into Hebrew by Paul B. Fenton (Jerusalem: Meqize Nirdamim, 1985).

CHAPTER 5

1. Hesiod, *Works and Days*, lines 170.
2. Hesiod, *Works and Days*, lines 109–120.
3. Jacques Barzun, *Classic, Romantic, Modern* (Boston: Little Brown, 1961), 131.
4. E.g., Hilary Putnam, "Reply to Tim Maudlin," in *The Philosophy of Hilary Putnam*, ed. Randall E. Auxier, Douglas R. Anderson, and Lewis Edwin Hahn (Chicago: Open Court, 2015), 502–509, at 504–506.

5. Here I am inspired by the comments found in Kalman P. Bland, *The Artless Jew: Medieval and Modern Affirmations and Denials of the Visual* (Princeton, NJ: Princeton University Press, 2000), 3–12.
6. See, for example, Ismar Schorsch, "The Religious Parameters of *Wissenschaft*: Jewish Academics at Prussian Universities," in his *From Text to Context*, 51–70; Nils Roemer, *Jewish Scholarship and Culture in Nineteenth-Century Germany* (Madison: University of Wisconsin Press, 2005), 26–34; Brenner, *Prophets of the Past*, 9–12.
7. Important exceptions include Russell T. McCutcheon, *Manufacturing Religion: The Discourse on Sui Generis Religion and the Politics of Nostalgia* (New York: Oxford University Press, 1997), 27–50; Ivan Strenski, *Four Theories of Myth in Twentieth-Century History: Cassirer, Eliade, Levi Strauss and Malinowski* (Iowa City: University of Iowa Press, 1987); see also Daniel Dubuisson, *Twentieth Century Mythologies: Dumazil, Levi-Strauss, Eliade*, trans. Martha Cunningham (Sheffield: Equinox, 2006).
8. See, for example, the important collection of essays in *The Study of Religion under the Impact of Fascism*, ed. Horst Junginger (Leiden: Brill, 2008).
9. Susannah Heschel, *The Aryan Jesus: Christian Theologians and the Bible in Nazi Germany* (Princeton, NJ: Princeton University Press, 2008), 26–66.
10. See my "The Politics of Biblical Interpretation," 282–296.
11. See Sharada Sugirtharajah, *Imagining Hinduism: A Postcolonial Perspective* (London: Routledge, 2003), 47–48.
12. See the studies by Strenski and Dubuisson mentioned in n. 7.
13. Biemann, *Inventing New Beginnings*, 13.
14. On the use of this in the rise of modern Israeli consciousness, for example, see Yael Zerubavel, *Recovered Roots: Collective Memory and the Making of Israeli National Tradition* (Chicago: University of Chicago Press, 1995), 3–12.
15. McCutcheon, *Manufacturing Religion*, 43.
16. Mircea Eliade, *The Myth of the Eternal Return; or, Cosmos and History*, trans. Willard R. Trask (Princeton, NJ: Princeton University Press, 1954), 85.
17. Steven M. Wasserstrom, *Religion after Religion: Gershom Scholem, Mircea Eliade, and Henri Corbin at Eranos* (Princeton, NJ: Princeton University Press, 1999), 112–124.
18. Biemann, *Inventing New Beginnings*, 72.
19. See David N. Myers, *Resisting History*, 13–34.
20. Arthur McCalla, "When Is History Not History?" *Historical Reflections* 20.3 (1994): 435–452.
21. Heinrich Graetz, "The Structure of Jewish History," in Heinrich Graetz, *The Structure of Jewish History and Other Essays*, trans. and ed. Ismar Schorsch (New York: Jewish Theological Seminary of America, 1975), 65.
22. Graetz, "The Structure of Jewish History," 117.
23. Graetz, "The Structure of Jewish History," 111.
24. Wiese, *Challenging Colonial Discourse*, 82. See also my *The Study of Judaism*, 39–56.

25. Schorsch, "Jewish Studies from 1818–1919," in his *From Text to Context*, 352.
26. Graetz, "The Structure of Jewish History," 111. More recently, see the biography of Maimonides, while noting the telling subtitle— Joel L. Kraemer, *Maimonides: The Life and World of One of Civilization's Greatest Minds* (New York: Doubleday, 2008).
27. See my forthcoming *The Irrational Jew*.
28. Graetz, "The Structure of Jewish History," 115.
29. See my "Maimonides and the Pre-Maimonidean Jewish Philosophical Tradition According to Hermann Cohen," *Journal of Jewish Thought and Philosophy* 18.1 (2010): 1–26.
30. On the novelty of their approach, their break from tradition, and their use of history to accomplish their reformist ends, see Yerushalmi, *Zakhor*, 77–103; Shorsch, "The Emergence of Historical Consciousness in Modern Judaism" and "Scholarship in the Service of Reform," both of which may be found in his *From Text to Context*, 158–176 and 303–333.
31. See Marcus, "Beyond the Sephardic Mystique," 35–53; M. R. Cohen, *Under Crescent and Cross*, ch. 1; Hughes, "The Golden Age of Muslim Spain: Religious Identity and the Invention of a Tradition in Modern Jewish Studies," 51–74; and more recently John M. Efron, *German Jewry and the Allure of the Sephardic* (Princeton, NJ: Princeton University Press, 2015).
32. Goitein, *Jews and Arabs*, 130.
33. See the collected essays in *Sephardism: Spanish Jewish History and the Modern Literary Imagination*, ed. Yael Halevi-Wise (Stanford, CA: Stanford University Press, 2012).
34. Ismar Schorsch, "The Myth of Sephardic Supremacy," in his *From Text to Context*, 71.
35. It is probably no coincidence that many contemporary Arab intellectuals who now often emphasize the "golden age" of medieval Jewish-Muslim relations also think less about Judaism than they do about Islam's place in the modern world. The "Jew" thus functions—not unlike the "Muslim"—as a textual strategy to showcase a set of modern virtues.
36. See the classic study of Eliza May Butler, *The Tyranny of Greece over Germany* (Cambridge: Cambridge University Press, 1935).
37. Anthony La Vopa, "Specialists against Specialization: Hellenism as Professional Ideology in German Classical Studies," in *German Professions, 1800–1950*, ed. Geoffrey Cocks and Konrad H. Jarausch (New York: Oxford University Press, 1990), 30–36. Also, see the collection *Rediscovering Hellenism: The Hellenic Inheritance and the English Imagination*, ed. G. W. Clarke (Cambridge: Cambridge University Press, 1989).
38. For the towering scholar of Jewish philosophy, H. A. Wolfson, this all goes back to the figure of Philo. See his *Philo: Foundations of Religious Philosophy in Judaism, Christianity, and Islam*, 2 vols. (Cambridge, MA: Harvard University Press, 1947).

39. E. R. Dodds, *The Greeks and the Irrational* (Berkeley: University of California Press, 1966), vii–viii.
40. Here it is worth noting that the tem "aesthetics" also and uncoincidentally played a crucial role in the reformation of Judaism, which coincided with and fed the program associated with Wissenschaft des Judentums.
41. Marchand, *Down from Olympus*, 6.
42. Marchand, *Down from Olympus*, 6.
43. Edward W. Said, *Orientalism* (New York: Vintage, 1978), 3.
44. On the role of Jews in the study of Islam, see the collected essays in *The Jewish Discovery of Islam*, ed. Martin S. Kramer; and, more recently, Susannah Heschel, "Constructions of Jewish Identity through Reflections on Islam," in *Faithful Narratives: Historians, Religions, and the Challenge of Objectivity*, ed. Nina Caputo and Andrea Sterk (Ithaca, NY: Cornell University Press, 2014), 169–184; Heschel, "German-Jewish Scholarship on Islam as a Tool of De-Orientalization," *New German Critique* 117 (2012): 91–117.
45. See, for example, the works of Schorsch, Myers, Brenner, and Hughes cited previously.
46. Gershom Scholem, "The Science of Judaism—Then and Now," in his *The Messianic Idea in Judaism and Other Essays on Jewish Spirituality* (New York: Schocken, 1971), 304–313; Scholem, "Reflections on Modern Jewish Studies," in *On the Possibility of Mysticism in Our Time and Other Essays*, ed. Avraham Shapira and trans. Jonathan Chipman (Philadelphia: Jewish Publication Society of America, 1997), 51–71.
47. See my discussion in *Rethinking Jewish Philosophy*, 48–65.
48. Brenner, *Prophets of the Past*, 10.
49. Brenner, *Prophets of the Past*, 10–11.
50. I think here of many of the volumes that have appeared in the *Library of Contemporary Jewish Philosophy* that I have coedited with my colleague Hava Tirosh-Samuelson. This library documents, with several exceptions, the previous generation of people working in, broadly speaking, the field of Jewish philosophy. I would like to think that a new generation of Jewish philosophers, while building on the work of those collected in this library, will nonetheless question many of their operating assumptions about Judaism, philosophy, and the contours of rationality.
51. Teddy Kollek, "Decade of United Jerusalem," in *The Encyclopaedia Judaica Yearbook 1977/1978* (Jerusalem: Keter, 1979), 24–25.
52. Hava Lazarus-Yafeh, "Judeo-Arabic Culture," in *The Encyclopaedia Judaica Yearbook 1977/1978* (Jerusalem: Keter, 1979), 101–109, at 101–102.
53. Lazarus-Yafeh, "Judeo-Arabic Culture," 102.
54. Graetz, *History of the Jews*, 3:313–314.
55. Graetz, *History of the Jews*, 3:270.
56. For biographical sketch, see *Le-zikhro shel Yitzhak Baer*, ed. Haim Beinart, Joshua Prawer, and Samuel Ettinger (Jerusalem: ha-Akademiah ha-leumit ha-israelit le-madaim, 1983).

57. See Israel Jacob Yuval, "Yitzhak Baer and the Search for Authentic Judaism," in *The Jewish Past Revisited: Reflections on Modern Jewish Historians*, ed. David N. Myers and David B. Ruderman (New Haven, CT: Yale University Press, 1998), 77–87.
58. Yuval, "Yitzhak Baer and the Search for Authentic Judaism," 77.
59. Lazarus-Yafeh, "Judeo-Arabic Culture," 102.
60. Baer, *A History of the Jews in Christian Spain*, 1:37.
61. Baer, *A History of the Jews in Christian Spain*, 1:37.
62. On the tension between scholarly and agricultural Zionism, see Anita Shapira, "The Zionist Labor Movement and the Hebrew University," *Judaism* 45.2 (1996): 183–198.
63. Baer, *A History of the Jews in Christian Spain*, 1:37–38.
64. Yuval, "Yitzhak Baer and the Search for Authentic Judaism," 80–81.
65. I have examined the rise and misuse of the term "Abrahamic religions" in my *Abrahamic Religions*.
66. Several of the examples that I use in this section derive from my *Abrahamic Religions*, 131–139. In that context, my concern was less with the construction of an imagined trope for Jewish–Muslim relations than in how Muslim Spain figures highly in the discourses associated with Abrahamic religions.
67. Joan Rosenbaum, "Foreword," in *Convivencia*, ed. Vivian B. Mann, Thomas F. Glick, and Jerrilynn D. Dodds, vii.
68. Amir Hussain and Dorian Llywelyn SJ, "Foreword to the Bellarmine Forum," Online at http://bellarmine.lmu.edu/thebellarmineforum/pastforumsarchive/2008archive/forewardto2008bellarmineforum/.
69. Online at http://bellarmine.lmu.edu/thebellarmineforum/pastforumsarchive/2008archive/participants/.
70. Online at http://www.cordobainitiative.org/our-mission/.
71. Feisal Abdul Rauf, *What's Right with Islam: A New Vision for Muslims and the West*, foreword by Karen Armstrong (San Francisco: HarperCollins, 2004), 2.
72. Barbara Johnson, "Translator's Introduction" to Jacques Derrida, *Dissemination* (Chicago University of Chicago Press, 1981), xv.

CHAPTER 6

1. "While I have not undertaken my inquiry by means of Goitein's comprehensive sociographic overview, it is nevertheless the case that, even given my more limited investigation, our interpretations are complementary—for I have tried to interpret symbiosis as a creative means of making novelty, as the cultural machinery of newness, as worldmaking." In Wasserstrom, *Between Muslim and Jew*, 224.
2. See the comments in Wilfred Cantwell Smith, "Traditions in Contact and Change: Toward a History of Religion in the Singular," in *Traditions in Contact*

and Change: Selected Proceedings of the XIVth Congress of the International Association for the History of Religions, ed. Peter Slater and Donald Wiebe, with Maurice Boutin and Harold Coward (Waterloo, ON: Wilfrid Laurier University Press, 1983), 1–23, at 22.
3. David J. Wasserstein, "The Muslims and the Golden Age of Jews in al-Andalus," *Israel Oriental Studies* 17 (1997): 109–125.
4. Jacob Lassner, "Genizah Studies in the United States: Its Past and its Future Links to Near Eastern Historiography," in *A Mediterranean Society by S. D. Goitein: An Abridgement in One Volume*, 478.
5. Ross Brann, *Power in the Portrayal: Representations of Jews and Muslims in Eleventh- and Twelfth-Century Islamic Spain* (Princeton, NJ: Princeton University Press, 2002), 5.
6. Goitein, *Jews and Arabs*, 130.
7. George Lakoff and Mark Johnson, *Metaphors We Live By* (Chicago: University of Chicago Press, 1980), 3–6.
8. See, for example, Ross Brann, *The Compunctious Poet: Cultural Ambiguity and Hebrew Poetry in Muslim Spain* (Baltimore: Johns Hopkins University Press, 1991), 9–22; see, further, his *Power in the Portrayal*, 1–23.
9. See Etan Kohlberg, "The Term 'Rāfida' in Imāmī Shī'ī Usage," *Journal of the American Oriental Society* 99.4 (1979): 677–679.
10. Wasserstrom, *Between Muslim and Jew*, 94.
11. Wasserstrom, *Between Muslim and Jew*, 101.
12. On the legend of Ibn Sabā', see Israel Friedlander, "Abdallah b. Saba, der Begründer der Shiʿa, und sein jüdischer Ursprung." See also Maria Massi Dakake, *The Charismatic Community: Shi'ite Identity in Early Islam* (Albany: State University of New York Press, 2007), 262; William Frederick Tucker, *Mahdis and Millenarians: Shī'ite Extremists in early Muslim Iraq* (Cambridge: Cambridge University Press, 2008), 10–12.
13. Jonathan Z. Smith, "What a Difference a Difference Makes," in *"To See Ourselves as Others See Us": Christians, Jews, and "Others" in Late Antiquity*, ed. Jacob Neusner and Ernest S. Frerichs (Chico, CA: Scholars Press, 1985), 47.
14. Stillman, *The Jews of Arab Lands*, 63.
15. Stillman, *The Jews of Arab Lands*, 61.
16. See, for example, ch. 2 above.
17. See Stanley J. Tambiah, "Animals Are Good to Think and Good to Prohibit," *Ethnology* 8.4 (1969): 457. Tambiah, of course, is riffing off Claude Lévi-Strauss, *The Savage Mind* (Chicago University of Chicago Press, 1970), 204–208. See also Edmond Leach, "Anthropological Aspects of Language: Animal Categories and Verbal Abuse," in *New Directions in the Study of Language*, ed. E. H. Lenneberg (Cambridge, MA: MIT Press, 1964), 23–63; and Mary Douglas, *Purity and Danger: An Analysis of Concept of Pollution and Taboo*, rev. ed. (London: Routledge, 2002 [1966]), 1–7.

18. The equation of retrofitting and creation becomes not unlike that of inventing new beginnings. For treatments of these themes in literary studies consult, for example, Roland Barthes, "Where to Begin?," in his *New Critical* Essays, trans. Richard Howard (Berkeley: University of California Press, 1990), 79–90; Benjamin Harshav, *Language in Time of Revolution* (Berkeley: University of California Press, 1993), 24–32. On the relation to intertextuality, see Michael Riffaterre, *Fictional Truth* (Baltimore: Johns Hopkins University Press, 1990), 53–83.
19. Benedict Anderson, *Imagined Communities: Reflections on the Origins and Spread of Nationalism*, rev. ed. (London: Verso, 2006), 1–6.
20. Such as the likes of Abraham ibn Ezra (1089–1167), Judah Halevi (1075–1141), and Moses Maimonides (1135–1204) to be discussed later in this chapter.
21. Such as those of Bahya ibn Paqūda (b. 1050), Abraham Maimonides (1186–1237), and Obadya Maimonides (1228–1265) to be discussed later in this chapter.
22. Such as Shmuel Hanagid (993–1056), Judah Halevi (1075–1141), and Moshe ibn Ezra to be discussed later in this chapter.
23. Requisite biographical material may be found in Goitein, *A Mediterranean Society*, 5:448–468; Hayyim Schirmann, "The Life of Judah Halevi," (in Hebrew) *Tarbiz* 9 (1937–1939): 35–54, 219–240, 284–305; 10 (1938–1939): 237–239; 11 (1939–1940): 125.
24. Judah Halevi, *Kitāb al-radd wa'l-dalīl fī'l-dīn al-dhalīl* (al-kitāb al-khazarī), ed. David H. Baneth and Haggai Ben-Shammai (Jerusalem: Magnes Press, 1977); a rather poor English translation may be found in *The Kuzari: An Argument for the Faith of Israel*, trans. Hartwig Hirschfeld (New York: Schocken, 1964). A much better French translation is in *Le Kuzari: Apologie de la religion méprisée*, trans. Charles Touati (Paris: Verdier, 1994).
25. I present all the evidence in my *The Art of Dialogue in Jewish Philosophy* (Bloomington: Indiana University Press, 2008), 26–49. I refer the interested reader to this work. My reasons in the present chapter are much less technical: to show how Halevi's understanding of Judaism draws its inspiration from a Muslim subculture.
26. In addition to my *The Art of Dialogue in Jewish Philosophy*, see, for example, Shlomo Pines, "Shi'ite Terms and Conceptions in Judah Halevi's *Kuzari*," *Jerusalem Studies in Arabic and Islam* 2 (1980): 165–251; Yohanan Silman, *Philosopher and Prophet: Judah Halevi, the Kuzari, and the Evolution of His Thought*, trans. Lenn J. Schramm (Albany: State University of New York Press, 1995); Diana Lobel, *Between Mysticism and Philosophy: Sufi Language of Religious Experience in Judah Ha-Levi's Kuzari* (Albany: State University of New York Press, 2000).
27. Hughes, *The Art of Dialogue in Jewish Philosophy*, 32–35. See most recently Ehud Krinis, *God's Chosen People: Judah Halevi's 'Kuzari' and the Shī'ī Imām Doctrine* (Turnhout, Belgium: Brepols, 2014).
28. Hughes, *The Art of Dialogue in Jewish Philosophy*, 35–38.

29. Pines, "Shi'ite Terms and Conceptions in Judah Halevi's *Kuzari*," 167–172.
30. See the work mentioned in n. 25.
31. Pines, "Shi'ite Terms and Conceptions in Judah Halevi's *Kuzari*," 167–170. See also Lobel, *Between Mysticism and Philosophy*, 38.
32. *Kuzari* 1:44–47 (Hirschfeld, 49); see also 2:56 (Hirschfeld, 117).
33. *Kuzari* 1:1 (Hirschfeld, 35).
34. Requisite biographical details may be found in Israel Levin, *Abraham Ibn Ezra: His Life and Poetry* (in Hebrew) (Tel Aviv: Hakibbutz Hameuchad, 1969); Levin, *Abraham Ibn Ezra Reader* (in Hebrew) (New York and Tel Aviv: Israel Martz Hebrew Classics and Edward Kiev Library Fund, 1986). A brief English synopsis may be found in my *The Texture of the Divine*, 21–23 and "The Philosophical Thought of Ibn Ezra," *Iberia Judaica* 4 (2012): 59–72.
35. Twersky and Harris, *Rabbi Abraham Ibn Ezra: Studies in the Writings of a Twelfth-Century Jewish Polymath*.
36. The term "Neoplatonist" is notoriously imprecise and anachronistic. It was originally coined in the nineteenth century and was used pejoratively to denote later commentators to Plato and Aristotle, none of whom were thought to be as original as the great masters. Indeed, it was assumed that the very genre of commentary was unoriginal. The result is that today we label as "Neoplatonic" thinkers who did not see themselves as such and, because of this, we group them under the rubric "Neoplatonic" despite the fact that their thought may well have had very little in common. On the history of this term, see Maria Luisa Gatti, "Plotinus: The Platonic Tradition and the Foundation of Neoplatonism," in Lloyd P. Gerson, *The Cambridge Companion to Plotinus* (Cambridge: Cambridge University Press, 1996), 22–27.
37. It was published in the appendix to my aforementioned *Texture of the Divine*.
38. Avicenna's text is translated into English in Henry Corbin, *Avicenna and the Visionary Recital*, trans. Willard Trask (Princeton, NJ: Bollingen, 1960), 137–150.
39. See my "A Case of 12th-Century Plagiarism? Abraham ibn Ezra's *Hay ben Meqitz* and Avicenna's *Hayy ibn Yaqẓān*," *Journal of Jewish Studies* 55.2 (2004): 306–331.
40. The translation is mine and comes from *Texture of the Divine*, 190.
41. Genesis 24:65.
42. Song of Songs 4:1, 3.
43. Deuteronomy 34:7; Song of Songs 4:3.
44. Deuteronomy 34:7.
45. Avicenna's same description read as follows:

> Once when I had taken up residence in my city, I chanced to go out with my companions to one of the pleasure places that lie about the same city. Now, as we were coming and going, making a circle, suddenly in the distance appeared a Sage. He was beautiful; his person shone with a divine glory. Certainly he had tasted of years; long duration had passed over him. Yet there was seen in him only the freshness proper to young men; no weakness bowed his bearing,

no fault injured the grace of his stature. In short, no sign of old age was to be found in him, save the imposing gravity of old Sages. (Corbin, *Avicenna and the Visionary Recital*, 137)

46. See, e.g., Brann, who deftly connects this to cultural ambiguity in *The Compunctious Poet*, 23–58.
47. See, for example, the classic work by Georges Vajda, *L'Amour de Dieu dans la théologie juive du Moyen Âge* (Paris: J. Vrin, 1957). More recent studies include Henry Corbin, *Creative Imagination in the Sufism of Ibn Arabi*, trans. Ralph Manheim (Princeton, NJ: Princeton University Press, 1969); Elliot R. Wolfson, *Through a Speculum That Shines: Vision and Imagination in Medieval Jewish Mysticism* (Princeton, NJ: Princeton University Press, 1994); also Hughes, *Texture of the Divine*, 82–114.
48. See, for example, Wolfson, *Through a Speculum That Shines*, 52–73.
49. For one of the most articulate expressions of this, see Elliot R. Wolfson, *Language, Eros, Being: Kabbalistic Hermeneutic and Poetic Imagination* (New York: Fordham University Press, 2005), 190–260; see further Elliot R. Wolfson, *Venturing Beyond: Law and Morality in Kabbalistic Mysticism* (Oxford: Oxford University Press, 2006).
50. Lobel, *A Jewish–Sufi Dialogue*.
51. Baḥya ibn Paqūda, *The Book of Directions to the Duties of the Heart*, trans. Menahem Mansoor (London: Routledge and Kegan Paul, 1973), 89.
52. Georges Vajda, *La Théologie ascétique de Baḥya ibn Paqūda* (Paris: Imprimerie Nationale, 1947), 131–137.
53. See the comments in Moshe Idel, *Kabbalah: New Perspectives* (New Haven, CT: Yale University Press, 1988), 59–73.
54. Baḥya, *The Book of Directions to the Duties of the Heart*, 443–444.
55. See, for example, Shlomo Pines, "Maimonides' Halakhic Works and the *Guide of the Perplexed*," in *Maimonides and Philosophy*, ed. S. Pines and Y. Yovel (Dordrecht: Martinus Nijhoff, 1986), 9–11.
56. Maimonides, *The Guide of the Perplexed*, 2 vols., trans. Shlomo Pines (Chicago: University of Chicago Press, 1963), III. 51 (2:618–628).
57. *Guide*, III. 51 (623).
58. See, for example, Elliot R. Wolfson, "Beneath the Wings of the Great Eagle: Maimonides and Thirteenth-Century Kabbalah," in *Moses Maimonides (1138–1204)—His Religious, Scientific, and Philosophical Wirkungsgeschichte in Different Cultural Contexts*, ed. G. K. Hasselhoff and Otfried Fraisse (Würzburg: Ergon Verlag, 2004), 209–237; and his "Via Negativa in Maimonides and Its Impact on Thirteenth-Century Kabbalah," *Maimonidean Studies* 5 (2008): 363–412. See also Menachem M. Kellner, *Maimonides' Confrontation with Mysticism* (London: Littman Library, 2011).
59. *Guide*, III. 51 (628).
60. See Wolfson, *Through a Speculum That Shines*, 3–12.

61. E.g., Alfred Ivry, "Neoplatonic Currents in Maimonides' Thought," in *Perspectives on Maimonides: Philosophical and Historical Studies*, ed. Joel L. Kraemer (Oxford: Oxford University Press for the Littman Library, 1991), 115–140.
62. See the recent study of Elisha Fishbane, *Judaism, Sufism, and the Pietists of Medieval Egypt: A Study of Abraham Maimonides and His Times* (New York: Oxford University Press, 2015), 1–42.
63. For biographical details, see Samuel Rosenblatt, *The High Ways to Perfection of Abraham Maimonides* (New York: Columbia University Press, 1927), 40–58; Shlomo Dov Goitein, "Abraham Maimonides and his Pietist Circle," in *Jewish Medieval and Renaissance Studies*, ed. Alexander Altmann (Cambridge, MA: Harvard University Press, 1967), 145–164.
64. Rosenblatt, *The High Ways to Perfection of Abraham Maimonides*, 50.
65. Fishbane, *Judaism, Sufism, and the Pietists of Medieval Egypt*, 135–157.
66. Rosenblatt, *The High Ways to Perfection of Abraham Maimonides*, 51.
67. Rosenblatt, *The High Ways to Perfection of Abraham Maimonides*, 134–135.
68. Rosenblatt, *The High Ways to Perfection of Abraham Maimonides*, 138–139.
69. Paul Fenton, *The Treatise of the Pool: Al-Maqala al-Hawdiyya* (London: Octagon Press, 1981), 115. I modify Fenton's translation somewhat here.
70. Fenton, *The Treatise of the Pool*, 13.
71. Fenton, *The Treatise of the Pool*, 12.
72. See Shlomo Dov Goitein, "New Documents from the Cairo Geniza," in *Homenaje a Millas-Vallicrosa* (Barcelona: Consejo Superior de Investigaciones Científicas, 1954), 1:707–720.
73. Fenton, *The Treatise of the Pool*, 115. Again, I modify Fenton's translation somewhat here.
74. See Shlomo Dov Goitein, "A Jewish Addict to Sufism in the time of Nagid David II Maimonides," *Jewish Quarterly Review* 44 (1953–1954): 37–49; Paul Fenton, "The Literary Legacy of David ben Joshua, Last of the Maimonidean Nĕgīdim," *Jewish Quarterly Review* 75.1 (1984): 1–56.
75. Paul Fenton, "Judeo-Arabic Mystical Writings of the XIIIth–XIVth Centuries," in *Judaeo-Arabic Studies: Proceedings of the Founding Conference of the Society for Judaeo-Arabic Studies*, ed. Norman Golb (Amsterdam: Harwood, 1997), 87–102.
76. The influence of Islamic mysticism on Jewish thought was not confined to al-Andalus and the Western Mediterranean basin, however. After the expulsion from Spain in 1492, the development of Jewish mysticism took place virtually exclusively in Islamic lands. See, for example, Paul Fenton, "Shabbatay Sebi and the Muslim Mystic Muhammad an-Niyazi," in *Approaches to Judaism in Medieval Times*, vol. 3, ed. David R. Blumenthal (Atlanta, GA: Scholars Press, 1988), 81–88; Fenton, "A New Collection of Sabbatian Hymns," in *The Sabbatian Movement and Its Aftermath: Messianism, Sabbatianism and Frankism*, vol. 1, ed. Rachel Elior (Jerusalem: Magnes Press, 2001), 329–351 (in Hebrew); Fenton, "Influences soufies sur le développement de la Qabbale à Safed: L'Exemple de

la visitation des tombes," in *Etudes sur les terres saintes et les pèlerinages dans les religions monothéistes*, ed. D. Tollet (Paris: Librairie Honoré Champion, 2012), 201–230.

One such individual is one of the most controversial figures in later Lurianic mysticism—the self-declared messiah, Shabbetai Zvi (d. 1676). This individual spent some of his formative years in Salonika (today northeastern Greece), a city that was renowned for its Sufis, the majority of whom were Mevlevis, the school associated with Jalāl al-Dīn Rūmī, in addition to being a major center of kabbalah and of rabbinic scholarship. After Shabbetai Zvi converted to Islam, his not insignificant followers—from as far away as Yemen in the South and Amsterdam in the North—had three options. The majority realized that he was not the Messiah and returned to their previous lives and professions, where they now presumably practiced normative Judaism. Another group remained Jews but still referred to him as the Messiah. These individuals became known as Sabbateans. And a small number converted to Islam along with their Messiah. These individuals became known as the *Dönmeh*, a group that was—using the categories of the *ẓāhir/bāṭin* utilized earlier—externally Muslim, but internally Jewish. These "crypto-Jews," while presumably having nothing to do with normative Jews, remained open to Muslim influence, especially that of Sufism. See, for example, Gershom Scholem, "Sprouting of the Horn of the Son of David: A New Source from the Beginnings of the Doenme Sect in Salonica," in *In the Time of Harvest: Essays in Honor of Abba Hillel Silver*, ed. Daniel Jeremy Silver (New York: Macmillan, 1963), 385; and more recently, Marc David Baer, *The Dönme: Jewish Converts, Muslim Revolutionaries, and Secular Turks* (Stanford, CA: Stanford University Press, 2010), 5–12.

CONCLUSION

1. Amos Oz, "For Its Survival, Israel Must Abandon the One-State Option," *Los Angeles Times*, March 7, 2015. Online at http://www.latimes.com/opinion/op-ed/la-oe-oz-two-state-solution-peace-israel-palestinians-20150308-story.html.
2. David Grossman, "Swiss Mountain View: A Story," in his *The Yellow Wind*, trans. Haim Watzman (New York: Picador, 1988), 127–144, at 144.
3. Lewis, *The Jews of Islam*, 190.
4. One does not have far to look for the latter either, however. See, in this regard, Mark Tessler, *A History of the Israeli–Palestinian Conflict*, 2d ed. (Bloomington: Indiana University Press, 2009), 185–264.
5. See Benny Morris, *Righteous Victims: A History of the Zionist–Arab Conflict, 1881–2001* (New York: Vintage, 2001), 676–694.
6. Smith, *Drudgery Divine*, 46.

Bibliography

Abrahamov, Binyamin. *Islamic Theology: Traditionalism and Rationalism*. Edinburgh: Edinburgh University Press, 1998.
Ackerman-Lieberman, Phillip. *The Business of Identity: Jews, Muslims, and Economic Life in Medieval Egypt*. Stanford, CA: Stanford University Press, 2014.
Adang, Camilla. *Muslim Writers on Judaism and the Hebrew Bible: From Ibn Rabban to Ibn Hazm*. Leiden: Brill, 1996.
Ahrens, K. "Christliches im Koran." *ZDMG* 60 (1930): 15–16, 148–190.
Alcalay, Ammiel. *After Jews and Arabs: Remaking Levantine Culture*. Minneapolis: University of Minnesota Press, 1992.
Anderson, Benedict. *Imagined Communities: Reflections on the Origins and Spread of Nationalism*. Rev. ed. London: Verso, 2006.
Anidjar, Gil. *The Jew, the Arab: The History of the Enemy*. Stanford, CA: Stanford University Press, 2003.
Arjomand, Said Amir. "'Abd Allah Ibn al-Muqaffa' and the Abbasid Revolution." *Religion and Society in Islamic Iran during the Pre-Modern Era* 27.1 (1994): 9–36.
Arnal, William E., and Russell T. McCutcheon. *The Sacred Is the Profane: The Political Nature of "Religion."* New York: Oxford University Press, 2013.
Asatryan, Mushegh. *Cosmology and Community in Early Shi'i Islam: The Ghulat and Their Literature*. London: I. B. Tauris, 2016.
Ashtor, Eliyahu. *The Jews of Moslem Spain*. Translated by Aaron Klein and Jenny Machlowitz Klein. 3 vols. Philadelphia: Jewish Publication Society of America, 1973–1984.
Assaf, Simha. *Tekufat ha-geonim ve-sifrutah*. Jerusalem: Mossad ha-Rav Kook, 1955.
Astren, Fred. *Karaite Judaism and Historical Understanding*. Columbia: University of South Carolina Press, 2004.
Attwood, Bain. *The Making of Aboriginees*. Sydney: Allen and Unwin, 1989.
al-Azmeh, Aziz. *The Emergence of Islam in Late Antiquity: Allāh and His People*. Cambridge: Cambridge University Press, 2014.

Azra, Azyumardi. "Trialogue of Abrahamic Faiths: Toward an Alliance of Civilizations." In *The Meeting of Civilizations: Muslim, Christian, and Jewish*, edited by Moshe Maoz, 20–29. Eastbourne, UK: Sussex Academic Press, 2009.

Bachrach, Bernard S. *Early Medieval Jewish Policy in Western Europe*. Minneapolis: University of Minnesota Press, 1977.

Bäck, Samuel. *Die Geschichte des jüdischen Volkes und seiner Literatur vom babylonischen Exil bis auf die Gegenwart*. 3d ed. Frankfurt am Main: J. Kauffmann, 1906.

Baer, Marc David. *The Dönme: Jewish Converts, Muslim Revolutionaries, and Secular Turks*. Stanford, CA: Stanford University Press, 2010.

Baer, Yitzhak. *A History of the Jews in Christian Spain*. 2 vols. Philadelphia: Jewish Publication Society of America, 1961–1966.

Barnett, Richard D., ed. *The Sephardi Heritage*. Vol. 1. London: Vallentine and Mitchell, 1971.

Baron, Salo W. "Saadia's Communal Activities." *Saadia Anniversary Volume* (1943): 9–74.

Baron, Salo W. *A Social and Religious History of the Jews*. 18 vols. New York: Columbia University Press, 1952–1983.

Barth, J. *Midraschische Elemente in der muslimischen Tradition*. Berlin: Druck von H. Itzkowski, 1903.

Barth, J. *Studien zur Kritik und Exegese des Qorans*. Strassberg: Karl J. Trübner, 1915.

Barthes, Roland. "Where to Begin?." In his *New Critical Essays*, translated by Richard Howard, 79–90. Berkeley: University of California Press, 1990.

Barzun, Jacques. *Classic, Romantic, Modern*. Boston: Little Brown, 1961.

Bashear, Suliman. "Apocalyptic and Other Materials in Early Muslim-Byzantine Wars: A Review of Arabic Sources." *Journal of the Royal Asiatic Society*, n.s., 1–2 (1991): 173–207.

Baudrillard, Jean. *Simulacra and Simulation*. Translated by Sheila Faria Glaser. Ann Arbor: University of Michigan Press, 1995.

Beard, Mary, John A. North, and S. R. F. Price. *Religions of Rome*. Cambridge: Cambridge University Press, 1998.

Becker, C. H. *Christentum und Islam*. Tübingen: Mohr, 1907.

Beinart, Haim. *The Expulsion of the Jews from Spain*. Translated by Jeffrey M. Green. London: Littman Library of Jewish Civilization, 2005.

Beinart, Haim, Joshua Prawer, and Samuel Ettinger, eds. *Le-zikhro shel Yitzhak Baer*. Jerusalem: ha-Akadamiah ha-leumit ha-israelit le-madaim, 1983.

Ben Shammai, Haggai. "A Note on Some Karaite Copies of Muʿtazilite Writings." *Bulletin of the School of Oriental and African Studies* 37 (1974): 295–304.

Ben Shammai, Haggai. "The Attitude of Some Early Karaites Towards Islam." In *Studies in Medieval Jewish History*, edited by Isadore Twersky, 2:3–40. Cambridge, MA: Harvard University Press, 1984.

Ben-Shammai, Haggai. "The Karaite Controversy: Scripture and Tradition in Early Karaism." In *Religionsgespräche im Mittelalter*, edited by Bernard Lewis and Friedrich Niewöhner, 11–26. Wiesbaden: Otto Harrassowitz, 1992.

Ben Shammai, Haggai. "Between Ananites and Karaties: Observations on Early Muslim–Jewish Sectarianism." *Studies in Medieval Jewish–Islamic Relations* 1 (1993): 19–31.

Ben Shammai, Haggai. "Kalām in Medieval Jewish Philosophy." In *History of Jewish Philosophy*, edited by Daniel H. Frank and Oliver Leaman, 114–148. London: Routledge, 1997.

Ben-Zeev, I. *Ha-yehudim be-'Arav*. Jerusalem, 1931.

Berman, Joshua A. *Created Equal: How the Bible Broke with Ancient Political Thought*. New York: Oxford University Press, 2008.

Biemann, Asher D. *Inventing New Beginnings: On the Idea of Renaissance in Modern Judaism*. Stanford, CA: Stanford University Press, 2009.

Bland, Kalman P. *The Artless Jew: Medieval and Modern Affirmations and Denials of the Visual*. Princeton, NJ: Princeton University Press, 2000.

Boccaccini, Gabrielle. *Roots of Rabbinic Judaism: An Intellectual History, from Ezekiel to Daniel*. Grand Rapids, MI: Eerdmans, 2002.

Bowersock, Glen Warren. *Empires in Collision in Late Antiquity*. Waltham, MA: Brandeis University Press, 2012.

Bowersock, Glen Warren. *The Throne of Adulis: Red Sea Wars on the Eve of Islam*. New York: Oxford University Press, 2013.

Boyarin, Daniel. *The Jewish Gospels: The Story of the Jewish Christ*. New York: New Press, 2012.

Boyarin, Daniel. *Border Lines: The Partition of Judaeo-Christianity*. Philadelphia: University of Pennsylvania Press, 2014.

Brakke, David. *The Gnostics: Myth, Ritual, and Diversity in Early Christianity*. Cambridge, MA: Harvard University Press, 2011.

Brann, Ross. *The Compunctious Poet: Cultural Ambiguity and Hebrew Poetry in Muslim Spain*. Baltimore: Johns Hopkins University Press, 1991.

Brann, Ross. *Power in the Portrayal: Representations of Jews and Muslims in Eleventh- and Twelfth-Century Islamic Spain*. Princeton, NJ: Princeton University Press, 2002.

Brenner, Michael, *Prophets of the Past: Interpreters of Jewish History*. Translated by Steven Rendall. Princeton, NJ: Princeton University Press, 2010.

Brockelmann, C. *History of the Islamic Peoples*. London: G. P. Putnam's Sons, 1950.

Brockopp, Jonathan. "Islamic Origins and Incidental Normativity." *Journal of the American Academy of Religion* 84.1 (2016): 28–43.

Brody, Robert. *The Geonim of Babylonia and the Shaping of Medieval Jewish Culture*. New Haven, CT: Yale University Press, 1998.

Brody, Robert. *Sa'adiyah Gaon*. Translated by Betsy Rosenberg. Oxford: Littman Library of Jewish Civilization, 2013.

Bulliet, Richard W. *Islam: The View from the Edge*. New York: Columbia University Press, 1994.

Butler, Eliza May. *The Tyranny of Greece over Germany*. Cambridge: Cambridge University Press, 1935.

Cameron, Averil. "The Eastern Provinces in the Seventh Century: Hellenism and the Emergence of Islam." In *Hellēnismos: Quelques jalons pour une histoire de l'identité grecque: Actes du Colloque de Strasbourg. 25–27 octobre, 1989*, edited by Suzanne Saïd, 287–313. Leiden: Brill, 1991.

Cameron, Averil. *The Mediterranean World in Late Antiquity: ad 395–700*. 2d ed. London: Routledge, 2012.

Castro, Américo. *The Spaniards*. Translated by Williard F. King and Selma Margaretten. Berkeley: University of California Press, 1971.

Chidester, David. *Savage Systems: Colonialism and Comparative Religion in Southern Africa*. Charlottesville: University of Virginia Press, 1996.

Chidester, David. *Empire of Religion: Imperialism and Comparative Religion*. Chicago: University of Chicago Press, 2014.

Chittester, Joan, Murshod Saadi Shakur Christi, and Rabbi Arthur Waskow. *The Tent of Abraham: Stories of Hope and Peace for Jews, Christians, and Muslims*. Foreword by Karen Armstrong. Boston: Beacon Press, 2006.

Clarke, Graeme W., ed. *Rediscovering Hellenism: The Hellenic Inheritance and the English Imagination*. Cambridge: Cambridge University Press, 1989.

Cohen, Gerson. "The Reconstruction of Gaonic History." In *Texts in Jewish History and Literature*, vol. 1, edited by Jacob Mann, 1:xiii–xcvii. New York: Ktav, 1972.

Cohen, Gerson. "Rabbinic Judaism (2nd–18th Centuries)." *Encyclopedia Britannica*, 15th ed., 22:416–422. Chicago: Encyclopedia Britannica, 1974.

Cohen, Mark R. *Under Crescent and Cross: The Jews in the Middle Ages*. Princeton, NJ: Princeton University Press, 1994.

Cohen, Mark R. *Poverty and Charity in the Jewish Community of Medieval Egypt*. Princeton, NJ: Princeton University Press, 2005.

Cohen, Shaye J.D. *The Beginnings of Jewishness: Boundaries, Varieties, Uncertainties*. Berkeley: University of California Press, 2001.

Cohen, Shaye J. D. *From the Maccabees to the Mishnah*. 2d ed. Louisville, KY: Westminster John Knox Press, 2006.

Cook, David. *Studies in Muslim Apocalyptic*. Princeton, NJ: Darwin Press, 2002.

Cook, David. *Contemporary Muslim Apocalyptic Literature*. Syracuse, NY: Syracuse University Press, 2005.

Cook, Michael. "The Origins of the *Kalām*." *Bulletin of the School of Oriental and African Studies* 43 (1980): 32–43.

Cook, Michael. *Commanding Right and Forbidding Wrong in Islamic Thought*. Cambridge: Cambridge University Press, 2000.

Corbin, Henry. *Avicenna and the Visionary Recital*. Translated by Willard Trask. Princeton, NJ: Bollingen, 1960.

Corbin, Henry. *Creative Imagination in the Sufism of Ibn Arabi*. Translated by Ralph Manheim. Princeton, NJ: Princeton University Press, 1969.

Crone, Patricia. *Meccan Trade and the Rise of Islam*. Princeton, NJ: Princeton University Press, 1987.

Crone, Patricia. "Jewish Christianity and the Qur'ān." *Journal of Near Eastern Studies* 74 (2015): 225–253.
Crone, Patricia, and Michael Cook. *Hagarism: The Making of the Islamic World.* Cambridge: Cambridge University Press, 1979.
Dakake, Maria Massi. *The Charismatic Community: Shi'ite Identity in Early Islam.* Albany: State University of New York Press, 2007.
Davidson, Herbert A. *Alfarabi, Avicenna, and Averroes, on Intellect: Their Cosmologies, Theories of the Active Intellect, and Theories of Human Intellect.* New York: Oxford University Press, 1992.
Davidson, Israel. "The Study of Medieval Hebrew Poetry in the Nineteenth Century." *Proceedings of the American Academy for Jewish Research* 1 (1928): 33–48.
Delitzsch, Franz. *Zur Geschichte der jüdischen Poesie.* Leipzig: Tauchnitz, 1836.
Derrida, Jacques. *Writing and Difference.* Translated by Alan Bass. Chicago: University of Chicago Press, 1978.
Dodds, E.R. *The Greeks and the Irrational.* Berkeley: University of California Press, 1966.
Dodds, Jerrilynn D., María Rosa Menocal, and Abigail Krasner Balbale. *The Arts of Intimacy: Christians, Jews, and Muslims in the Making of Castilian Culture.* New Haven, CT: Yale University Press, 2008.
Dohrmann, Natalie, and Annette Yoshiko Reed. "Introduction." In *Jews, Christians, and the Roman Empire: The Poetics of Power in Late Antiquity*. Edited by N. Dohrmann and A. Y. Reed, 1–22. Philadelphia: University of Pennsylvania Press, 2013.
Donner, Fred. *Narratives of Islamic Origins: The Beginnings of Islamic Historical Writing.* Princeton, NJ: Darwin Press, 1998.
Donner, Fred. *Muhammad and the Believers: At the Origins of Islam.* Cambridge, MA: Harvard University Press, 2010.
Douglas, Mary. *Purity and Danger: An Analysis of Concept of Pollution and Taboo.* Rev. ed. London: Routledge: 2002 [1966].
Drory, Rina. "The Function of Karaite Literature in the Evolution of Tenth-Century Jewish Literature." (Hebrew) *Dappim le Mehqar be-Sifrut* 9 (1994): 101–110.
Dubuisson, Daniel. *Twentieth Century Mythologies: Dumazil, Levi-Strauss, Eliade.* Translated by Martha Cunningham. Sheffield: Equinox, 2006.
Efron, John M. "Orientalism and the Jewish Historical Gaze." In *Orientalism and the Jews*, edited by Ivan Davidson Kalmar and Derek J. Penslar, 80–93. Stanford, CA: Stanford University Press, 2005.
Efron, John M. *German Jewry and the Allure of the Sephardic.* Princeton, NJ: Princeton University Press, 2015.
Einbinder, Susan L. *Beautiful Death: Jewish Poetry and Martyrdom in Medieval France.* Princeton, NJ: Princeton University Press, 2002.
El-Badawi, Emran. *The Qur'an and the Aramaic Gospel Traditions.* London: Routledge, 2013.

Eliade, Mircea. *The Myth of the Eternal Return: Or, Cosmos and History*. Translated by Willard R. Trask. Princeton, NJ: Princeton University Press, 1954.

Elm, Susana. "Orthodoxy and the True Philosophical Life: Julian and Gregory of Nazianus." *Studia Patristica* 37 (2001): 69–85.

Erder, Yoram. "The Negation of the Exile in the Messianic Doctrine of the Karaite Mourners of Zion." *Hebrew Union College Annual* 68 (1997): 109–140.

Ess, Joseph van. *The Flowering of Muslim Theology*. Translated by Jane Marie Todd. Cambridge, MA: Harvard University Press, 2006.

Feiler, Bruce. *Abraham: A Journey to the Heart of Three Faiths*. New York: HarperCollins, 2002.

Feiner, Shmuel. *The Jewish Enlightenment*. Translated by Chaya Naor. Philadelphia: University of Pennsylvania Press, 2002.

Feldman, Louis H. *Jew and Gentile in the Ancient World: Attitudes and Interactions from Alexander to Justinian*. Princeton, NJ: Princeton University Press, 1993.

Fenton, Paul, trans. and ed. *The Treatise of the Pool: Al-Maqala al-Hawdiyya*. London: Octagon Press, 1981.

Fenton, Paul. "The Literary Legacy of David ben Joshua, Last of the Maimonidean Nēgīdim." *Jewish Quarterly Review* 75.1 (1984): 1–56.

Fenton, Paul. "Shabbatay Sebi and the Muslim Mystic Muhammad an-Niyazi." In *Approaches to Judaism in Medieval Times*, vol. 3, edited by David R. Blumenthal, 81–88. Atlanta, GA: Scholars Press, 1988.

Fenton, Paul. "Judeo-Arabic Mystical Writings of the XIIIth–XIVth Centuries." In *Judaeo-Arabic Studies: Proceedings of the Founding Conference of the Society for Judaeo-Arabic Studies*, edited Norman Golb, 87–102. Amsterdam: Harwood, 1997.

Fenton, Paul. "A New Collection of Sabbatian Hymns" (in Hebrew). In *The Sabbatian Movement and Its Aftermath: Messianism, Sabbatianism and Frankism*, vol. 1, edited by Rachel Elior, 329–351. Jerusalem: Magnes Press, 2001.

Fenton, Paul. "Influences soufies sur le développement de la Qabbale à Safed: L'Exemple de la visitation des tombes." In *Etudes sur les terres saintes et les pèlerinages dans les religions monothéistes*, edited by D. Tollet, 201–230. Paris: Librairie Honoré Champion, 2012.

Fernandez-Morera, Dario. *The Myth of Andalusian Paradise: Muslims, Christians, and Jews under Islamic Rule in Muslim Spain*. Wilmington, DE: ISI Books, 2016.

Firestone, Reuven. *Journeys in Holy Lands: The Evolution of the Abraham-Ishmael Legends in Islamic Exegesis*. Albany: State University of New York Press, 2000.

Fishbane, Elisha. *Judaism, Sufism, and the Pietists of Medieval Egypt: A Study of Abraham Maimonides and His Times*. New York: Oxford University Press, 2015.

Fishman, Talya. *Becoming the People of the Talmud: Oral Torah as Written Tradition in Medieval Jewish Cultures*. Philadelphia: University of Pennsylvania Press, 2001.

Fitzgerald, Timothy. *The Ideology of Religious Studies*. New York: Oxford University Press, 2000.

Foucault, Michel. *The Order of Things: An Archaeology of the Human Sciences.* New York: Random House, 1970.

Frank, Daniel. "The *Shoshanim* of Tenth-Century Jerusalem: Karaite Exegesis, Prayer, and Communal Identity." In *The Jews of Medieval Islam: Community, Society, and Identity*, edited by Daniel Frank, 199–245. Leiden: Brill, 1995.

Frank, Daniel. *Search Scripture Well: Karaite Exegesis and the Origins of the Jewish Bible Commentary in the Islamic East.* Leiden: Brill, 2004.

Franklin, Arnold E. *This Noble House: Jewish Descendants of King David in the Medieval East.* Philadelphia: University of Pennsylvania Press, 2013.

Freidenreich, David M. "Comparisons Compared: A Methodological Survey from 'A Magic Dwells' to *A Magic Still Dwells*." *Method and Theory in the Study of Religion* 16 (2004): 80–101.

Freidenreich, David M. *Foreigners and Their Food: Constructing Otherness in Jewish, Christian, and Islamic Law.* Berkeley: University of California Press, 2011.

Friedlander, Israel. "Abdallah b. Saba, der Begründer der Shiʿa, und sein jüdischer Ursprung." *Zeitschrift für Assyriologie* 23 (1909): 296–327 and 24 (1910): 1–46.

Friedlander, Israel. "The Jews of Arabia and the Gaonate." *Jewish Quarterly Review* 1 (1910–1911): 249–252.

Friedlander, Israel. "Jewish-Arabic Studies." *Jewish Quarterly Review* 1 (1910–1911): 183–215; 2 (1911–1912): 481–517; 3 (1912–1913): 235–300.

Friedman, Saul S. "The Myth of Arab Toleration." *Midstream* 16.1 (1970): 56–59.

Fudeman, Kirsten A. *Vernacular Voices: Language and Identity in Medieval French Jewish Communities.* Philadelphia: University of Pennsylvania Press, 2010.

Gager, John G. *Who Made Early Christianity?: The Jewish Lives of the Apostle Paul.* New York: Columbia University Press, 2015.

Gaon, Saadya. *See* Saadya Gaon

Gastfreund, I. *Mohammed nach Talmud und Midrasch.* Berlin: L. Gerschel, 1875.

Gatti, Maria Luisa. "Plotinus: The Platonic Tradition and the Foundation of Neoplatonism." In *The Cambridge Companion to Plotinus*, edited by Lloyd P. Gerson, 10–37. Cambridge: Cambridge University Press, 1996.

Geiger, Abraham. *Was hat Mohammed aus dem Judenthume aufgenommen?* Bonn: F. Baaden, 1833. English translation: *Judaism and Islam.* Translated by F. M. Young. Madras: MDCSPK Press, 1835; repr. New York: Ktav 1970.

Geiger, Abraham. *Das Judentum und seine Geschichte.* 2 vols. 2nd ed. Breslau: Schletter, 1871. English translation: *Judaism and Its History in Two Parts.* Hanover, NH: University Press of America, 1985.

Gerber, Jane S. "Judaism in the Middle East and North Africa since 1492." *Encyclopedia of Religion*, edited by Mircea Eliade, 8:157–164. New York: Macmillan, 1987.

Gerber, Jane S. *The Jews of Spain: A History of the Sephardic Experience.* Philadelphia: Jewish Publication Society of America, 1992.

Gil, Moshe. "The Constitution of Medina: A Reconsideration." *Israel Oriental Studies* 4 (1974): 44–66.

Gilbert, Martin. "The Jews of Islam: Golden Age or Ghetto?" *Jewish Chronicle Colour Magazine*, November 23, 1979, 56–60.

Goitein, Shlomo Dov. "A Jewish Addict to Sufism in the Time of Nagid David II Maimonides." *Jewish Quarterly Review* 44 (1953–1954): 37–49.

Goitein, Shlomo Dov. "New Documents from the Cairo Geniza." In *Homenaje a Millas-Vallicrosa*, 1:707–720. Barcelona: Consejo Superior de Investigaciones Científicas, 1954.

Goitein, Shlomo Dov. *Jews and Arabs: Their Contact through the Ages*. 3d rev. ed. New York: Schocken, 1955.

Goitein, Shlomo Dov. "The Rise of the Near Eastern Bourgeoisie in Early Islamic Times." *Journal of World History* 32 (1956–1957): 583–604.

Goitein, Shlomo Dov. "Abraham Maimonides and his Pietist Circle." In *Jewish Medieval and Renaissance Studies*, edited by Alexander Altmann, 145–164. Cambridge, MA: Harvard University Press, 1967.

Goitein, Shlomo Dov. *Temanim: Historyah, sidre hevrah, haye ha-ruah: Mivhar mehkarim*. Edited by Menahem Ben-Sason. Jerusalem: Mekhon Ben-Tsevi le-heker kehilot Yisra'el bamizrah, 1983.

Goitein, Shlomo Dov. *A Mediterranean Society: The Jewish Communities of the Arab World as Portrayed in the Documents of the Cairo Geniza*. Berkeley: University of California Press, 1967–1993.

Goitein, Shlomo Dov. *A Mediterranean Society: An Abridgment in One Volume*. Edited by Jacob Lassner. Berkeley: University of California Press, 1999.

Goldberg, Jessica. *Trade and Institutions in the Medieval Mediterranean: The Geniza Merchants and the Business World*. Cambridge: Cambridge University Press, 2011.

Goldziher, Ignaz. "Le Dénombrement des sects mohamétanes." *Revue de l'histoire des religions* 26 (1892): 129–137.

Goldziher, Ignaz. *Introduction to Islamic Theology and Law*. Translated by Andras and Ruth Hamori. Princeton, NJ: Princeton University Press, 1981.

Graetz, Heinrich. "*History of the Jews*. Vol. 3. Philadelphia: Jewish Publication Society of America, 1956.

Graetz, Heinrich. *The Structure of Jewish History and Other Essays*. Translated and edited by Ismar Schorsch. New York: Jewish Theological Seminary of America 1975.

Grossman, Avraham. *The Babylonian Exilarchate in the Gaonic Period* (in Hebrew). Jerusalem: Zalman Shazar Center, 1984.

Grossman, Avraham. "Aliya in the Seventh and Eighth Centuries." *Jerusalem Cathedra* 3 (1988): 65–94.

Grossman, David. "Swiss Mountain View: A Story." In his *The Yellow Wind*, translated by Haim Watzman, 127–144. New York: Picador, 1988.

Gruen, Erich S. *Rethinking the Other in Late Antiquity*. Princeton, NJ: Princeton University Press, 2011.

Grünbaum, M. *Neue Beiträge zur semitischen Sagenkunde*. Leiden: Brill, 1893.

Grunebaum, Gustav E. von. "Medieval Islam (in conversation with Norman Cantor)." In *Perspectives on the European Past*, edited by N. Cantor, 168–186. New York: Collier Macmillan, 1971.

Gutas, Dimitri. *Greek Thought, Arabic Culture: The Graeco-Arabic Translation Movement in Baghdad and Early ʿAbbasaid Society (2nd–4th/5th–10th c)*. London: Routledge, 1998.

Guttmann, Julius. *Philosophies of Judaism: A History of Jewish Philosophy from Biblical Times to Franz Rosenzweig*. Translated by David W. Silverman. New York: Schocken, 1964.

Halevi, Judah. *Kitāb al-radd wa'l-dalīl fīʾl-dīn al-dhalīl* (al-kitāb al-khazarī). Edited by David H. Baneth and Haggai Ben-Shammai. Jerusalem: Magnes Press, 1977. English translation: *The Kuzari: An Argument for the Faith of Israel*. Translated by Hartwig Hirschfeld. New York: Schocken, 1964. French translation: *Le Kuzari: Apologie de la religion méprisée*. Translated by Charles Touati. Paris: Verdier, 1994.

Halevi-Wise, Yael, ed. *Sephardism: Spanish Jewish History and the Modern Literary Imagination*. Stanford, CA: Stanford University Press, 2012.

Hallaq, Wael. *The Origins and Evolution of Islamic Law*. Cambridge: Cambridge University Press, 2005.

Hamidullah, Muhammad. *The First Written Constitution in the World: An Important Document of the Time of the Holy Prophet*. 3d rev. ed. Lahore, Pakistan: Sh. Muhammad Ashraf, (1394) 1975.

Harshav, Benjamin. *Language in Time of Revolution*. Berkeley: University of California Press, 1993.

Hawting, Gerald R. *The Idea of Idolatry and the Rise of Islam: From Polemic to History*. Cambridge: Cambridge University Press, 1999.

Hazony, Yoram. *The Philosophy of Hebrew Scripture*. Cambridge: Cambridge University Press, 2012.

Hegedus, Gyonghi. "Theological Summae." In *The Literary Forms of Medieval Jewish Philosophy*, edited by Aaron W. Hughes and James T. Robinson. Bloomington: Indiana University Press, forthcoming.

Heschel, Susannah. *Abraham Geiger and the Jewish Jesus*. Chicago: University of Chicago Press, 1998.

Heschel, Susannah. "How the Jews Invented Jesus and Muhammad: Christianity and Islam in the Work of Abraham Geiger." In *Ethical Monotheism, Past and Present: Essays in Honor of Wendell S. Dietrich*, edited by Theodore M. Vial and Mark A. Hadley, 49–73. Providence, RI: Brown Judaic Studies, 2001.

Heschel, Susannah. *The Aryan Jesus: Christian Theologians and the Bible in Nazi Germany*. Princeton, NJ: Princeton University Press, 2008.

Heschel, Susannah. "German-Jewish Scholarship on Islam as a Tool of De-Orientalization." *New German Critique* 117 (2012): 91–117.

Heschel, Susannah. "Constructions of Jewish Identity through Reflections on Islam." In *Faithful Narratives: Historians, Religions, and the Challenge of Objectivity*, edited by Nina Caputo and Andrea Sterk, 169–184. Ithaca, NY: Cornell University Press, 2014.

Hezser, Catherine. *The Social Structure of the Rabbinic Movement in Roman Palestine*. Tübingen: Mohr Siebeck, 1997.

Hezser, Catherine. "Roman Law and Rabbinic Legal Composition." In *The Cambridge Companion to the Talmud and Rabbinic Literature*, edited by Charlotte E. Fonrobert and Martin S. Jaffee, 144–164. Cambridge: Cambridge University Press, 2007.

Hirschberg, H. Z. *Yisra'el be-ʿArav*. Tel Aviv: Bialik Foundation, 1946.

Hodgson, Marshall G. S. *The Venture of Islam: Conscience and History in a World Civilization*. 3 vols. Chicago: University of Chicago Press, 1974.

Howard-Johnston, James. *Witnesses to a World Crisis: Historians and Histories of the Middle East in the Seventh Century*. Oxford: Oxford University Press, 2011.

Hoyland, Robert. *Arabia and the Arabs: From the Bronze Age to the Coming of Islam*. London: Routledge, 2001.

Hoyland, Robert, trans. *Theophilus of Edessa's Chronicle and the Circulation of Historical Knowledge in Late Antiquity and Early Islam*. Liverpool: Liverpool University Press, 2011.

Hughes, Aaron W. "A Case of 12th-Century Plagiarism? Abraham ibn Ezra's *Hay ben Meqitz* and Avicenna's *Hayy ibn Yaqzān*." *Journal of Jewish Studies* 55.2 (2004): 306–331.

Hughes, Aaron W. *The Texture of the Divine: Imagination in Medieval Islamic and Jewish Thought*. Bloomington: Indiana University Press, 2004.

Hughes, Aaron W. "The 'Golden Age' of Muslim Spain: Religious Identity and the Invention of a Tradition in Modern Jewish Studies." In *Historicizing "Tradition" in the Study of Religion*, edited by Steven Engler and Gregory P. Grieve, 51–74. Berlin: Walter de Gruyter, 2005.

Hughes, Aaron W. "Epigone, Innovator, or Apologist?: The Case of Judah Abravanel." In *Epigonism and the Dynamics of Jewish Culture*, edited by Shlomo Berger and Irene Zweip, 109–125. Louvain: Peeters, 2007.

Hughes, Aaron W. *Situating Islam: The Past and Future of an Academic Discipline*. London: Equinox, 2007.

Hughes, Aaron W. *The Art of Dialogue in Jewish Philosophy*. Bloomington: Indiana University Press, 2008.

Hughes, Aaron W. "Maimonides and the Pre-Maimonidean Jewish Philosophical Tradition According to Hermann Cohen." *Journal of Jewish Thought and Philosophy* 18.1 (2010): 1–26.

Hughes, Aaron W. *Abrahamic Religions: On the Uses and Abuses of History*. New York: Oxford University Press, 2012.

Hughes, Aaron W. "'Medieval' and the Politics of Nostalgia: Ideology, Scholarship and the Creation of the Rational Jew." In *Encountering the Medieval in Modern Jewish Thought*, edited by James A. Diamond and Aaron W. Hughes, 17–40. Leiden: Brill, 2012.

Hughes, Aaron W. "The Philosophical Thought of Ibn Ezra." *Iberia Judaica* 4 (2012): 59–72.
Hughes, Aaron W. *Theorizing Islam: Disciplinary Deconstruction and Reconstruction.* London: Routledge, 2012.
Hughes, Aaron W. *Muslim Identities: An Introduction to Islam.* New York: Columbia University Press, 2013.
Hughes, Aaron W. *The Study of Judaism: Identity, Authenticity, Scholarship.* Albany: State University of New York Press, 2013.
Hughes, Aaron W. *Rethinking Jewish Philosophy: Beyond Particularism and Universalism.* New York: Oxford University Press, 2014.
Hughes, Aaron W. *Islam and the Tyranny of Authenticity: An Inquiry in Disciplinary Apologetics and Self-Deception.* Sheffield: Equinox, 2015.
Hughes, Aaron W. "The Politics of Biblical Interpretation: A Review Essay." *Critical Research on Religion* 3.3 (2015): 282–296.
Hughes, Aaron W. "Review of *The Religious and Spiritual Life of the Jews of Medina* by Haggai Mazuz." *Journal of the American Academy of Religion* 83.2 (2015): 580–582.
Hughes, Aaron W. "Theology: The Articulation of Orthodoxy." In *The Routledge Companion of Muslim–Jewish Relations*, edited by Josef Meri, 77–94. New York: Routledge, 2016.
Husik, Isaac. *A History of Mediaeval Jewish Philosophy.* Philadelphia: Jewish Publication Society of America, 1941.
Hutchison, John, and Anthony Smith. *Ethnicity.* Oxford: Oxford University Press, 1996.
Idel, Moshe. *Kabbalah: New Perspectives.* New Haven, CT: Yale University Press, 1988.
Ivanow, Vladimir. *Ibn al-Qaddah: The Alleged Founder of Ismailism.* 2d ed. Bombay: Ismaili Society Press, 1957.
Ivry, Alfred. "Neoplatonic Currents in Maimonides' Thought." In *Perspectives on Maimonides: Philosophical and Historical Studies*, edited by Joel L. Kraemer, 115–140. Oxford: Oxford University Press for the Littman Library, 1991.
Ivry, Alfred L. "Review of *Moses Maimonides* by Oliver Leaman." *AJS Review* 18.2 (1993): 306–308.
Jacobs, Andrew S. *Christ Circumcised: A Study in Early Christian History and Difference.* Philadelphia: University of Pennsylvania Press, 2012.
Jenkins, Richard. *Rethinking Ethnicity.* London: Sage, 2008.
Johnson, Barbara. "Translator's Introduction." In *Dissemination*, by Jacques Derrida, vii–xxxiii. Chicago: University of Chicago Press, 1981.
Jospe, Raphael. *Jewish Philosophy: Foundations and Extensions*, vol. 1: *General Questions and Considerations.* Lanham, MD: University Press of America, 2008.
Junginger, Horst, ed. *The Study of Religion under the Impact of Fascism.* Leiden: Brill, 2008.
Junod (Arbell), Dominique-D. *Convivencia and Its French and English Equivalents: The Word and the Concept.* Translated by Martin Hemmings. n.p.: Editions Florent HUET, 2012.

Katsh, Abraham I. *Judaism in Islam: Biblical and Talmudic Backgrounds of the Koran and Its Commentaries*. New York: Sepher-Hermon Press, 1954.

Katz, Solomon. *The Jews in the Visigothic and Frankish Kingdoms of Spain and Gaul*. Cambridge, MA: Monographs of the Medieval Academy of America, 1937.

Kohlberg, Etan. "The Term 'Rāfiḍa' in Imāmī Shī'ī Usage." *Journal of the American Oriental Society* 99.4 (1979): 677–679.

Kollek, Teddy. "Decade of United Jerusalem." In *The Encyclopaedia Judaica Yearbook 1977/1978*, edited by Cecil Roth, 24-25. Jerusalem: Keter, 1979.

Koltun-Fromm, Ken. *Abraham Geiger's Liberal Judaism: Personal Meaning and Religious Authority*. Bloomington: Indiana University Press, 2006.

Kraemer, Joel L. *Maimonides: The Life and World of One of Civilization's Greatest Minds*. New York: Doubleday, 2008.

Kramer, Martin S., ed. *The Jewish Discovery of Islam: Studies in Honor of Bernard Lewis*. Tel Aviv: Moshe Dayan Center, 1999.

Krinis, Ehud. *God's Chosen People: Judah Halevi's 'Kuzari' and the Shī'ī Imām Doctrine*. Turnhout, Belgium: Brepols, 2014.

Kugle, James L. *In Potiphar's House: The Interpretive Life of Biblical Texts*. Cambridge, MA: Harvard University Press, 1990.

Kuschel, Karl-Josef. *Abraham: Sign of Hope for Jews, Christians, and Muslims*. Translated by John Dowden. New York: Continuum, 1995.

La Vopa, Anthony. "Specialists Against Specialization: Hellenism as Professional Ideology in German Classical Studies." In *German Professions, 1800–1950*, edited by Geoffrey Cocks and Konrad H. Jarausch, 30–36. New York: Oxford University Press, 1990.

Lakoff, George. *Women, Fire, and Dangerous Things: What Categories Reveal about the Mind*. Chicago: University of Chicago Press, 1987.

Lakoff, George, and Mark Johnson. *Metaphors We Live By*. Chicago: University of Chicago Press, 1980.

Laoust, Henri. "L'Hérésiographie musulmane sous les Abbassides." *Cahiers de civilization medieval* 19 (1967): 157–178.

Laskier, Michael M. and Yaacov Lev, eds. *The Convergence of Judaism and Islam: Religious, Scientific, and Cultural Dimensions*. Gainesville: University Press of Florida, 2011.

Laskier, Michael M. and Yaacov Lev, eds. *The Divergence of Judaism and Islam: Interdependence, Modernity, and Political Turmoil*. Gainesville: University Press of Florida, 2011.

Lazarus-Yafeh, Hava. "Judeo-Arabic Culture." In *The Encyclopaedia Judaica Yearbook 1977/1978*, edited by Cecil Roth, 101–109. Jerusalem: Keter, 1979.

Leach, Edmond. "Anthropological Aspects of Language: Animal Categories and Verbal Abuse." In *New Directions in the Study of Language*, edited E. H. Lenneberg, 23–63. Cambridge, MA: MIT Press, 1964.

Leaman, Oliver. *Moses Maimonides*. London: Routledge, 1990.

Leaman, Oliver. *Jewish Thought: An Introduction*. London: Routledge, 2006.
Lecker, Michael. *Muslims, Jews, and Pagan: Studies in Early Islamic Medina*. Leiden: Brill, 1995.
Lecker, Michael. "Did Muḥammad Conclude Treaties with the Jewish Tribes Naḍir, Qurayẓa, and Qaynuqāʿ?" *Israel Oriental Society* 17 (1997): 29–36.
Lecker, Michael. *The Constitution of Medina: Muḥammad's First Legal Document*. Princeton, NJ: Darwin, 2004.
Lecker, Michael. "Were the Jewish Tribes in Arabia Clients of Arab Tribes?" In *Patronate and Patronage in Early and Classical Islam*, edited by Monique Bernards and John Nawas, 50–69. Leiden: Brill, 2005.
Lévi-Strauss, Claude. *The Savage Mind*. Chicago University of Chicago Press, 1970.
Levin, Israel, ed. *Abraham Ibn Ezra: His Life and Poetry* (in Hebrew). Tel Aviv: Hakibbutz Hameuchad, 1969.
Levin, Israel, ed. *Abraham Ibn Ezra Reader* (in Hebrew). New York and Tel Aviv: Israel Martz Hebrew Classics and Edward Kiev Library Fund, 1986.
Lewis, Bernard. "An Apocalyptic Vision of Islamic History." *BSOAS* 13 (1950): 308–338.
Lewis, Bernard. *The Jews of Islam*. Princeton, NJ: Princeton University Press, 1984.
Lewis, Bernard. *The Kingly Crown*. South Bend, IN: University of Notre Dame Press, 2002.
Limberis, Vasiliki. "'Religion' as the Cipher for Identity: The Case of Emperor Julian, Libianius, and Gregory Nazianzus." *Harvard Theological Review* 93.4 (2000): 373–400.
Livne-Kafri, Ofer. "The Early Shiʿa and Jerusalem." *Arabica* 48 (2001): 112–120.
Livne-Kafri, Ofer. "Jerusalem in Early Islam: The Eschatological Aspect." *Arabica* 53 (2006): 382–403.
Lobel, Diana. *Between Mysticism and Philosophy: Sufi Language of Religious Experience in Judah Ha-Levi's Kuzari*. Albany: State University of New York Press, 2000.
Lobel, Diana. *A Sufi–Jewish Dialogue: Philosophy and Mysticism in Baḥya Ibn Paquda's Duties of the Heart*. Philadelphia: University of Pennsylvania Press, 2007.
Lowney, Chris. *A Vanished World: Muslims, Christians, and Jews in Medieval Spain*. New York: Oxford University Press, 2005.
Lyotard, Jean-François. *The Postmodern Condition: A Report on Knowledge*. Translated by Geoff Bennington and Brian Massumi. Minneapolis: University of Minnesota Press, 1984.
Lyotard, Jean-François, and Eberhard Gruber. *The Hyphen: Between Judaism and Christianity*. Translated by Pascal-Anne Brault and Michael Naas. Amherst, NY: Humanity Books, 1999.
Maimonides, David b. Joshua. *Al-Murshid ilā-l-tafarrud wa-l-murfid ilā-l-tagarrud*. Edited and translated into Hebrew by Paul B. Fenton. Jerusalem: Meqize Nirdamim, 1985.
Maimonides, Moses. *The Guide of the Perplexed*. 2 vols. Translated by Shlomo Pines. Chicago: University of Chicago Press, 1963.

Maimonides, Moses. *Epistles of Maimonides: Crisis and Leadership*. Translated by Abraham Halkin. Philadelphia: Jewish Publication Society of America, 1985.

Malter, Henry. *Saadia Gaon: His Life and Works*. Philadelphia: Jewish Publication Society of America, 1921.

Manekin, Charles. "Introduction." In *Medieval Jewish Philosophical Writings*, edited by Charles Manekin, vii–xxxi. Cambridge: Cambridge University Press, 2007.

Mann, Vivian, Thomas Glick, and Jerrilyn Dodds, eds. *Convivencia: Jews, Muslims, and Christians in Medieval Spain*. New York: George Braziller, 1992.

Marchand, Suzanne L. *Down from Olympus: Archaeology and Philhellenism in Germany, 1750–1970*. Princeton, NJ: Princeton University Press, 1996.

Marcus, Ivan G. "Beyond the Sephardic Mystic." *Orim: A Jewish Journal at Yale* 1 (1985): 35–53.

Margoliouth, D. S. *Relations between Arabs and Israelites Prior to the Rise of Islam*. London: Oxford University Press for the British Academy, 1924.

Margoliouth, D. S. *Mohammed*. London: Blackie, 1939; repr. Westport, CT: Hyperion Press, 1982.

Masuzawa, Tomoko. *The Invention of World Religions: Or, How European Universalism Was Preserved in the Language of Pluralism*. Chicago: University of Chicago Press, 2005.

Mazuz, Haggai. *The Religious and Spiritual Life of the Jews of Medina*. Leiden: Brill, 2014.

McCalla, Arthur. "When Is History Not History?." *Historical Reflections* 20.3 (1994): 435–452.

McCutcheon, Russell T. *Manufacturing Religion: The Discourse on Sui Generis Religion and the Politics of Nostalgia*. New York: Oxford University Press, 1997.

Meddeb, Abdelwahab, and Benjamin Stora, eds. *A History of Jewish–Muslim Relations: From the Origins to the Present Day*. Paris and Princeton, NJ: Albin Michel and Princeton University Press, 2013.

Melchert, Christopher. *The Formation of Sunni Schools of Law, 9th–10th Centuries c.e.* Leiden: Brill, 1997.

Mendes-Flohr, Paul, and Jehuda Reinharz, eds. *The Jew in the Modern World: A Documentary History*. 3d ed. New York: Oxford University Press, 2011.

Menocal, María Rosa. *The Ornament of the World: How Muslims, Jews, and Christians Created a Culture of Tolerance in Medieval Spain*. New York: Back Bay Books, 2002.

Meyerson, Mark D. *A Jewish Renaissance in Fifteenth-Century Spain*. Princeton, NJ: Princeton University Press, 2004.

Moberg, A. *Über eine christliche Legende in der islamischen Tradition*. Lund: H. Ohlssons Buchdruckerei, 1930.

Momen, Moojan. *An Introduction to Shi'i Islam*. New Haven, CT: Yale University Press, 1985.

Morris, Benny. *Righteous Victims: A History of the Zionist–Arab Conflict, 1881–2001*. New York: Vintage, 2001.

Motzki, Harald, ed. *The Biography of Muhammad: The Issue of the Sources*. Leiden: Brill, 2000.

Muffs, Yochanan. *Studies in the Aramaic Legal Papyri from Elephantine*. Leiden: Brill, 2013.

Myers, David N. *Re-inventing the Jewish Past: European Jewish Intellectuals and the Zionist Return to History*. New York: Oxford University Press, 1995.

Myers, David N. *Resisting History: Historicism and Its Discontents in German-Jewish Thought*. Princeton, NJ: Princeton University Press, 2003.

Nemoy, Leon. "Anan ben David: A Re-appraisal of the Historical Data." In *Karaite Studies*, edited by Philip Birnbaum, 309–318. New York: Hermon Press, 1971.

Nemoy, Leon. *Karaite Anthology: Excerpts from the Early Literature*. New Haven, CT: Yale University Press, 1980.

Neusner, Jacob. "The History of Earlier Rabbinic Judaism: Some New Approaches." *History of Religions* 16.3 (1977): 216–236.

Neusner, Jacob. *Judaism: The Classical Statement. The Evidence of the Bavli*. Chicago: University of Chicago Press, 1986.

Neusner, Jacob. *Judaism States Its Theology: The Talmudic Re-Presentation*. Atlanta, GA: Scholars Press, 1993.

Neusner, Jacob, and Tamara Sonn. *Comparing Religions through Law: Judaism and Islam*. London: Routledge, 1999.

Nevo, Yehuda D., and Judith Koren. *Crossroads to Islam: The Origins of the Arab Religion and the Arab State*. Amherst, NY: Prometheus, 2003.

Newby, Gordon D. *A History of the Jews of Arabia: From Ancient Times to Their Eclipse under Early Islam*. Columbia: University of South Carolina Press, 1988.

Nirenberg, David. *Communities of Violence: Persecution of Minorities in the Middle Ages*. Princeton, NJ: Princeton University Press, 1996.

Nongbri, Brent. *Religion before Religion: A History of a Modern Concept*. New Haven, CT: Yale University Press, 2013.

Oberman, J. "Islamic Origins." In *The Arab Heritage*, edited by N. A. Faris, 58–120. Princeton, NJ: Princeton University Press, 1944.

el-Omari, Racha. "The *Mu'tazilite* Movement: The Origins of the *Mu'tazila*." In *The Oxford Handbook of Islamic Theology*, edited Sabine Schmidtke, 130–141. New York: Oxford University Press, 2016.

Paqūda, Bahya ibn. *The Book of Directions to the Duties of the Heart*. Translated by Menahem Mansoor. London: Routledge and Kegan Paul, 1973.

Parfitt, Tudor, ed. *Israel and Ishmael: Studies in Muslim–Jewish Relations*. New York: St. Martins Press, 2000.

Penn, Michael Philip. *Envisioning Islam: Syriac Christians and the Early Muslim World*. Philadelphia: University of Pennsylvania Press, 2015.

Perlmann, Moshe, ed. and trans. *Ibn Kammūna's Examination of the Three Faiths: A Thirteenth-Century Essay in the Comparative Study of Religion*. Berkeley: University of California Press, 1971.

Peters, Francis E. *Muhammad and the Origins of Islam*. Albany: State University of New York Press, 1994.

Peters, Francis E. *The Children of Abraham: Judaism, Christianity, Islam*. New ed. Princeton, NJ: Princeton University Press, 2006.

Peters, Francis E. *The Monotheists: Jews, Christians, and Muslims in Conflict and Competition*. 2 vols. Princeton, NJ: Princeton University Press, 2006.

Pines, Shlomo. "The Jewish Christians of the Early Centuries of Christianity according to a New Source." *Proceedings of the Israel Academy of Sciences and Humanities* 2.13 (1966): 237–310.

Pines, Shlomo. "Shi'ite Terms and Conceptions in Judah Halevi's *Kuzari*." *Jerusalem Studies in Arabic and Islam* 2 (1980): 165–251.

Pines, Shlomo. "Notes on Islam and on Arabic Christianity and Judaeo-Christianity." *Jerusalem Studies in Arabic and Islam* 4 (1985): 135–152.

Pines, Shlomo. "Maimonides' Halakhic Works and the *Guide of the Perplexed*." In *Maimonides and Philosophy*, edited by S. Pines and Y. Yovel, 1–14. Dordrecht: Martinus Nijhoff, 1986.

Polliack, Meira. *The Karaite Tradition of Arabic Bible Translation: A Linguistic and Exegetical Study of Karaite Translations of the Pentateuch from the Tenth and Eleventh Centuries c.e.* Leiden: Brill, 1997.

Polliack, Meira, ed. *Karaite Judaism: A Guide to Its History and Literary Sources*. Leiden: Brill, 2003.

Porton, Bezlalel, et al. *The Elephantine Papyri in English: Three Millennia of Cross-Cultural Continuity and Change*. Rev. ed. Leiden: Brill, 1996.

Pourjavady, Reza, and Sabine Schmidtke, eds. *A Jewish Philosopher of Baghdad: 'Izz al-Dawla Ibn Kammūna (d. 683/1284) and His Writings*. Leiden: Brill, 2009.

Powers, David S. *Muhammad Is Not the Father of Any of Your Men: The Making of the Last Prophet*. Philadelphia: University of Pennsylvania Press, 2009.

Pregill, Michael. "The Hebrew Bible and the Quran: The Problem of the Jewish 'Influence' on Islam." *Religion Compass* 1.6 (2007): 643–659.

Pregill, Michael. "Isra'iliyyat, Myth, and Pseudepigraphy: Wahb b. Munabbih and the Early Islamic Versions of the Fall of Adam and Eve." *Jerusalem Studies in Arabic and Islam* 34 (2008): 215–284.

Putnam, Hilary. "Reply to Tim Maudlin." In *The Philosophy of Hilary Putnam*, edited by Randall E. Auxier, Douglas R. Anderson, and Lewis Edwin Hahn, 502–509. Chicago: Open Court, 2015.

Rauf, Feisal Abdul. *What's Right with Islam: A New Vision for Muslims and the West*. Foreword by Karen Armstrong. San Francisco: HarperCollins, 2004.

Reynolds, Gabriel Said, and Samir Khalil Samir, ed., trans., and ann. *Abd al-Jabbār: A Critique of Christian Origins*. Provo, UT: Brigham Young University Press, 2010.

Riffaterre, Michael. *Fictional Truth*. Baltimore: Johns Hopkins University Press, 1990.

Bibliography

Rivlin, J. J. *Gesetz im Koran: Kultus und Ritus*. Jerusalem: Bamberger und Wahrmann, 1934.

Robin, Christopher Julien. "Himyar et Israël." *Comptes-Rendus de l'Académie des Inscriptions et Belles-Lettres* (2004): 831–908.

Robinson, James T., ed. and trans. *Asceticism, Eschatology, Opposition to Philosophy: The Arabic Translation and Commentary of Salmon b. Yeroham on Qohelet (Ecclesiastes)*. Leiden: Brill, 2012.

Robinson, James T., ed. and trans. *The Arabic Translation and Commentary of Yefet b. 'Eli the Karaite on the Book of Joshua*. Leiden: Brill, 2014.

Roemer, Nils. *Jewish Scholarship and Culture in Nineteenth-Century Germany*. Madison: University of Wisconsin Press, 2005.

Rosenblatt, Samuel. *The High Ways to Perfection of Abraham Maimonides*. New York: Columbia University Press, 1927.

Rosenthal, Franz. *The Classical Heritage in Islam*. London: Routledge, 1992 [1975].

Roth, Cecil. *The Jews in the Renaissance*. Philadelphia: Jewish Publication Society of America, 1977.

Rubin, Uri. "The 'Constitution of Medina': Some Notes." *Studia Islamica* 62 (1985): 5–23.

Ruiz, Teofilo F. *The Terror of History: On the Uncertainties of Life in Western Civilization*. Princeton, NJ: Princeton University Press, 2011.

Rustow, Marina. *Heresy and Politics of Community: The Jews of the Fatimid Caliphate*. Ithaca, NY: Cornell University Press, 2008.

Saadya Gaon. *Kitāb amānāt wa'l-i'tiqādāt*. Edited by S. Landauer. Leiden: Brill, 1880. Translated into English as *The Book of Beliefs and Opinions*. Translated by Samuel Rosenblatt. New Haven, CT: Yale University Press, 1976.

Saadya Gaon. *Ha-Egron: Kitāb 'usūl al-sh'ir al-'ibrānī*. Critical edition with introduction and commentary by Nehemya Allony. Jerusalem: Academy of the Hebrew Language, 1969.

Saadya Gaon. *Sefer Yezirah 'im perush Rabbeinu Saadya ben Yosef Fayyumi*. Arabic text and Hebrew translation by Yosef Kafiḥ. Jerusalem: Mossad ha-Rav Kook, 1972.

Saadya Gaon. *Or rishon bi-ḥokhmah ha-lashon: Sefer siḥot lashon ha-ivrim le-rav saadya gaon*. Edited by A. Dotan. Jerusalem: World Union of Jewish Studies, 1997.

Saadya Gaon. *Mpirushei Rav Saadya Gaon la-mikra*. Jerusalem: Mossad ha-Rav Kook, 2004.

Said, Edward W. *Orientalism*. New York: Vintage, 1978.

Schirmann, Hayyim. "The Life of Judah Halevi" (in Hebrew). *Tarbiz* 9 (1937–1939): 35–54, 219–240, 284–305; 10 (1938–1939): 237–239; 11 (1939–1940): 125.

Scholem, Gershom. "Sprouting of the Horn of the Son of David: A New Source from the Beginnings of the Doenme Sect in Salonica." In *In the Time of Harvest: Essays in Honor of Abba Hillel Silver*, edited by Daniel Jeremy Silver, 368–386. New York: Macmillan, 1963.

Scholem, Gershom. "The Science of Judaism—Then and Now." In *The Messianic Idea in Judaism and Other Essays on Jewish Spirituality*, by Gershom Scholem, 304–313. New York: Schocken, 1971.

Scholem, Gershom. "Reflections on Modern Jewish Studies." In *On the Possibility of Mysticism in Our Time and Other Essays*, edited by Avraham Shapira and translated by Jonathan Chipman, 51–71. Philadelphia: Jewish Publication Society of America, 1997.

Schorsch, Ismar. *From Text to Context: The Turn to History in Modern Judaism*. Hanover, NH: University Press of New England, 1994.

Schwartz, Seth. *Imperialism and Jewish Society from 200 B.C.E. to 640 C.E.* Princeton, NJ: Princeton University Press, 2001.

Secunda, Shai. *The Iranian Talmud: Reading the Bavli in Its Sasanian Context*. Philadelphia: University of Pennsylvania Press, 2014.

Shapira, Anita. "The Zionist Labor Movement and the Hebrew University." *Judaism* 45.2 (1996): 183–198.

Sharon, Moshe. *Black Banners from the East: The Establishment of the Abbasid State: Incubation of a Revolt*. Jerusalem: Magnes Press and Brill, 1983.

Shoemaker, Stephen J. *The Death of a Prophet: The End of Muhammad's Life and the Beginnings of Islam*. Philadelphia: University of Pennsylvania Press, 2012.

Silman, Yohanan. *Philosopher and Prophet: Judah Halevi, the Kuzari, and the Evolution of His Thought*. Translated by Lenn J. Schramm. Albany: State University of New York Press, 1995.

Silver, Daniel Jeremy. *Maimonidean Criticism and the Maimonidean Controversy, 1180–1240*. Leiden: Brill, 1965.

Silverstein, Adam J., and Guy G. Stroumsa, eds. *The Oxford Handbook to the Abrahamic Religions*. New York: Oxford University Press, 2015.

Sirat, Colette. *A History of Jewish Philosophy in the Middle Ages*. Cambridge and Paris: Cambridge University Press and Editions de la Maison de l'Homme, 1985.

Sivertsev, Alexei M. *Households, Sects, and the Origins of Rabbinic Judaism*. Leiden: Brill, 2005.

Smith, H. P. *The Bible and Islam, or, the Influence of the Old and New Testaments on the Religion of Mohammed*. New York: Scribner's, 1897.

Smith, Jonathan Z. *Map Is Not Territory: Studies in the History of Religions*. Chicago: University of Chicago Press, 1978.

Smith, Jonathan Z. *Imagining Religion: From Babylon to Jonestown*. Chicago: University of Chicago Press, 1982.

Smith, Jonathan Z. "What a Difference a Difference Makes." In *"To See Ourselves as Others See Us": Christians, Jews, and "Others" in Late Antiquity*, edited by Jacob Neusner and Ernest S. Frerichs, 3–49. Chico, CA: Scholars Press, 1985.

Smith, Jonathan Z. "Connections." *Journal of the American Academy of Religion* 58.1 (1990): 1–15.

Bibliography

Smith, Jonathan Z. *Drudgery Divine: On the Comparison of Early Christianities and the Religions of Late Antiquity*. Chicago: University of Chicago Press, 1990.

Smith, R. B. *Mohammed and Mohammedanism*. London: Smith, Elder, and Co, 1889.

Smith, Wilfred Cantwell. "Traditions in Contact and Change: Toward a History of Religion in the Singular." In *Traditions in Contact and Change: Selected Proceedings of the XIVth Congress of the International Association for the History of Religions*, edited by Peter Slater and Donald Wiebe, with Maurice Boutin and Harold Coward, 1–23. Waterloo, ON: Wilfrid Laurier University Press, 1983.

Spencer, Robert, ed. *The Myth of Islamic Tolerance: How Islamic Law Treats Non-Muslims*. Amherst, NY: Prometheus Books, 2005.

Speyer, Heinrich. "Von den biblischen Erzählungen im Koran." *Korrespondenzblatt* (1923–1924): 7–26.

Stark, Rodney. *One True God : Historical Consequences of Monotheism*. Princeton, NJ: Princeton University Press, 2003.

Steinschneider, Moritz. "Apocalypsen mit polemischer Tendenz." *ZDMG* 28 (1874): 627–659.

Stillman, Norman. *The Jews of Arab Lands: A History and a Sourcebook*. Philadelphia: Jewish Publication Society of America, 1979.

Stillman, Norman, ed. *Encyclopedia of Jews in the Islamic World*. 5 vols. Leiden: Brill, 2010.

Strenski, Ivan. *Four Theories of Myth in Twentieth-Century History: Cassirer, Eliade, Levi Strauss and Malinowski*. Iowa City: University of Iowa Press, 1987.

Stroumsa, Guy G. "Gnostics and Manichaeans in Byzantine Palestine." In *Studia Patristica* 18, edited by Elizabeth A. Livingston, 273–278. Kalamazoo, MI: Cistercian Press, 1985.

Stroumsa, Guy G. "Jewish Christianity and Islamic Origins." In *Islamic Cultures, Islamic Contexts: Essays in Honor of Patricia Crone*, edited by Behnam Sadeghi, Asad Q. Ahmed, Adam Silverstein, and Robert Hoyland, 72–96. Leiden: Brill, 2015.

Stroumsa, Guy G. *The Making of Abrahamic Religions in Late Antiquity*. New York: Oxford University Press, 2015.

Stroumsa, Sarah. *Dāwūd Ibn Marwān al-Muqammiṣ's Twenty Chapters ('Ishrun al-Maqāla)*. Leiden: Brill, 1989.

Stroumsa, Sarah. *Maimonides in His World: Portrait of a Mediterranean Thinker*. Princeton, NJ: Princeton University Press, 2011.

Sugirtharajah, Sharada. *Imagining Hinduism: A Postcolonial Perspective*. London: Routledge, 2003.

Tambiah, Stanley J. "Animals Are Good to Think and Good to Prohibit." *Ethnology* 8.4 (1969): 423–459.

Tessler, Mark. *A History of the Israeli–Palestinian Conflict*. 2d ed. Bloomington: Indiana University Press, 2009.

Trible, Phyllis, and Letty M. Russell, eds. *Hagar, Sarah, and Their Children: Jewish, Christian, and Muslim Perspectives*. Louisville, KY: Westminster John Knox Press, 2006.

Tucker, William Frederick. *Mahdis and Millenarians: Shī'ite Extremists in Early Muslim Iraq*. Cambridge: Cambridge University Press, 2008.

Twersky, Isadore, and Jay M. Harris, eds. *Rabbi Abraham Ibn Ezra: Studies in the Writings of a Twelfth-Century Jewish Polymath*. Cambridge, MA: Harvard University Press, 1994.

Vajda, Georges. *La Théologie ascétique de Baḥya ibn Paqūda*. Paris: Imprimerie Nationale, 1947.

Vajda, Georges. *L'Amour de Dieu dans la théologie juive du Moyen Âge*. Paris: J. Vrin, 1957.

Wallman, Sandra. "Introduction: The Scope for Ethnicity." In *Ethnicity at Work*, edited by Sandra Wallman, 1–14. London: MacMillan, 1979.

Wansbrough, John. *Quranic Studies: Sources and Methods of Scriptural Interpretation*. Oxford: Oxford University Press, 1977.

Wansbrough, John. *The Sectarian Milieu: Content and Composition of Islamic Salvation History*. Oxford: Oxford University Press, 1978.

Wansbrough, John. "Review of Josef van Ess, Anfänge muslimischer Theologie: Zwei antiqadaritische Traktate aus dem ersten Jahrhundert der Higra." *Bulletin of the School of Oriental and African Studies* 43 (1980): 361–363.

Wansbrough, John. *Res Ipsa Loquitur: History and Mimesis*. Jerusalem: Israel Academy of Sciences and Humanities, 1987.

Wasserstein, David J. "The Muslims and the Golden Age of Jews in al-Andalus." *Israel Oriental Studies* 17 (1997): 109–125.

Wasserstrom, Steven M. "Islamicate History of Religions?." *History of Religions* 27 (1988): 405–411.

Wasserstrom, Steven M. "The Isawiyya Revisited." *Studia Islamica* 75 (1992): 57–80.

Wasserstrom, Steven M. *Between Muslim and Jew: The Problem of Symbiosis under Early Islam*. Princeton, NJ: Princeton University Press, 1995.

Wasserstrom, Steven M. *Religion after Religion: Gershom Scholem, Mircea Eliade, and Henri Corbin at Eranos*. Princeton, NJ: Princeton University Press, 1999.

Watt, W. Montgomery. *Muhammad at Mecca*. Oxford: Clarendon Press, 1953.

Webb, Peter. *Imagining the Arabs: Arab Identity and the Rise of Islam*. Edinburgh: Edinburgh University Press, 2016.

Wellhausen, Julius. "Muhammads Gemeindeordnung von Medina." In *Skizzen und Vorarbeiten*, edited by Julius Wellhausen, 4:65–83. Berlin: G. Reimer, 1889.

Wellhausen, Julius. *Reste arabischen Heidentums*. Berlin: G. Reimer, 1897.

Wiese, Christian. *Challenging Colonial Discourse: Jewish Studies and Protestant Theology in Wilhelmine Germany*. Translated by Barbara Harshav and Christian Wiese. Leiden: Brill, 2005.

Winckler, Hugo. "Arabisch-semitisch-orientalisch: Kulturgeschichtlich-mythologische Untersuchung." *Mitteilungen der vorderasiatischen Gesellschaft* 6 (1901): 222–225.

Wokoeck, Ursula. *German Orientalism: The Study of the Middle East and Islam from 1800–1945*. London: Routledge, 2009.

Wolfson, Elliot R. *Through a Speculum that Shines: Vision and Imagination in Medieval Jewish Mysticism*. Princeton, NJ: Princeton University Press, 1994.

Wolfson, Elliot R. "Beneath the Wings of the Great Eagle: Maimonides and Thirteenth-Century Kabbalah." In *Moses Maimonides (1138–1204)—His Religious, Scientific, and Philosophical Wirkungsgeschichte in Different Cultural Contexts*, edited by G. K. Hasselhoff and Ottfried Fraisse, 209–237. Würzburg: Ergon Verlag, 2004.

Wolfson, Elliot R. *Language, Eros, Being: Kabbalistic Hermeneutic and Poetic Imagination*. New York: Fordham University Press, 2005.

Wolfson, Elliot R. *Venturing Beyond: Law and Morality in Kabbalistic Mysticism*. Oxford: Oxford University Press, 2006.

Wolfson, Elliot R. "Via Negativa in Maimonides and Its Impact on Thirteenth-Century Kabbalah." *Maimonidean Studies* 5 (2008): 363–412.

Wolfson, Harry Austryn. Philo: Foundations of Religious Philosophy in Judaism, Christianity, and Islam. 2 vols. Cambridge, MA: Harvard University Press, 1947.

Wolfson, Harry Austryn. *Philo: Foundations of Religious Philosophy in Judaism, Christianity, and Islam*. Cambridge, MA: Harvard University Press, 1948.

Wolfson, Harry Austryn. *Repercussions of the Kalam in Jewish Philosophy*. Cambridge, MA: Harvard University Press, 1979.

Yerushalmi, Yosef Hayim. *Zakhor: Jewish History and Jewish Memory*. Seattle: University of Washington Press, 1982.

Yuval, Israel Jacob. "Yitzhak Baer and the Search for Authentic Judaism." In *The Jewish Past Revisited: Reflections on Modern Jewish Historians*, edited by David N. Myers and David B. Ruderman, 77–87. New Haven, CT: Yale University Press, 1998.

Zellentin, Holger. *The Qur'ān's Legal Culture: The Didascalia Apostolorum as a Point of Departure*. Tübingen: Mohr Siebeck, 2013.

Zerubavel, Yael. *Recovered Roots: Collective Memory and the Making of Israeli National Tradition*. Chicago: University of Chicago Press, 1995.

Ziai, Hossein, and Ahmed Alwishah, eds. *Ibn Kammūna: Al-Tanqīḥāt fī sharḥ al-talwīḥāt. Refinement and Commentary on Suhrawardī's Intimations. A Thirteenth Century Text on Natural Philosophy and Psychology*. Costa Mesa, CA: Mazda Publishers, 2003.

Zunz, Leopold. "Die Zukunft der jüdischen Wissenschaft." *Hebraische Bibliographie* 9 (1869): 76–78.

Index

Abbāsid Caliphate 67, 71–72, 75–76
Abner of Burgos 33
Abraham 6, 36, 37, 38, 39–40, 41, 132
Abrahamic Religions 5, 28, 36, 37, 38–43, 121–123
Abu Bakr 56
Ahrens, K. 49
Albo, Joseph 114
Alfarabi 28, 33
Alī 71, 77, 80, 127
amal/niyya (actions/intentions) 132
American Israel Public Affairs Committee (AIPAC) 34
amr ilāhī 132–133
Ananites 78, 79, 80
al-Andalus. *See* Muslim Spain
Andalusi 33, 110, 111, 114, 118, 125, 126
Anderson, Benedict 130
apartheid wall 15, 16, 145
apocalypticism 4, 6, 9, 10, 14, 44, 45, 57, 58–59, 70, 71, 72, 76, 77, 78, 85, 149
Arabia 1, 6, 26, 34, 37, 40, 46, 47, 48, 49, 50, 51, 52, 53, 54, 57, 59, 63, 117, 12
Arabian Jews 6, 26, 46, 47, 51, 52, 53–58, 63, 84
Arabian Peninsula 4, 5, 6, 8, 9, 13, 14, 20, 22, 26, 37, 39, 42, 44, 46, 49, 57, 59, 71, 82, 116, 144

Arabic 5, 14, 50, 73, 92, 94, 101, 128, 135, 143
  Jews and 27, 68, 83, 87, 95, 98, 100, 108, 109, 126, 127, 131, 133, 146
  and Judeo-Arabic 33, 63, 65, 93, 100, 117
Arabness 1, 57
Arabophone. *See* Arabic
Arabs x, 8, 24, 34, 40–43, 49, 50, 51, 52, 53, 55, 57–58, 111, 121, 146, 147. *See also* Bedouin, Jewish Arabs, pre-Islamic Arabs
Ashkenazic 22, 23, 31–33, 110, 120
Ashtor, E. 63
Association for Jewish Studies (AJS) 33
Avicenna 28, 33, 133–135

Babylonia 14, 26, 45, 47, 48, 49, 53, 54, 57, 59, 66, 67, 68, 69, 108. *See also* Geonim, Talmud
Bachrach, Bernard S. 63
Bäck, Samuel 23
Baer, Yitzhak 63, 119–121
Baghdad 4, 62, 49, 67, 68, 75, 81, 88, 91, 95
Banū Naḍir 60
Banū Qaynuqāʿ 60
Banū Qurayẓa 45, 60
Barnett, Richard D. 63

Baron, Salo Wittmayer 79–80
Barth, J. 48
Barzun, Jacques 105
Becker, C. H. 49
Bedouin 22, 40, 49
Beinart, Haim 63
Ben David, Anan 69, 78, 79
Ben-Zeev, I. 49
Biemann, Asher 106, 107
Big Lebowski (*The*) 44
biology 4, 5, 18, 24, 28, 29, 35, 126
boundaries x, 4, 10, 11, 12, 13, 14, 18, 19, 59, 77, 86, 89, 117, 121, 124, 126, 129, 143
Boyarin, Daniel 4, 85–86, 88
Brakke, David 89
Brann, Ross 125
Brenner, Michael 115
Brockelmann, C. 49
Brockopp, Jonathan 55
Bulliet, Richard 8, 53

Cairo Geniza 3, 24, 35, 102
Cameron, Averil 71
Castro, Américo 30
Chidester, David 20
Christianity ix, x, 4, 7, 12, 17, 20, 24, 30–33, 38, 56, 57, 62, 66, 85, 88, 93, 119, 122
Christian origins 89–90, 149
Clinton, William Jefferson 17, 18, 23, 121
Cohen Mark R. 34, 63
commensalism 13, 25, 30
commensality 18, 27–29
comparison xi–xii, 11, 20, 30–33, 85, 149
convergence 13, 18, 27–29, 35
conversion 45, 46, 56, 93, 93, 94
convivencia 2, 18, 29–30, 122–123, 124
Crone, Patricia, and Michael Cook 58

Delitzsch, Franz 21
Doctrina Iacobi 58, 71, 74

Dodds, E. R. 112
Donner, Fred 9
Drory, Rina 80

Einbinder, Susan L. 32–33
Elephantine (Island of) 44
Eliade, Mircea 106, 107
essentialism 2, 37
ethnicity 6, 8, 12, 50, 55, 59
Exilarch 64, 69, 80

Fenton, Paul 143
Fernandez-Morera, Dario 34
Frank, Daniel 80
Friedlander, Israel 70, 72
Friedman, Saul S. 34

Gaon, Saadya 5, 14, 19, 63, 65, 66, 67–70, 79, 80, 81, 84, 87, 94, 95–100, 103, 114
Gastfreund, I. 48
Geiger, Abraham 21, 37, 46–50, 51, 52, 53, 56, 118, 119
Geonic Period 59, 69
Geonim 64, 66, 67–69, 88, 92–93
Gerber, Jane S. 63–64
Ghassān 8
ghulāt 20, 71, 72, 77, 78
Goitein, Shlomo Dov ix–x, 2, 3, 24–27, 35, 36, 41–42, 48, 62, 68, 83–84, 88, 110, 112, 118, 119, 125, 126, 127, 130, 143
"golden age" ix, 1, 6, 21, 31, 63, 104–124, 146
Goldziher, Ignaz 91
Graetz, Heinrich 21, 22, 31, 47, 50–51, 52, 56, 68, 107–110, 111, 118–119
Green Line 13, 145
Greun Erich S. 11
Grossman, David 146
Grünbaum, M. 48

Index

Hagar 6, 39
halakhah 74, 79, 86, 109, 110
Halevi, Judah 5, 15, 21, 33, 114, 131–133, 139
Hebrew Bible 40, 48
heresiography 20, 64, 98
Hesiod 104–105
heterodoxy 5, 7, 20, 64, 65, 66, 67, 70, 71, 74, 82, 88, 89, 97, 92, 98, 99, 126, 142, 149
Ḥijāz 6, 8, 26, 43, 46, 50, 53, 54, 86
hijra 59
Hirschberg, H. Z. 49
history xi, xii, 1, 2, 8, 11, 18, 25, 30, 36–37, 54, 61, 64, 65, 78, 107–108, 112, 145
   history of religions 3–4, 128
   Islamic history 40, 53–54, 55, 59, 71, 98
   Jewish history 34, 47, 50, 63, 74, 83, 86, 115, 119–120
Hodgson, Marshall G. S. 25, 99
Holocaust 54
Hoyland, Robert 57–58
al-Ḥusaynī, Amīn 34

Ibn Ezra, Abraham 15, 67, 133–135, 139
Ibn Ezra, Moshe 19, 33
Ibn Gabriol, Shlomo 21, 33, 119
Ibn Ḥazm 100
Ibn Kammūna 100–102
Ibn Paqūda, Baḥya 15, 100, 114, 135–138, 139, 140
ibn Sabā', Abd Allah 127
Ibn Tibbon 95
identity xi, 6, 16, 22, 57, 89, 113, 120, 127, 143
   assumed stability of 22, 26, 44, 47, 53, 117, 128, 148
   fluidity of 57–58, 84–85, 124
   late antique notions of 11–12, 40, 60
influences 10, 13, 48, 65–66, 71, 73–74, 83, 89

Isaac 6, 38, 39
Isawiyya 64, 70–78, 80, 85, 88, 98
al-Iṣfahānī, Abū ʿĪsā 71–74
Ishmael 6, 39
Ishmaelites 40
Islamicate 25, 66, 98–99
Islamic Judaism 14, 15, 83, 109, 130, 131, 135, 139
Ismāʿīlism 5, 20, 130, 132–133, 139
Israel (State of) 7, 16, 34, 118, 120, 122, 145
Israel-Palestine xi, 145–146

Jacob 38
Jacobs, Andrew 12
Jerusalem 24, 34, 45, 46, 47, 49, 50, 58, 71, 76, 77, 79, 84, 117–118, 145
Jesus 12, 20, 74, 102, 106
Jewish Arabs 45, 47, 52, 63
Jewishness 10–11, 26, 85, 88
   Arab Jewishness 26, 51
Jewish philosophy 5, 19, 111
Jewish pride 48
Jewish studies 21, 33, 63, 107, 108
Jewish tribes 8, 59, 60
Jewmuslims xii, 82, 84, 138, 148
Josephus 40–41
Judeo-Arabic 63, 65, 68, 93, 100, 117

Kabbalah 23, 142
Kalām 14, 90–102
   Jewish Kalām 92–94
Karaites 64, 68, 69, 70, 73, 74, 78–80, 88, 98
Katsh, Abraham I. 49
Katz, S. 63
Khārijites 71, 90
Khazars 70, 80, 88
Kollek, Teddy 117

Lakhm 8
Lakoff, George and Mark Johnson 126

Laoust, Henri 98
larceny 14, 43–47, 50–53
Laskier, Michael M. and Yaakov Lev, 27–29
Lassner, Jacob 125
late antiquity ix, xi, 11, 30, 47, 63, 68, 81, 84, 92, 149
Lazarus-Yafeh, Hava 117–118
Lecker, Michael 60–61
Lewis, Bernard 24, 30, 32, 34, 57, 63, 147–148
Lincoln, Bruce 3

Maimonides, Abraham 139–141, 142
Maimonides, David b. Joshua 100–102
Maimonides, Moses 15, 19, 21, 28, 33, 74–75, 92–93, 100, 109–110, 114, 138–139
Maimonides, Obadya 141–143
Malter, Henry, 67
Marchand, Suzanne 113
Margoliouth, D. S. 9, 51–53
Mazuz, Haggai 49, 55–57
McCutcheon, Russell T. 3, 106
Mecca 6, 39, 43, 44, 45, 59–60, 84, 86, 102
Medina (Yathrib) 6, 43, 45, 46, 48, 49, 50, 52, 55, 56, 57, 59–60, 86
  Constitution of 59–60
  Jews of 45, 49–50, 52, 55, 56, 57
Mediterranean 11, 18, 24, 26, 44, 48, 53, 58, 65, 67
Menocal, María Rosa 30
metaphors 18, 28, 29, 48, 126, 129
  biological 25, 27–28, 48
Metatron 76
midwife ix, xi, 5, 6, 10, 21, 26, 27, 46, 85
Mishnah 52, 54
Moberg, A. 49
monotheism 19, 36, 46, 48, 49, 50, 57, 60, 62, 83, 90, 115, 129

Moses 38
Muʿāwiyah 71
Muhammad ix, 1, 8, 14, 20, 21, 26, 38, 44–46, 56, 57, 59, 62, 63, 70, 81, 84, 87, 101–102, 144
Müller, F. Max 106
al-Muqammiṣ, Dāwūd 93–94, 95, 99–100
Murjiʾites 90
Muslimjews xii, 60, 82, 138, 148
Muslimness 11, 85, 88
Muslim Spain ix, 1, 6, 14, 21, 22–23, 29–30, 63–64, 82, 85, 105, 108–110, 121–124, 138, 146
mutakallimūn 19, 66, 90–102
Muʿtazila 5, 65, 67–68, 80, 92–96, 100
mutualism 25, 26

Neoplatonism 3, 133, 134, 135, 137
Newby, Gordon D. 49, 53–55
normativity 7, 43, 55–56, 62, 65, 66, 68, 70, 83, 84, 85, 89, 90, 91, 92, 95, 129, 130, 148
nostalgia 104, 105, 106–107, 110, 118, 121, 146

Oberman, J. 49
occupation 7, 145–146
Oral Torah 20, 68, 69, 78, 79, 97
Orientalism 13, 37, 51–52
orthodoxy 5, 7, 67, 88, 89–90, 127, 129–130, 149
orthopraxy 5, 85, 88, 98
Oslo Accords 17
Oz, Amos 145

parasitism 24–25
Pharisees 90
Philo 92
Pines, Shlomo 71–72, 132
post-1948 35, 143
post-symbiotic 4, 27, 102, 149

Index

pre-Islamic Arabs ix, 6, 42
Princeton 3, 24
proto-Shīʿī 71, 78
Pulcher, Isaac 33
Putnam, Hilary 105

qibla 46
al-Qūmisī, Daniel 78
Qurʾān 20, 26, 40, 48, 56, 127, 137

Rabbinic Judaism 4, 8, 43, 63, 65, 68, 78, 85, 87–88, 130
Rabinyan, Dorit 16
rationalism 111–116
religion 1, 2, 12, 17
religious studies 1, 3
righteous victimhood 147
Roman Empire 87
Rubin, Uri 60

Sadducees 90
ṣafwa 132
Said, Edward W. 113
Saraceni 58
Sarah 6, 39
Schorsch, Ismar 110–111
Second Temple 46, 54, 56, 70, 90, 113
Secrets of Rabbi Shimon bar Yoḥai 58, 74, 75–77
sectarianism 20, 49, 64, 66, 68, 71–73, 75, 77, 78, 81, 121
security fence 15, 145
Sephardism 110, 114
September 11, 2001 29–30
al-Shahrastānī 73, 75
sharīʿa 86, 141
Sharon, Ariel 145
Shīʿism 4, 20, 65, 72, 77, 78, 81, 85, 127, 130, 133
Six Day War 7, 34
Smith, H. P. 49

Smith, Jonathan Z. 3, 31, 127–128, 149
Smith, Robertson 42, 48
Speyer, H. 49
Steinschneider, Moritz 21
Stillman, Norman A. 63, 128–129
Sufism 100, 102, 136–137, 138–143
Sunni Islam 4, 65, 78, 81, 127, 133
symbiosis x, xi, 13, 18, 24–27, 41–42, 83, 95, 118, 125, 129, 138, 147

Talmud 23, 43, 47–48, 53, 55, 56, 57, 59, 67, 68, 69, 108, 109, 147
Tambiah, Stanley 129
Ṭayyāyē 58
theft. *See* larceny
theology. *See* Kalām
tolerance 29–30

Umayyad Caliphate 71, 75

Vajda, George 137

Wansbrough, John 55, 86
Wasserstein, David 125
Wasserstrom, Steven M. 2, 3–4, 65, 69–71, 73, 77, 98, 106–107, 125
Webb, Peter 1, 8, 40
Wellhausen, Julius 42, 49
West Bank 16
Winckler, Hugo 52
Wissenschaft des Judentums 21–24, 31, 109, 111, 114–116, 118–119

Yemen 6, 24, 44, 50, 57
Yom Kippur 46
Yom Kippur War 7

zāhir/bāṭin (exoteric/esoteric) 130, 132, 136, 141
Zionism 7, 34, 120–121, 147
Zunz, Leopold 108